Teach Yourself VISUALLY™

Salesforce.com®

by Justin Davis and
Richard Wentk

Visual™

A Wiley Brand

Teach Yourself VISUALLY™ Salesforce.com®

Published by

John Wiley & Sons, Inc.
10475 Crosspoint Boulevard
Indianapolis, IN 46256

www.wiley.com

Published simultaneously in Canada

Copyright © 2013 by John Wiley & Sons, Inc., Indianapolis, Indiana

Wiley publishes in a variety of print and electronic formats and by print-on-demand. Some material included with standard print versions of this book may not be included in e-books or in print-on-demand. If this book refers to media such as a CD or DVD that is not included in the version you purchased, you may download this material at http://booksupport.wiley.com. For more information about Wiley products, visit www.wiley.com.

Library of Congress Control Number: 2013935669

ISBN: 978-1-118-55159-2

Manufactured in the United States of America

10 9 8 7 6 5 4 3 2 1

Trademark Acknowledgments

Contact Us

For general information on our other products and services please contact our Customer Care Department within the U.S. at 877-762-2974, outside the U.S. at 317-572-3993 or fax 317-572-4002.

For technical support please visit www.wiley.com/techsupport.

Sales | Contact Wiley at (877) 762-2974 or fax (317) 572-4002.

Credits

Acquisitions Editor
Aaron Black

Project Editor
Lynn Northrup

Technical Editor
Christopher Rodriguez

Copy Editor
Lauren Kennedy

Editorial Director
Robyn Siesky

Business Manager
Amy Knies

Senior Marketing Manager
Sandy Smith

Vice President and Executive Group Publisher
Richard Swadley

Vice President and Executive Publisher
Barry Pruett

Senior Project Coordinator
Kristie Rees

Graphics and Production Specialists
Jennifer Mayberry
Rashell Smith

Quality Control Technician
Melissa Cossell

Proofreading and Indexing
BIM Indexing & Proofreading Services
Potomac Indexing, LLC

About the Authors

Justin Davis is the chief operating officer of MK Partners, a full-service Salesforce consulting and implementation firm in Los Angeles. Developing on the Salesforce platform for more than five years, he has overseen 600+ Salesforce implementations for corporate, non-profit, and government clients throughout the United States. You can reach his firm at www.mkpartners.com.

Richard Wentk is the author of ten books, five iPhone apps, and countless magazine features about technology. He writes regularly for leading international web and IT publications and covers topics for a broad range of readers, from basic beginners to professional developers. He lives in the UK and works online. You can find out more at www.zettaboom.com.

Authors' Acknowledgments

Justin Davis: Aaron Black was instrumental in assembling the team for this publication, which includes my co-author Richard Wentk, and project editor Lynn Northrup. Most importantly, I want to acknowledge the wonderful support of my wife Monica, who provided determination and encouragement throughout this project.

Richard Wentk: First and foremost, I'd like to thank my co-author, Justin Davis, for his patience and professionalism in getting this title out the door. Much appreciation is also due to Aaron Black, for overseeing the project, and to project editor Lynn Northrup, for her avid attention to detail. Finally, I'd like to acknowledge the invaluable contribution of Annette Saunders, for nights out at the opera and other incidental music.

How to Use This Book

Who This Book Is For

This book is for the reader who has never used this particular technology or software application. It is also for readers who want to expand their knowledge.

The Conventions in This Book

① Steps

This book uses a step-by-step format to guide you easily through each task. **Numbered steps** are actions you must do; **bulleted steps** clarify a point, step, or optional feature; and **indented steps** give you the result.

② Notes

Notes give additional information — special conditions that may occur during an operation, a situation that you want to avoid, or a cross-reference to a related area of the book.

③ Icons and Buttons

Icons and buttons show you exactly what you need to click to perform a step.

④ Tips

Tips offer additional information, including warnings and shortcuts.

⑤ Bold

Bold type shows command names or options that you must click or text or numbers you must type.

⑥ Italics

Italic type introduces and defines a new term.

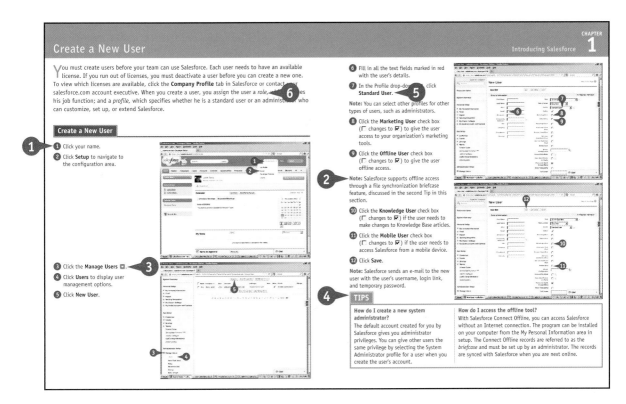

Table of Contents

Chapter 3 — Using the Service Cloud

Chapter 4 — Using the AppExchange

Table of Contents

Chapter 6 — Collaborating

Table of Contents

Chapter 7   Configuring Security

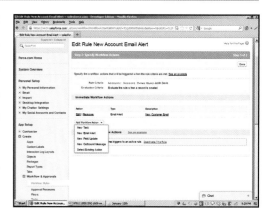

Foreword

Nearly 14 years ago, I worked as a system administrator at a small software company in the Bay Area. A large portion of my daily routine was spent performing maintenance on our servers (installing software updates, performing backups to tape, restoring lost data from backups, etc.). One day, I was assigned the seemingly mundane task of finding a new CRM application to replace our outdated, custom-built one. I had no idea at the time that this task would alter my perception of the world and change my life forever.

After much research, I narrowed down the contenders to a short list, at the top of which was Salesforce. The product met the majority of our requirements, provided additional features we had not even considered, and eliminated my mundane duties of server maintenance. As part of my research I signed up for a free 30-day trial of Salesforce and was able to easily configure changes to the application. I saw the future, one where I did not have deal with tape backups or restart servers daily, and I liked it. Unfortunately, my employer had other ideas and decided to ignore my recommendation and keep me performing server maintenance.

As you may have guessed, it was not long after that time that I said good-bye to the server maintenance world and took a position working at salesforce.com. My role was to guide customers through making the transition, like I had, from old servers to software-as-a-service. As you are soon to discover, this transition is shockingly simple. Instead of spending days installing software and configuring settings, you can sign up for a new account and be up and running in seconds. Configuration changes are made just as easily and quickly. Once you have experienced the ease of Salesforce, I am confident that, like me, you will never look back. It is only fitting that an application as easy to configure as Salesforce be documented in a book as easy to understand as this one.

As an early adopter, I benefited greatly and went on to found a cloud consulting firm, author books on cloud technologies, and train hundreds of individuals on cloud technology and development. Over the years I have had the privilege of working with many talented individuals, but none so much as Justin Davis. Justin is an amazing consultant and a gifted developer. He has a mastery of all aspects of Salesforce that is rivaled by few. I cannot think of a better person for the job of training tens of thousands of readers on how to configure and administer Salesforce.

As a developer, I often explore new technologies and read step-by-step guides for instructions. I am constantly frustrated by the large gap between the printed instructions and the actual experience. As an author, I am very familiar with the limitations of the printed medium, and how hard it is to ensure that your readers will interpret your words as intended. As a trainer, I have seen first-hand how much better we learn through demonstration than through mere reading. This book bridges the gap between printed instruction and in-person training. It is a fundamentally different kind of book that allows the authors to literally "show" you how to do something. If a mere picture is worth a thousand words, then this book is priceless!

—Matt Kaufman, CTO, MK Partners; and co-author, *Salesforce.com For Dummies*

CHAPTER 1

Introducing Salesforce

Salesforce is the world's premier sales and business management tool.
It is used by major corporations and small businesses to automate,
streamline, and track sales processes, increasing the efficiency and
productivity of your staff and maximizing your business' value.

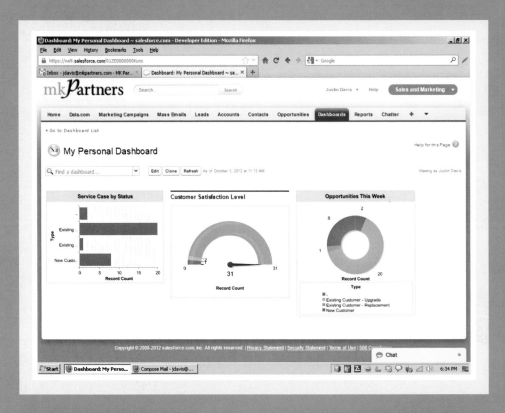

Choose an Edition of Salesforce

To provide you with the best return on your investment, Salesforce offers five editions. Price points and features are outlined at www.salesforce.com/crm/editions-pricing.jsp.

When you contact a salesforce.com account executive, he or she will ask questions to help you choose the edition that best suits your needs. You can upgrade to an edition with more features at any time by sending an electronic order to salesforce.com. Activation takes approximately a day. Note that you cannot downgrade editions.

Contact Manager Edition

Contact Manager offers basic contact, task, and event management for up to five users. This edition includes integration with Outlook and mobile access. Note that Gmail is only supported through a third-party add-on.

Group Edition

Group Edition includes all the features Contact Manager does, plus a web-to-lead management form, reports, opportunity lists, dashboards for tracking performance, and the option to install one of the applications from the AppExchange, salesforce.com's add-on marketplace.

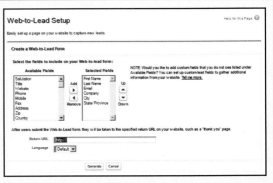

Professional Edition

Professional Edition offers all the features Group Edition does, plus the ability to send mass e-mails, manage marketing campaigns and products, create customizable personalized dashboards, add custom tabs and objects to Salesforce, and manage cases for customer service tracking. This edition includes up to five AppExchange applications and is ideal for most small businesses because it offers comprehensive analytics and custom reports.

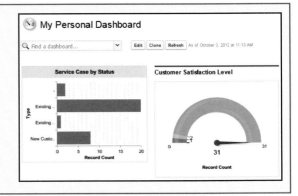

Enterprise Edition

Enterprise Edition is salesforce.com's flagship product. It includes all the features Professional Edition does, plus approval processes; field-level security; workflow rules; a sandbox for testing changes in a developer environment; additional AppExchange packages; record types, which provide the flexibility of using object records for more than one purpose; customized page layouts;, and an API (Application Programming Interface) for integration with outside systems. You can manage virtually any business process with Enterprise Edition, because it allows you to create custom applications in addition to the standard sales and customer-service features available out of the box.

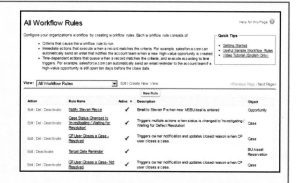

Unlimited Edition

Unlimited Edition includes all the features Enterprise Edition does, plus a Premier Success+ Plan; 24/7 technical support; unlimited online training; multiple sandboxes, including a full copy option; increased data storage from 1GB to 24.3GB; increased API limits; and mobile support. Administration services are also available to help you make customizations, which include using more tabs and creating custom objects.

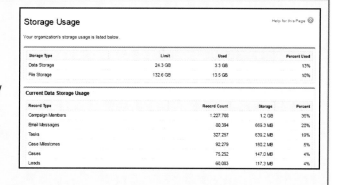

Choose Your Support Plan

Salesforce offers three different support packages for its various products. The Standard Success Plan comes with a self-service portal and knowledge base, online case submissions, and access to the online community. The Premier Success Plan provides 24 × 7 support, online or phone case submissions, and access to a trained technician who can assist you with making customizations. The Premier+ Success Plan offers all the features listed previously as well as a dedicated system administrator who responds to questions or customization requests within an hour for critical issues.

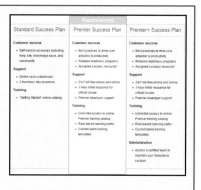

Understanding the Home Page

The home page gives you quick access to the most useful Salesforce features. You can use the links on this page to access your calendar, create records for prospects and contacts, and define sales tasks. You can also access the Salesforce Chatter feed to post news and files. This page includes a Recycle Bin feature that stores deleted files temporarily, but you can undelete them if you need to.

The ten most-recently viewed items also appear on the sidebar for convenient access. Additionally, you can perform global searches at the top of the home page.

Understanding the Home Page

Ⓐ Show Feed

Displays your Chatter feed — the Salesforce instant messaging system.

Ⓑ New Event

Creates a new entry in your Salesforce calendar.

Ⓒ Multi-User Display

Changes the calendar from a single-user view to a multi-user view.

Ⓓ Week View

Displays one week of calendar events.

Ⓔ Create New Record

Creates new records for prospects and contacts.

Ⓕ Create New Task

Creates a new sales task.

Calendar

You use the calendar to create and manage a list of events. You can view the time/date of each event, and list a subject and links to associated records. You can also view events in a more familiar graphical format. Click **Single-User View** to see only your events. Click **Multi-User View** to show your coworkers' calendars. You can also view events for the current day (Agenda), week, or month.

My Tasks

The Task area displays your to-do list. To organize tasks, click the **Date**, **Subject**, and **Name** column headers. You can also

associate one additional record with each task and display it under the Related To column. Click the check boxes in the Complete column to mark tasks as done when you complete them.

Recent Items

Recent Items shows a list of the last ten records you viewed. Items can include accounts, campaigns, cases, contacts, contracts, documents, ideas, questions, leads, opportunities, quotes, orders, solutions, and users. The list may show fewer than ten items if you delete any of the items that appear here.

Recycle Bin

The Recycle Bin keeps deleted records for fifteen days before it deletes them permanently. Most Salesforce instances have a limit of 25,000 records. If your organization exceeds this limit, Salesforce begins removing the oldest records from the Recycle Bin once they have been marked as deleted for at least two hours.

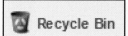

Customize the Home Page

You can customize the Salesforce home page to show items that are useful in your organization and hide items that are not. The changes are visible to all users.

You can access the customization features under the Home link in the App Setup menu. Select your items from a list of wide and narrow components, and then save your selection. Salesforce automatically updates the layout of the home page whenever you modify it.

Customize the Home Page

1 Click your name to display a submenu.

2 Click **Setup** to show the configuration area.

3 Click the **Customize** triangle (▼) to display additional options.

4 Click the **Home** ▼ to view options related to the home page.

5 Click **Home Page Layouts**.

6 Click **Edit**.

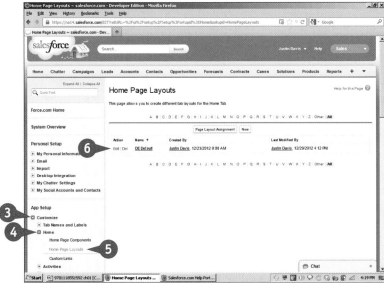

7 Click items to remove them from the home page (☑ changes to ☐).

8 Click items to add them to the home page (☐ changes to ☑).

9 Click **Next**.

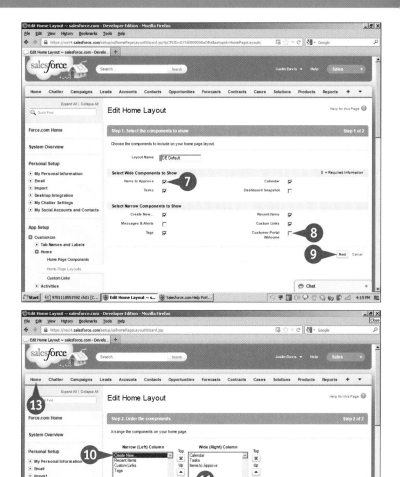

10 Select an item in either column.

11 Click the **Down** arrow (▼) to move the item down the list, or click the **Up** arrow (▲) to move the item higher in the list.

12 Click **Save**.

13 Click the **Home** tab to see your changes.

What is the difference between the wide and narrow components?

Two content areas appear on the home page — a wide components area in the middle of the page, and a narrow components area to its left. The wide area includes Tasks, Items to Approve, Dashboard Snapshot, and Calendar. The narrow components area contains Create New, Message & Alerts, Tags, Recent Items, and Custom Links. You can reorder these components by dragging them up or down in their respective areas.

Create a New User

You must create users before your team can use Salesforce. Each user needs to have an available license. If you run out of licenses, you must deactivate a user before you can create a new one. To view which licenses are available, click the **Company Profile** tab in Salesforce or contact your salesforce.com account executive. When you create a user, you assign the user a *role,* which defines his job function; and a *profile,* which specifies whether he is a standard user or an administrator who can customize, set up, or extend Salesforce.

Create a New User

1 Click your name.

2 Click **Setup** to navigate to the configuration area.

3 Click the **Manage Users** ⊟.

4 Click **Users** to display user management options.

5 Click **New User**.

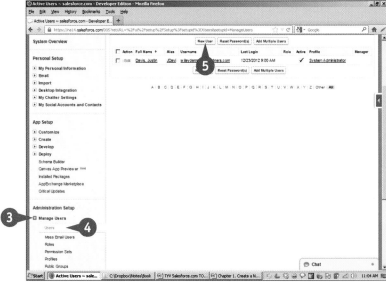

6 Fill in all the text fields marked in red with the user's details.

7 In the Profile drop-down list, click **Standard User**.

Note: You can select other profiles for other types of users, such as administrators.

8 Click the **Marketing User** check box (☐ changes to ☑) to give the user access to your organization's marketing tools.

9 Click the **Offline User** check box (☐ changes to ☑) to give the user offline access.

Note: Salesforce supports offline access through a file synchronization briefcase feature, discussed in the second Tip in this section.

10 Click the **Knowledge User** check box (☐ changes to ☑) if the user needs to make changes to Knowledge Base articles.

11 Click the **Mobile User** check box (☐ changes to ☑) if the user needs to access Salesforce from a mobile device.

12 Click **Save**.

Note: Salesforce sends an e-mail to the new user with the user's username, login link, and temporary password.

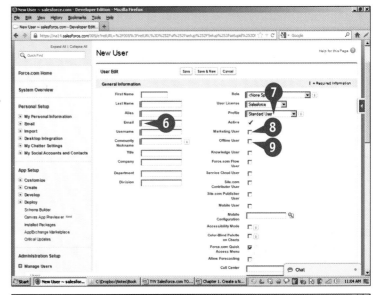

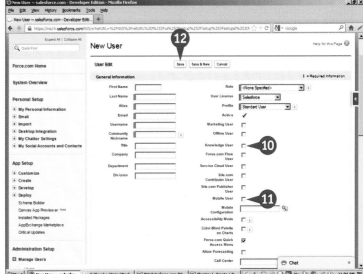

TIPS

How do I create a new system administrator?

The default account created for you by Salesforce gives you administrator privileges. You can give other users the same privilege by selecting the System Administrator profile for a user when you create the user's account.

How do I access the offline tool?

With Salesforce Connect Offline, you can access Salesforce without an Internet connection. The program can be installed on your computer from the My Personal Information area in setup. The Connect Offline records are referred to as the *briefcase* and must be set up by an administrator. The records are synced with Salesforce when you are next online.

Customize the Tabs

Users can customize the tabs in Salesforce. For example, they can simplify their experience by hiding tabs they never use. Users can work with this feature to make Salesforce easier to learn and to improve their efficiency.

Customize the Tabs

1 Click the plus sign (✚) at the end of the row of tabs.

2 Click the **View:** drop-down list and select **All Tabs** or **Select Tabs**.

Note: You can choose the tabs to customize using the Select Tabs option. Otherwise, Salesforce displays all available tabs.

3 Click **Customize My Tabs**.

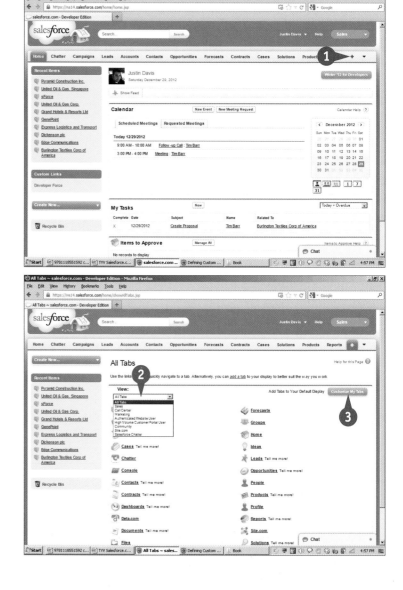

④ Click one or more of the available tabs.

Note: The Selected Tabs column on the right shows tabs that are already visible. The Available Tabs column on the left shows tabs you can add.

Note: This example adds the Ideas tab.

⑤ Click **Save**.

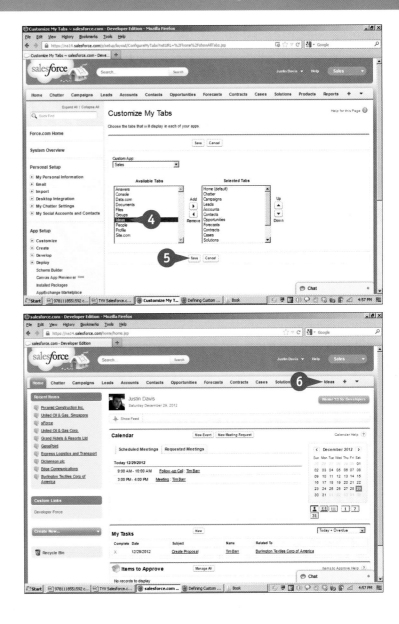

⑥ Click **Ideas**.

Salesforce displays your new tab configuration.

Can I turn certain tabs on or off for users in Salesforce?
Salesforce allows each user to customize his or her row of tabs, but each profile has different default tab settings. An administrator can set each tab to *default on* (visible), *default off* (invisible, but switchable), or *hidden* (invisible).

Upload a Company Logo

You can add a company logo to Salesforce. Users can insert this logo when creating apps, sending e-mails, or generating other documents. Typically users add the logo to templates for these documents. Salesforce then inserts the logo automatically.

Upload a Company Logo

1 Click the **Documents** tab.

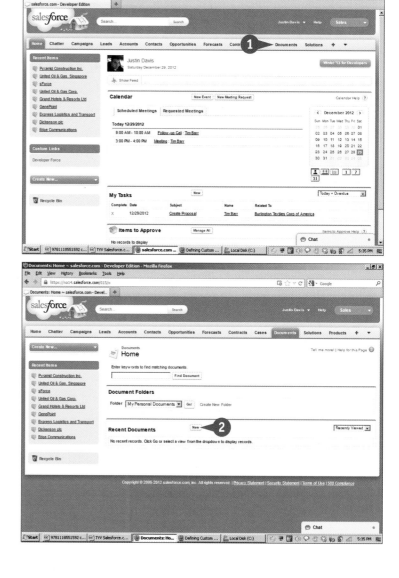

Salesforce displays the Documents area.

2 Click **New**.

Note: The logo is stored in a new document.

3 Type **Logo** in the Document Name field.

Note: You will use another name if your organization has a different naming convention.

4 Click the **Externally Available Image** check box (☐ changes to ☑).

Note: The document is now available outside the Documents area.

5 Click **Browse** and navigate to your logo file.

6 Click **Save**.

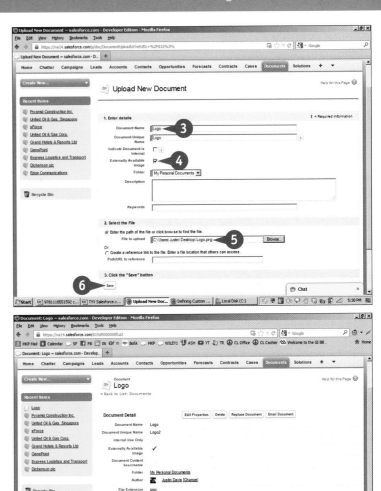

7 Salesforce uploads the logo and makes it available for use in other documents.

TIP

What size should my logo be?
The logo must be 255 × 55 pixels and smaller than 20K.

Create an App

A n *app* (short for *application*) in Salesforce is a collection of tabs that provides useful features to a team or department. Salesforce comes with standard apps such as Sales and Chatter, a social networking tool. You can get more from Salesforce by creating your own custom tab collections. The apps available in Salesforce are listed in the Force.com app menu. You can view this list on every page in Salesforce. When you select an app, Salesforce automatically changes the tabs you see. For example, if you switch from a sales app to a customer service app, Salesforce removes the leads and opportunities tabs and shows the cases and console tabs.

Create an App

① Click your name.

② Click **Setup**.

③ Click the **Create** ▾.

④ Click the **Apps** link.

⑤ Click **New**.

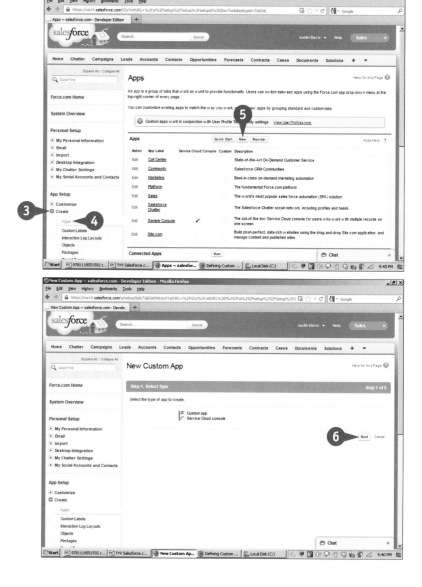

⑥ Click **Next**.

Note: The default option is Custom app. You do not usually need to change this.

7 In the App Label field, type the name of your organization or department.

8 Click **Next**.

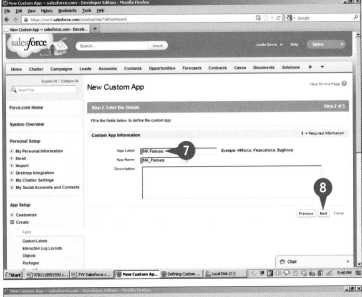

9 Click **Insert an Image**.

10 In the pop-up dialog box, select the logo you uploaded in the previous section.

Note: You can use any other image you have uploaded to the Documents area, such as a team, department, or project logo.

11 Click **Next**.

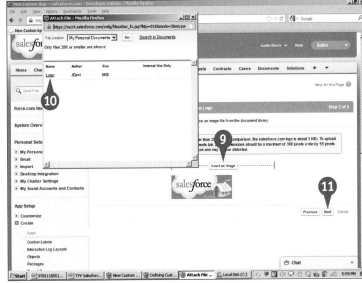

TIP

What are custom apps commonly used for?

Custom apps are typically created for each department or business unit. For examples a sales team might have lead, contact, account, opportunities, Chatter, and dashboard tabs. An executive app might have Chatter, reports, and dashboards. The key benefit is you can filter information so users can concentrate on the data they need.

continued ▶

After you create an app, you can associate it with one or more profiles to control which users can work with it. You can also create an app for a specific team and make it the team's login default; this way the app appears automatically to all members of the team when they sign in to Salesforce.

Create an App (continued)

⑫ Left-click the tabs you want to add and remove to select multiple tabs.

⑬ For each item, click the **Add** (▶) and **Remove** (◀) arrows to move tabs from the Available Tabs column to the Selected Tabs column, and vice versa.

⑭ Click **Next**.

⑮ Click the **Visible** check box (☐ changes to ☑).

Note: The app is now visible to all the users in your organization.

⑯ Click **Save**.

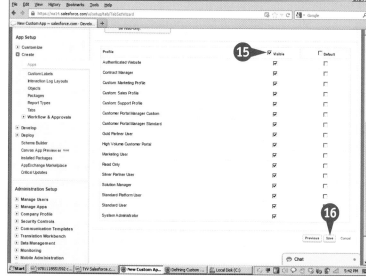

17 Click the default Sales app to display a list of apps.

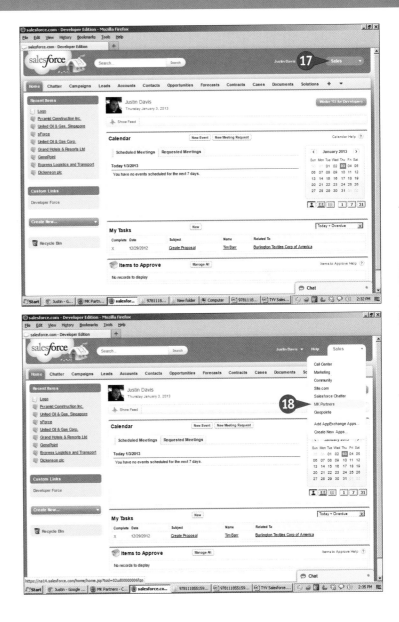

Salesforce displays a list of all the apps.

Note: Apps are collected in an area known as Force.com.

18 Look for the name of the app you used in Step **7**.

Note: For example, if the App Label name were Customer Service, you would choose the Customer Service app from the menu of options.

Note: It can take Salesforce up to five minutes to process the changes before they appear.

What is the AppExchange for?
An app has two meanings in Salesforce. In this chapter, an app is a collection of tabs. The apps available on the AppExchange marketplace are more complex and use custom code and features. They may also include tab collections, but the two concepts are different. For more information on the AppExchange, see Chapter 4.

Understanding the Company Information Page

You can use the Company Information page — also known as the *Company Profile page* — to view and change important Salesforce settings and to check usage and resource statistics. To view the page, click **Setup**, and then choose **Company Profile Area** from the drop-down list that appears. Settings include the default locale, organization ID, and fiscal year.

Salesforce administrators can check system-performance and resource-allocation information in a subpage called the *System Overview*. This subpage displays information about available licenses, the total data available and document storage, and API — external feature — limits. If your instance exceeds these limits, certain features may respond more slowly or become unavailable until you purchase further resources.

Organization Detail

The Organization Detail section displays basic contact information, including your organization's name, address, phone, and fax numbers. You can set up the Primary Contact field to define the main technical contact for Salesforce support in your organization. This section also includes fiscal year and locale settings, including language and currency. Use these settings to localize billings and reports so they match your operating territory. You can also set up the distribution of various newsletters and control the display of system-maintenance and downtime alerts.

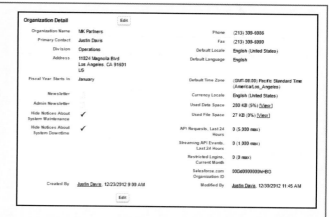

Used Data Space

The Used Data Space section displays the total space used by records in the system and a percentage of the available space. Click the **View** link next to Data Space to see which records occupy the most space, and which users own the most records. Record count is cumulative — one account with two records counts as three records in total. Most instances of Salesforce have a limit of 512,000 records.

Current File Storage Usage

Used File Space displays the total number of documents and attachments in the system, including Word documents, Excel spreadsheets, PDFs, images, and so on. The total is calculated using simple addition; for example, two 20KB files use 40KB of file space.

Current File Storage Usage

Record Type	Record Count	Storage	Percent
Documents	1	6 KB	22%
Photos	4	21 KB	78%

User Licenses

The User Licenses section displays the number of basic access licenses you can use in your edition of Salesforce. The standard license is known as *Salesforce* and is the same for all editions. Other licenses, including partner licenses, may have special features or may be limited in various ways. For a full list of license options, contact your salesforce.com account executive.

User Licenses   User Licenses Help

Name	Status	Total Licenses	Used Licenses	Remaining Licenses	Expiration Date
Salesforce Platform	Active	3	0	3	
Authenticated Website	Active	10	0	10	
High Volume Customer Portal	Active	10	0	10	
Force.com - Free	Active	2	0	2	
Customer Portal Manager Standard	Active	5	0	5	
Customer Portal Manager Custom	Active	5	0	5	
Gold Partner	Active	3	0	3	
Silver Partner	Active	2	0	2	
Chatter Free	Active	5,000	0	5,000	
Chatter External	Active	500	0	500	
Salesforce	Active	2	2	0	

Feature Licenses

The Feature Licenses area shows extra add-on licenses for other salesforce.com products, such as Service Cloud User or Knowledge User. For more information about these options, visit the salesforce.com site or contact your salesforce.com account executive. You can give any user access to any license by accessing his or her user record and selecting check boxes for the licenses from the list of options.

Feature Licenses   Feature Licenses Help

Feature Type	Status	Total Licenses	Used Licenses	Remaining Licenses
Marketing User	Active	2	2	0
Apex Mobile User	Active	2	1	1
Offline User	Active	2	2	0
Knowledge User	Active	2	1	1
Force.com Flow User	Active	3	0	3
Service Cloud User	Active	2	1	1
Live Agent User	Active	2	0	2
Site.com Contributor User	Active	1	0	1
Site.com Publisher User	Active	2	0	2
Salesforce CRM Content User	Active	2	0	2

Understanding the System Overview Page

The System Overview page duplicates some of the information shown on the Company Information page, but displays it graphically. It also displays more information of interest to technical users, including system administrators, developers, and consultants. These users can access this page to check critical resource limits, such as the number custom objects and custom settings.

Salesforce displays an alert when usage exceeds 95 percent of any resource limit. You can order more resources by talking to your salesforce.com account executive.

Schema

A *schema* is a virtual object that defines how information is organized. The Schema area shows statistics about custom objects, custom settings, and the overall data storage used by your records. You cannot create any further records if you exceed 110 percent of your data storage limit. Click the information box (i) next to each item to view more details about that item.

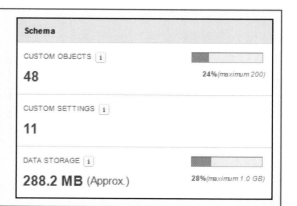

Schema

CUSTOM OBJECTS [i]

48   24%(maximum 200)

CUSTOM SETTINGS [i]

11

DATA STORAGE [i]

288.2 MB (Approx.)   28%(maximum 1.0 GB)

API Usage

The API Usage area shows how often your other applications, such as external databases or messaging tools, access Salesforce. For example, you will see the API usage increase if many users sync their Outlook accounts with Salesforce simultaneously. You can purchase additional API resources if you exceed your limits.

API Usage

API REQUESTS, LAST 24 HOURS

15   0%(maximum 14,000)

Business Logic

The Business Logic area displays Salesforce's automation and custom code features. Workflow rules trigger automated actions, such as e-mail alerts or data updates, when users perform a set action in Salesforce. This area also displays information about the Apex custom code system. Developers can use Apex to create custom add-ons and processes for Salesforce. Resource information for these add-ons appears here.

User Interface

The User Interface area displays messages about custom apps, active Force.com sites, active flows, custom tabs, and Visualforce pages. Custom apps organize tabs and logos to suit each department. Force.com sites list the number of Visualforce pages — standard web pages with HTML, JavaScript, and other standard web features — that can be viewed on a public-facing website. Flows allow administrators to create applications in a wizard-based format. Each feature has resource limits. The user interface page shows you how close your organization is to reaching them.

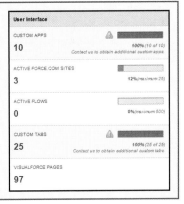

Most Used Licenses

The Most Used Licenses area summarizes the number of licenses your instance of Salesforce is using. It also includes specialized license information that does not appear elsewhere. For example, External Who licenses are created by Salesforce for internal use and do not count against your standard license limit. Salesforce Platform licenses offer limited access and are designed to be used with custom objects and code rather than by team members.

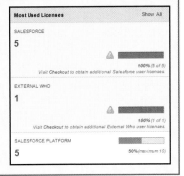

Modify the Fiscal Year

All businesses and accounting practices use a fixed time frame. You can set the fiscal year in Salesforce to match your organization's existing quarterly and annual account periods. You should do this before you begin using Salesforce for commercial projects because changing this information after you have created records and data is difficult, and you may lose important information.

Modify the Fiscal Year

1 Click your name.

Salesforce displays more options.

2 Click **Setup**.

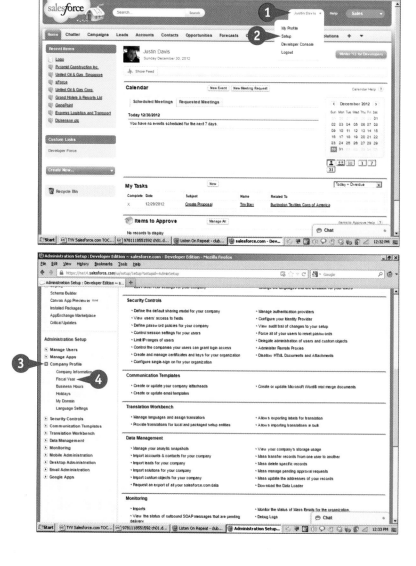

3 Click the **Company Profile**.

4 Click the **Fiscal Year** link.

5 In the Fiscal Year Start Month drop-down list, select a month for the start of your organization's fiscal year.

6 Confirm the correct Fiscal Year is Based On radio button is selected for your organization, and change the option if it is not.

7 Click **Save**.

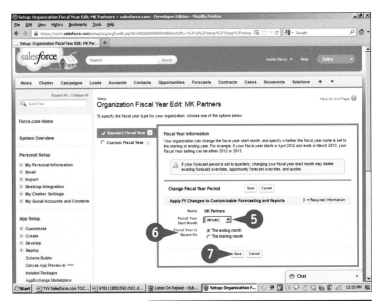

8 In the Are you sure? dialog box that appears, click **OK** to confirm the change.

TIP

What happens when I modify the fiscal year?
Modifying the fiscal year after using Salesforce for some time has two effects. First, user quota data is reset. You need to create and export a quota report before changing the fiscal year setting. Afterward, a system administrator should re-enter the user quota data by hand. Second, all reports and dashboards will use the new settings — which is usually the intended outcome.

Modify Business Hours

The Business Hours setting defines how your customer support team interacts with Salesforce. Issues submitted on your company website are handled differently during normal office hours than they are at other times. The support process is partially automated by Salesforce; the Business Hours option enables you to select the rules and tools used to log, escalate, measure, and process support requests.

Modify Business Hours

1 Click your name.

2 Click **Setup**.

3 Click the **Company Profile** ▼.

4 Click the **Business Hours** link.

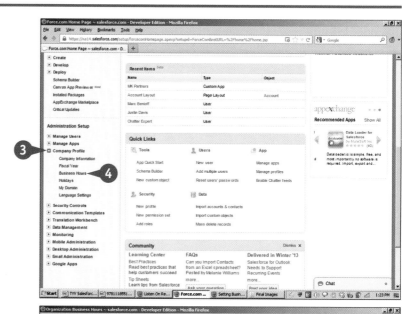

5 Click **Edit**.

Note: Salesforce shows more than one entry in this table if you create more than one set of business hours. Click the **Edit** link next to the hours you want to change.

6 Click the **Use these business hours as the default** check box (☐ changes to ☑).

A This check box confirms the hours set on this page apply to the entire organization by default.

B Leave this box unselected to specify different hours for different teams, offices, or departments.

7 Check the time zone setting for your organization.

C This option is set when you subscribe to Salesforce. You do not usually need to change it, unless your organization moves to a different country or area.

8 Click the **24 hours** check box to deselect it (☑ changes to ☐).

9 Select a start and end time for each day to match your business hours.

10 Click **Save**.

TIP

What about holidays?
Once the Business Hours record has been created, click **Add/Remove** at the bottom in the Holidays section. You can add new holidays and associate them with business hours records you created earlier. This affects support teams who rely on service-level agreements and entitlements to provide support to customers.

Log a Technical Support Case

Ⅰf you subscribe to the Premier Success Plan, you can call salesforce.com for support. Customers on the Standard Success Plan must use a web form.

Rate your issues on a four-point scale. Level 1 (critical) issues are ones that prevent contact with Salesforce staff, create data corruption, or prevent normal use. Level 2 (urgent) issues create serious operating problems. Level 3 (high) indicate a problem that only affects some users. Level 4 (medium) issues are routine technical problems with obvious work-arounds. After you submit a case, a salesforce.com technical support agent will contact you by phone or e-mail.

Log a Technical Support Case

1 Click the **Help link.**

2 Click **Contact Support.**

3 Click **Open a Case.**

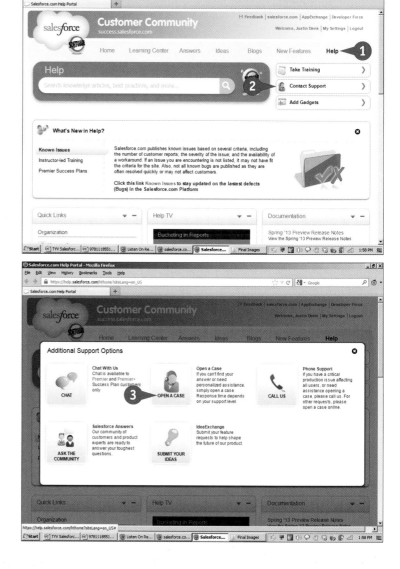

④ In the I need assistance with drop-down list, choose the Salesforce feature that is not working for you.

Note: CRM (customer relationship management) is often the correct choice.

⑤ In the Product Topics drop-down list, choose a product topic that matches your issue.

⑥ Type a subject.

Note: You can request help with features as well as report bugs and issues.

⑦ Type a description in the Description field.

Note: For a technical issue, include steps to re-create the problem if you know them.

Note: You can add more comments to a case after you submit it — for example, include more details if you remember them later.

⑧ Select a severity level from the menu.

Note: Most users select Level 4 - Medium for most issues. Select a higher level if the issue has an obvious and serious impact on your organization.

⑨ Fill in the Business Impact field with supporting information.

Note: Completing this section is optional, but it can help escalate a serious case, thereby resolving it more quickly.

⑩ Click **Next**.

Salesforce submits the case.

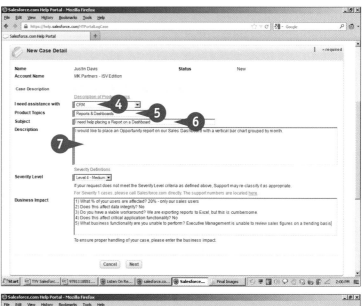

TIP

What is the response time for Salesforce technical support?

The quoted response time is 48 hours during the work week, but the typical time is often 24 hours. For a quicker response, you can subscribe to the optional Premier or Premier+ Success Plan. The Premier+ Success Plan gives you very fast access to a dedicated support agent.

Deactivate a User

When a team member leaves your organization or changes roles, you can deactivate his or her Salesforce account. Deactivating a user frees a license that can be used by another member of your organization. If a user has multiple licenses for multiple products, you must perform the deactivation process separately for each license.

Only active users can own and edit records. Salesforce prompts you to change the ownership of a deactivated user's records before you can edit them.

Deactivate a User

1 In the Setup area, click the **Manage Users** 🔽.

2 Click **Users**.

3 In the View drop-down list, choose **Active Users**.

4 Click **Edit** next to the user you wish to deactivate.

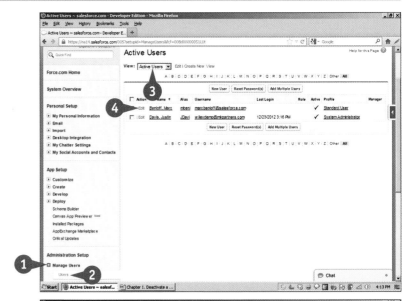

5 Click the **Active** check box to deselect it (☑ changes to ☐).

Salesforce warns you that deactivating a user removes him or her from active groups and removes the user's sharing privileges.

6 Click **OK** to confirm (not shown).

7 Click **Save**.

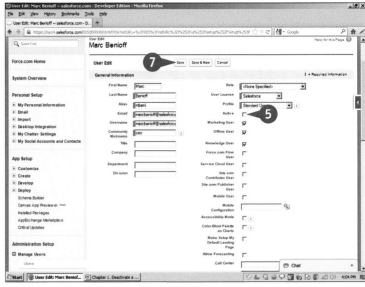

View the Learning Center

The Learning Center provides training and documentation on a wide range of topic areas, such as Setup, Sales & Marketing, Chatter, Reports & Dashboards, Service, Extending Salesforce, and User Adoption. This area provides training videos, best practices, tip sheets, and webinars.

View the Learning Center

1 Click the **Help** link in the top-right corner of Salesforce.

2 Click **Learning Center**.

3 Click any topic to find out more about it.

Salesforce displays training materials for that topic.

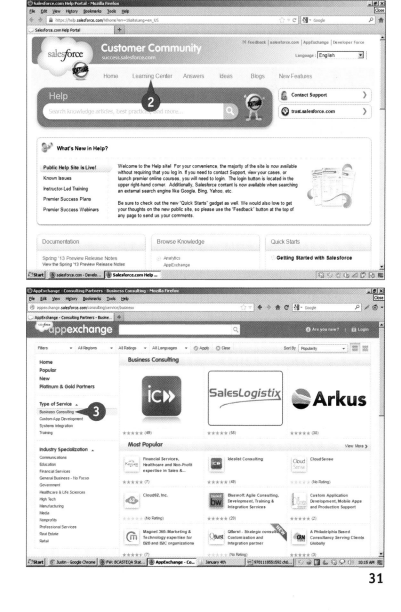

CHAPTER 2

Using the Sales Cloud

The Salesforce Sales Cloud provides complete support for sales and marketing professionals. Campaign, lead, and opportunity management records create a foundation for selling and marketing products and services. These Salesforce automation tools track and provide insight into converted leads, show visibility into the opportunity pipeline, and report your organization's marketing return on investment.

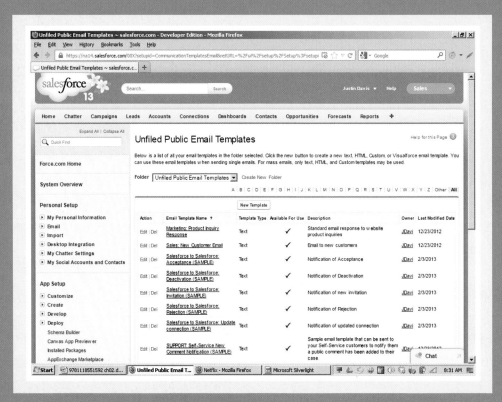

Create a New Lead

*L*eads are individuals or organizations who may be interested in the products and services you offer. Leads can come from a variety of sources, such as networking events, trade shows, and purchased lead lists.

You can use the leads area in Salesforce to manage and qualify leads, check and monitor their status as possible customers, and convert them into prospects.

Create a New Lead

1 Click the **Leads** tab.

2 Click **New**.

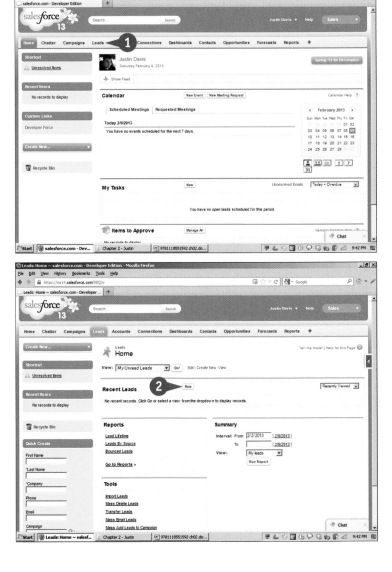

3 Enter the first name of the lead.

4 Enter the last name of the lead.

5 Enter the name of a company for the lead, if relevant.

6 Click **Save**.

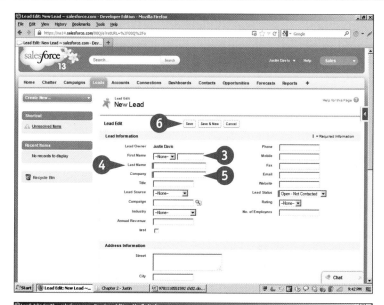

7 Salesforce saves your lead and displays the details on a new page in the lead list.

Note: To avoid duplicating leads, click **Find Duplicates** before you click **Save**.

TIPS

Who uses leads?

Leads are a key revenue-generating resource for any individual or team working in sales or marketing. Other departments, such as customer support and engineering, can also generate leads, although they often require help and training to collect opportunities and pass them to sales and marketing.

What is lead ownership?

In Salesforce, a lead is owned by one individual or group — usually, but not always, the person or team who first added it. The owner is expected to progress the lead, qualifying it to determine if the lead is a firm sales prospect. Leads can also be moved to a queue until they are qualified. For more on queue creation, see "Create a Lead Queue," later in this chapter.

Convert a Lead

When a lead is qualified as a firm prospect, you can convert it to an account, contact, and opportunity. Conversion creates a clear line between unqualified prospective leads, and qualified and active customers, called *accounts*.

When you convert a lead, you can create additional customers who may be involved with a sale. Converting a lead also creates an opportunity that appears on forecasting reports.

Convert a Lead

1 Click the **Leads** tab.

2 Click a lead to select it.

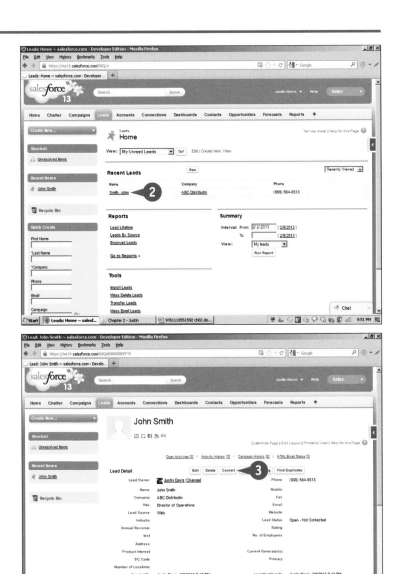

3 Click **Convert**.

④ Enter a name for the opportunity.

Note: Typically you enter a company name — the company is the opportunity; the individual lead is a contact.

⑤ Click **Convert**.

⑥ Salesforce displays the company name as the account name.

⑦ Salesforce displays the first and last name of the lead in the Contact Name field for the account.

TIP

Can I mass convert leads?

Mass conversion is unusual because it can be difficult to mass qualify leads. Salesforce does not have a mass convert option at this time. However, you can use optional supporting products such as DemandTools to add this feature. You can also export leads and reimport them as contacts and accounts. This is an advanced task and is usually performed by a developer or data specialist.

Create a New Account

You can use accounts to keep track of your customers in Salesforce. Contact and opportunity records are both included in accounts.

An account holds information about an organization you are selling to or supporting from a previous purchase. Accounts are typically a business entity such as a corporation, but can also be a non-profit, government department, or educational institution. The fields of an account record should only include information about the organization.

Create a New Account

1 Click the **Accounts** tab.

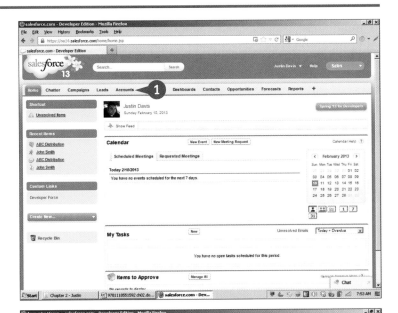

2 Click **New**.

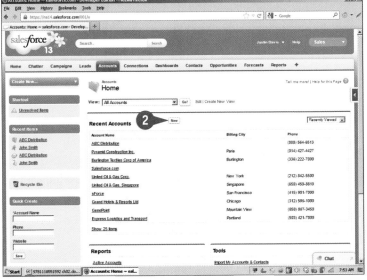

③ Type a name for the account.

④ Type additional information, such as the phone number.

⑤ Click **Save**.

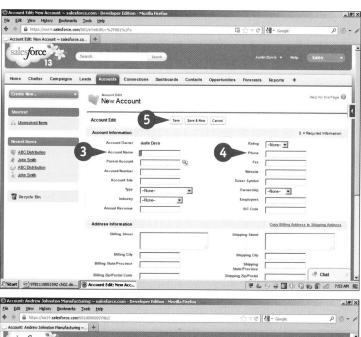

⑥ Salesforce saves the account.

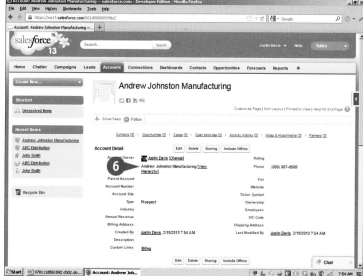

TIP

Can I merge duplicate accounts?

Yes. Click the **Accounts** tab, scroll to the bottom, click **Merge Accounts**, and then type the name of the duplicate account. Salesforce displays various options that define which account is the master, and how it should merge the information from the other accounts. You can merge only three records at a time. To merge additional duplicates, repeat the process.

Create a New Contact

Contact records are individuals who are in the market for the products or services you are selling. You can use contact records to store their personal and business details, including their titles, phone numbers, departments, and e-mail addresses.

Contacts are typically associated with an account. Each account can have more than one contact. For example, you may want to sell to two different departments in the same organization.

Create a New Contact

1 Click the **Contacts** tab.

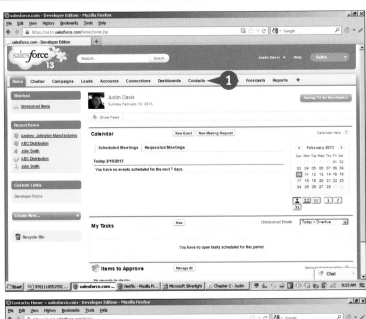

2 Click **New**.

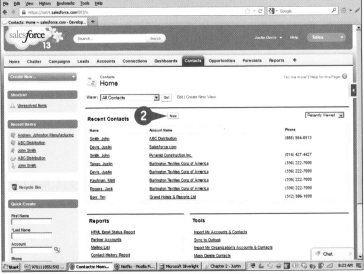

③ Type the first name of the contact.

④ Type the last name for the contact.

⑤ Type the name of the account for the contact.

Note: You can also click the magnifying glass icon (🔍) to search the available accounts.

⑥ Click **Save**.

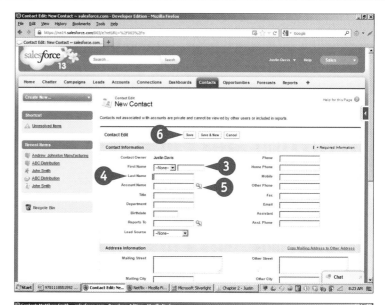

⑦ Salesforce displays the contact.

⑧ The contact is linked to the account you specified in Step 5.

Can I create a contact without creating a lead first?

You do not have to create a lead and convert it. If an account already has a contact, you can add as many further contacts as you need. For example, you can create a contact for the executive assistant in charge of scheduling meetings with an executive whom you qualified as a lead, and whom is your primary contact.

Create a List View

You can use list views to simplify access to the data in Salesforce. You can edit records directly without having to click them, open them, edit them, and save them. You can also drag and drop the columns in a list view to prioritize the information you want to see.

Examples of useful list views include active customers, active opportunities, and lists of follow-up tasks waiting for completion. List views can use up to 10 filters to select data, and they can display up to 11 columns.

Create a List View

① Click the **Accounts** tab.

② Click **Create New View**.

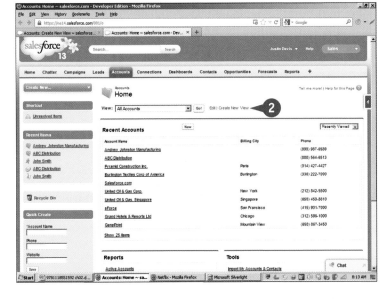

③ Type a descriptive name for this list view.

④ Click the **Field** drop-down list, and then click **None** to access the list of fields available for filtering.

⑤ Choose a field to filter on.

⑥ Type a value for the filter.

Note: This example selects records where the Billing State/Province equals CA.

Note: You can define up to 10 filters. Records appear in the list view only if all filters return True.

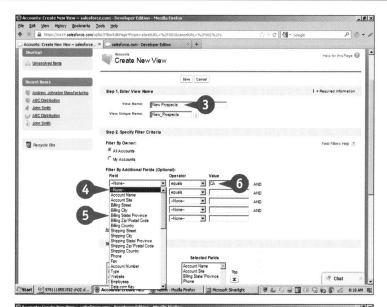

⑦ Select a field from the available fields to add it to the list view.

⑧ Click the **Add** arrow (▶).

⑨ Click the **Visible to All Users** radio button (○ changes to ◉).

Note: You can select up to 11 fields.

⑩ Click **Save**.

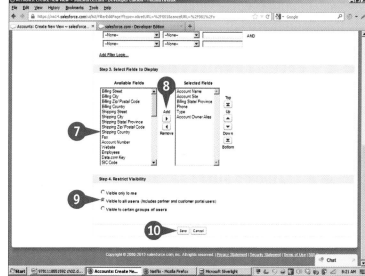

TIP

Can I sort list views?
Yes. To sort a list view, click any column header. The first click sorts the column in ascending order. Clicking again sorts the column in descending order. You can sort any column. However, you can sort only one column a time.

Create an E-mail Template

You can use e-mail templates to create prepopulated form e-mails. Salesforce supports four types. *Plain text* is compatible with all e-mail clients but does not support colored text or graphics. *HTML with letterhead* supports fonts and images and uses a standard letterhead. *Visualforce* uses Apex code to generate content. *Custom* provides full HTML support without the letterhead.

Create an E-mail Template

1 Click your name.

2 Click **Setup**.

3 Click the **Communication Templates** triangle (▼).

4 Click **Email Templates**.

44

5 Click **New Template**.

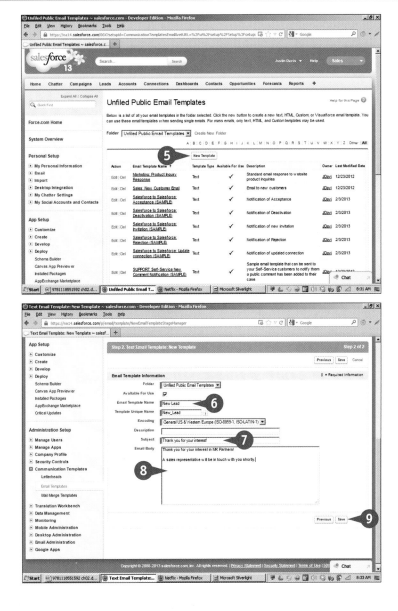

6 Type a descriptive name for the template.

7 Type a subject.

8 Type the body text of the e-mail.

9 Click **Save**.

How do I decide which e-mail template to use?

Typically plain text e-mails are reserved for internal use. The HTML and HTML without letterhead options are perfect for newsletters, invitations, and other marketing materials. Visualforce e-mail templates are typically used for customized content. For example, you can create an e-mail reminder for inactive customers with details of their last three orders.

Send a Single E-mail

Sales professionals rely on e-mail for contact with regular and prospective customers. You can send e-mail to a contact from the Activities area in Salesforce. You must include the recipient's name and a subject in your e-mail. Body text is optional, but recommended. Salesforce sends e-mails as soon as you click the Send button. The Reply to field includes the e-mail address in your Salesforce user record. When you send an e-mail, Salesforce logs it to the activity history for a contact so other users can see it. This helps avoid duplicate efforts and also summarizes e-mail activity for managers.

Send a Single E-mail

1 Click the **Leads** tab.

2 Select the lead who will receive your e-mail.

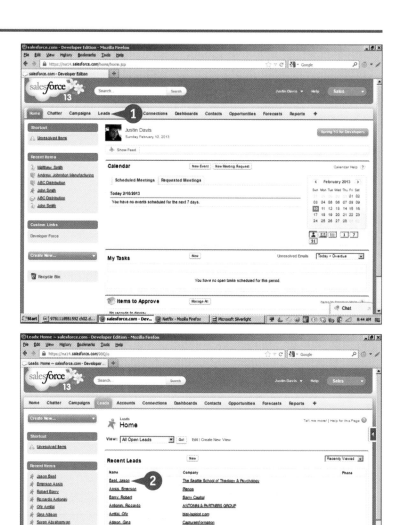

3 Click **Send an Email.**

4 Type a subject for the e-mail.

5 Type the body text for the e-mail.

6 Click **Send.**

TIP

Can I use an e-mail template?
You can use any template with the Available for Use check box selected. To use a template, click the **Select Template** button, select a template, and then click **OK.** After a few seconds, Salesforce loads the template and copies its text into the subject and body of your e-mail. You can then edit or extend the standard content.

Send a Mass E-mail

Marketing professionals can use the mass e-mail features in Salesforce to send out bulk mail to customers and prospects, and to send internal memos and updates. You can e-mail to up to 1,000 external addresses and an unlimited number of internal addresses per day. Professional Edition customers can queue up 250 e-mail addresses at a time, Enterprise Edition customers can queue up to 500, and Unlimited Edition customers can queue up to 1,000. Duplicated addresses count against these limits. You can use most templates for mass e-mails, but Visualforce templates are not supported.

Send a Mass E-mail

1 Click the **Leads** tab.

2 Click **Mass Email Leads**.

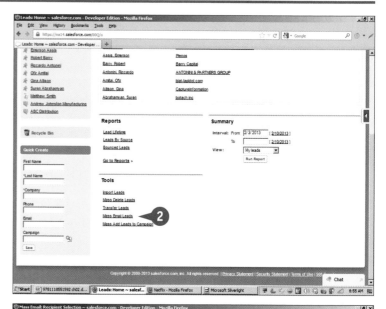

3 Select the recipients for the e-mail by selecting their check boxes (☐ changes to ☑).

4 Click **Send**.

5 Click an e-mail template to select it
(○ changes to ⦿).

6 Click **Next**.

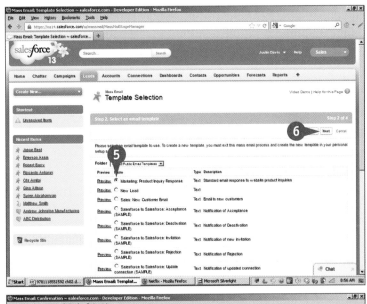

7 Type a descriptive name for this
mass e-mail.

Note: The name is for internal reference
only. Recipients do not see it.

8 Choose **Send now** if you want
to send the e-mail immediately
(○ changes to ⦿).

Note: You can also use the Schedule for
delivery options to schedule delivery at
a later date and time.

9 Select the **Store an activity
for each message** check box
(☐ changes to ☑).

Note: This option logs the e-mail to the
activity history log.

10 Click **Send**.

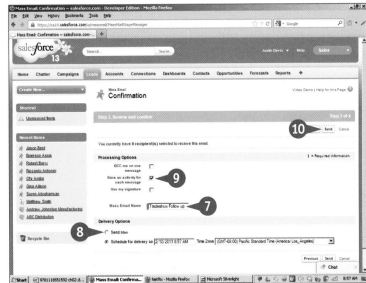

TIP

What will my From address be if I send a mass e-mail from Salesforce?
In order to increase deliverability and reduce abuse, outbound e-mail from Salesforce displays an "on behalf of" statement in the From field. To display your true address, deselect **Enable Compliance**. Choose **Setup**, **Email Administration**, and **Deliverability**. Deselect both check boxes in the compliance section, and then click **Save**. While this option displays your true address, it also makes it more likely your e-mail will be tagged as spam.

Create a New Opportunity

Opportunities represent sales and potential sales in Salesforce. Opportunities can include quotes, proposals, and orders. You typically create an opportunity after a salesperson communicates a value proposition to a prospective customer. For example, when a prospect is interested in reviewing a proposal, your salesperson creates an opportunity with a name, close date, stage, and dollar amount for the potential sale. You can then summarize this information in sales pipeline and forecasting reports. Linking opportunities to campaigns can also help determine campaign effectiveness.

Create a New Opportunity

1 Click the **Opportunities** tab.

2 Click **New**.

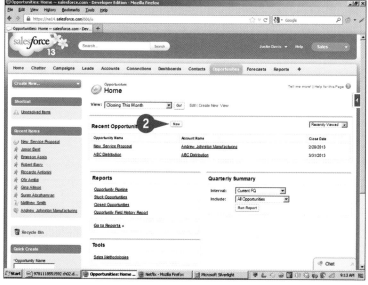

③ Type a descriptive name for the opportunity.

④ Choose a close date for the opportunity.

⑤ Type the account name associated with the opportunity.

⑥ Click **Save**.

⑦ Salesforce saves the opportunity and links it to the account.

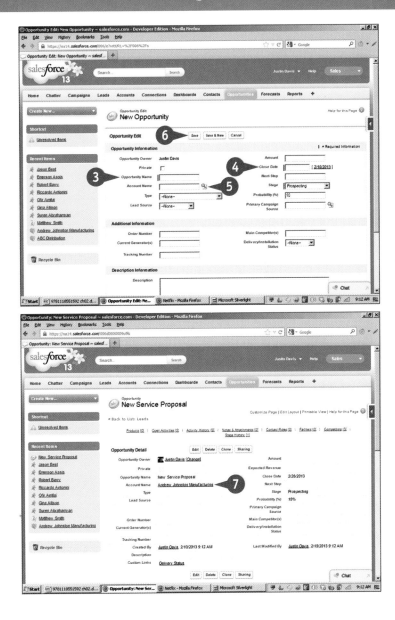

Create Products

The products object in Salesforce represents the products and services offered by your organization. Salesforce is flexible: a product record can include individual items, groups of products, and services in any combination. You can add product records to opportunities and to help generate visibility and demand reports for management. Products are typically shared with resellers and distributors via the Salesforce-to-Salesforce data sharing options described in Chapter 8. Data sharing helps keep partners aware of new product options and updated prices.

Create Products

1 Click the **Products** tab.

2 Click **New**.

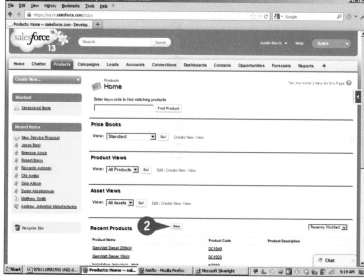

3 Type a descriptive name for the product.

4 Type a product description.

5 Click the **Active** check box (☐ changes to ☑).

6 Click **Save & Add Price**.

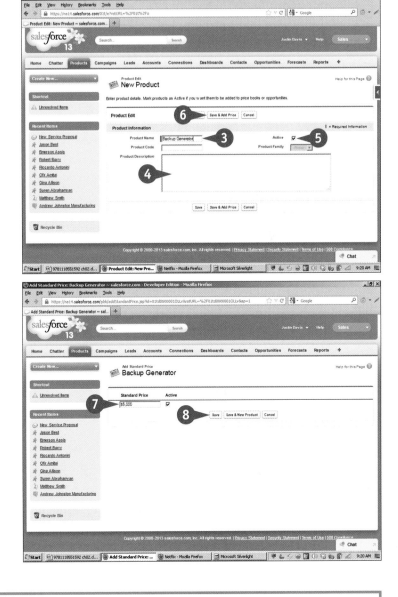

7 Type the list price for this product.

8 Click **Save**.

How are pricebooks related to products?

You must add products to pricebooks to make them available to opportunities. Many Salesforce customers use pricebooks to record list pricing for a calendar year, or define different prices for wholesalers, distributors, and other customers, with optional minimum orders. Companies that change prices every year can benefit from creating new pricebooks each year. This is more convenient than changing individual product prices, and also maintains a historical record of price changes.

Create Activities

*A*ctivities are tasks and events in Salesforce used to log and manage actions. For example, a salesperson can log when he or she makes a follow-up call to a lead, or a manager can create an event to schedule a weekly staff meeting. You can add activities to all standard and custom objects in Salesforce.

Create Activities

1 Click the **Leads** tab.

2 Click the name of a lead.

3 Click **New Task**.

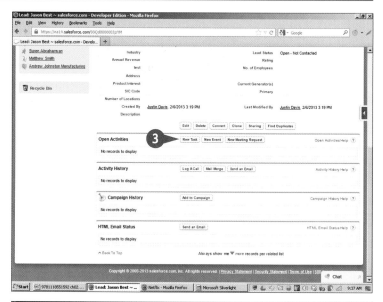

4 Type a subject (a descriptive title) for the task.

5 Click the **Status** drop-down arrow (⊡).

6 Select a status from the menu.

Note: The default status for new tasks is Not Started.

7 Type a due date.

Note: The due date is the date by which the task should be completed.

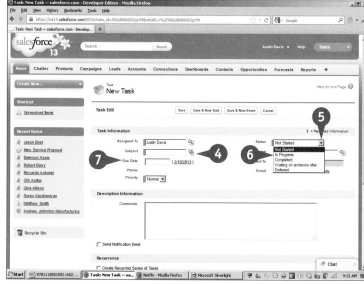

⑧ Choose a reminder date.

⑨ Choose a reminder time.

⑩ Click **Save**.

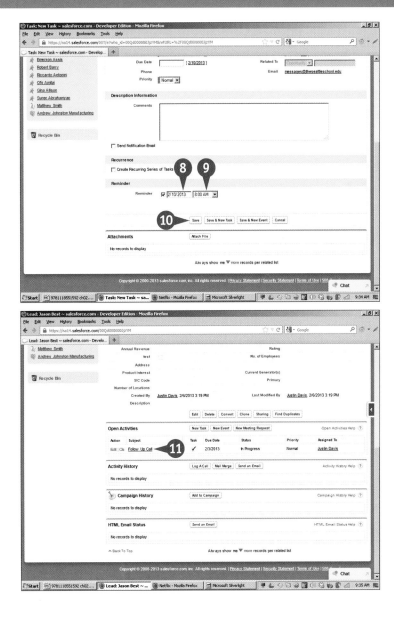

⑪ Salesforce displays the task with its due date and current status.

What is the difference between tasks and events?

Tasks are date-sensitive to-do items. They appear on the user's home page in the My Tasks section. Use tasks to list items due by a set date, which can be the end of the current workday. Events are like tasks, but include a start time and end time. Use events for items that have a defined schedule.

Modify a Quote Template

Salesforce provides an easy way to generate PDF copies of contracts, quotes, proposals, and other documents for prospects and current customers. You can save the PDFs to disk, or e-mail them to a customer.

The documents are known as *templates*. Before using a template, you can modify it to match your standard branding by adding a logo and other design elements. You can also add other elements such as product images, contract line items, and areas for signature, as needed.

Modify a Quote Template

1 Click **Setup**.

2 Click your name.

3 Click the **Customize** ▾.

4 Click the **Quotes** ▾.

5 Click **Settings**.

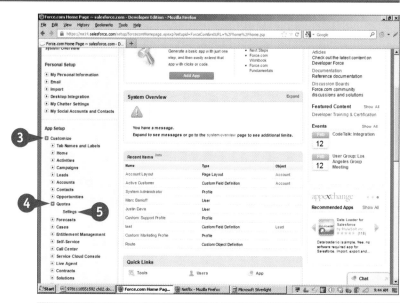

6 Click the **Enable Quotes** check box (☐ changes to ☑).

7 Click **Save**.

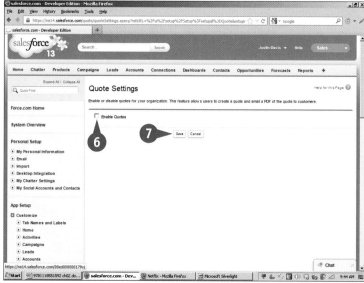

⑧ Click check box next to the
**Opportunity (Marketing)
Layout** (☐ changes to ☑).

Note: You can add quotes to
more than one layout at a time
by selecting the other check
boxes.

⑨ Click **Save**.

⑩ Click **Templates**.

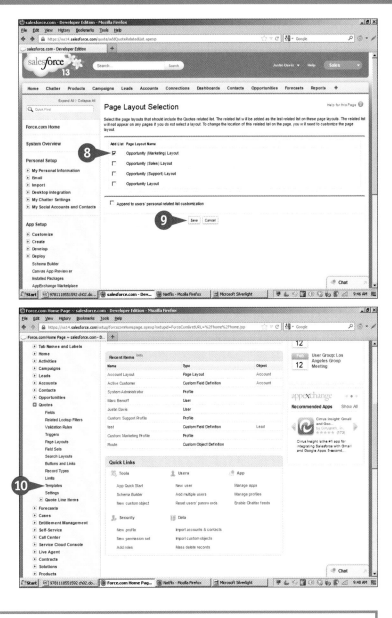

continued ▶

TIP

Can I use electronic signatures in quotes?
The Salesforce AppExchange hosts various providers of electronic signature solutions, including DocuSign
and EchoSign. You can add these products to your instance of Salesforce and integrate them with the quote
templates. When you generate a quote, it can include an electronic signature field that a prospect can
digitally sign.

Quotes can include images, such as product photos or a company logo. To include an image, drag the Image Field button to the quote. Click **Browse**, and choose an image. The image then appears in all the quotes the template generates.

You can add headers and footers in a similar way, and customize them to match the company letterhead and other documents used by your organization.

Modify a Quote Template (continued)

11 Click **Edit**.

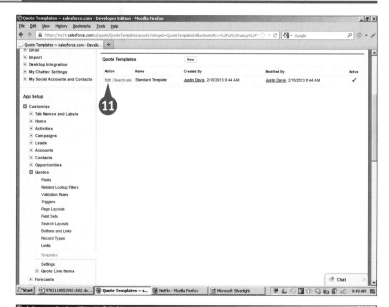

12 Click **Quote Template Properties**.

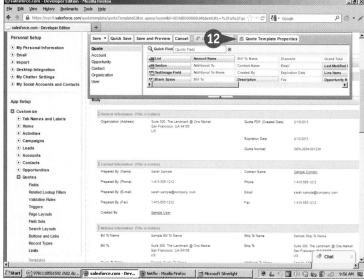

⑬ Type a descriptive name for the quote template.

⑭ Click **OK**.

⑮ Click **Save**.

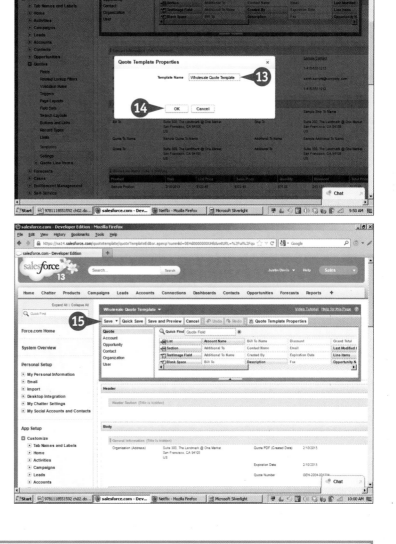

Do all fields appear in quotes?

When a user cannot see fields that are included on the quote template, those fields do not appear in the quote. Nor do blank fields with no values. Typically, users create multiple templates rather than creating a single template that does everything. For example, you might create one quote template with upfront payment terms, and another for payment due upon completion.

Build a Quote

After you create a quote template, you can use it to generate — *build* — a quote. Quotes always include line items selected from active and available products listings in Salesforce. Quote line items can also generate opportunity products on an opportunity page layout for upselling.

You can also *sync* a quote. This locks the value of the opportunity that receives the quote to the total quoted price.

Build a Quote

1 Click the **Opportunities** tab.

2 Select the opportunity that will receive the quote.

3 Click **New Quote**.

4 Type a descriptive name for the quote.

5 Click **Save**.

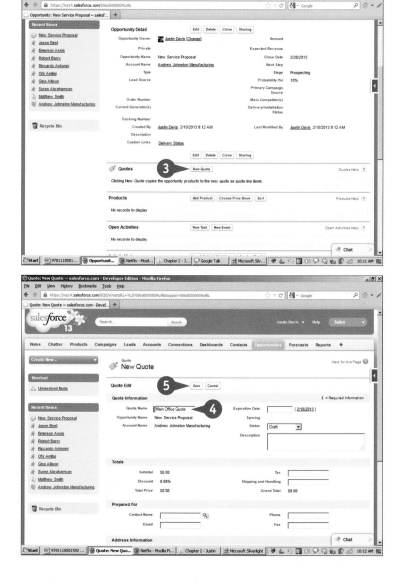

6 Click **Start Sync**.

7 Click **Sync**.

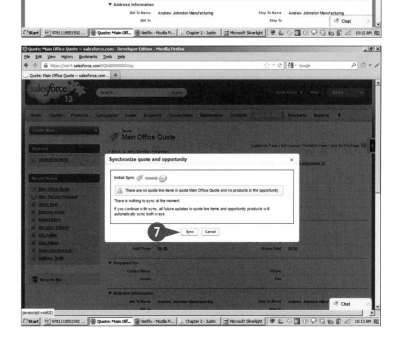

continued ►

TIP

Can I generate quotes in other file formats?
Salesforce generates quotes only in PDF format. If you need quotes in some other format, you can find solutions such as Conga Merge, which provides batch printing and a variety of output formats, on the App Exchange. You can also use mail merge templates to generate documents in Microsoft Word format from data on Salesforce records. You can then send the documents to your customer or further edit them in Word to customize them before you e-mail them. See the Salesforce help section for more information.

Build a Quote (continued)

You can add discounts to quotes by defining a discount percentage for a quote line item. The discount is automatically included in the final quoted price.

You can also add *lists* when you create and customize a quote template. Lists contain bullet points detailing the raw materials or parts that make up the products you sell. This is a useful option for products sold as packages.

Build a Quote (continued)

8 Click **Done**.

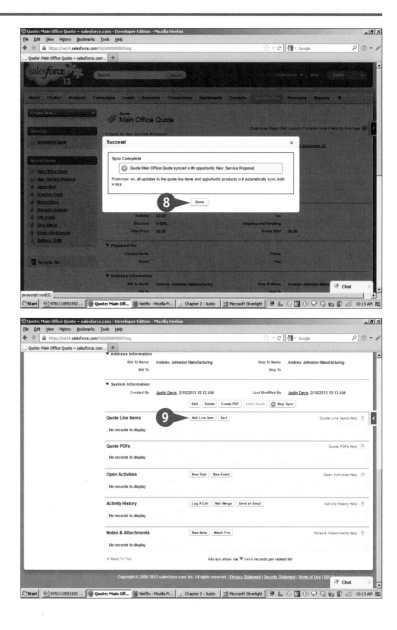

9 Click **Add Line Item**.

⑩ Click the check boxes to choose the items in the quote (☐ changes to ☑).

⑪ Click **Select**.

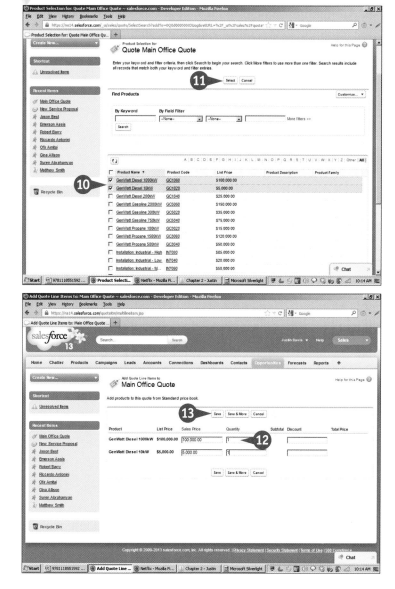

⑫ Type a product quantity for each item in the quote.

⑬ Click **Save**.

E-mail a Quote

After creating a quote, you can e-mail it to prospective customers, as long as they have a contact record with the e-mail field filled in. You can also send previous versions of quotes by clicking the **Email** link next to each saved version.

E-mail a Quote

1 Click the **Opportunities** tab.

2 Click an opportunity.

3 Click the quote you want to send to the opportunity.

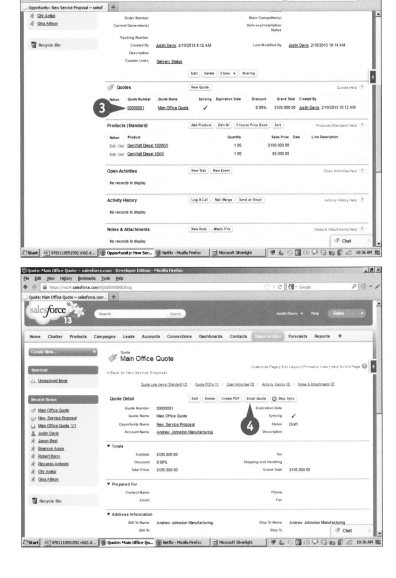

4 Click **Email Quote**.

5 Type the name of a contact at the opportunity.

6 Type a descriptive subject for the e-mail.

7 Type the body text of the e-mail.

8 Click **Send**.

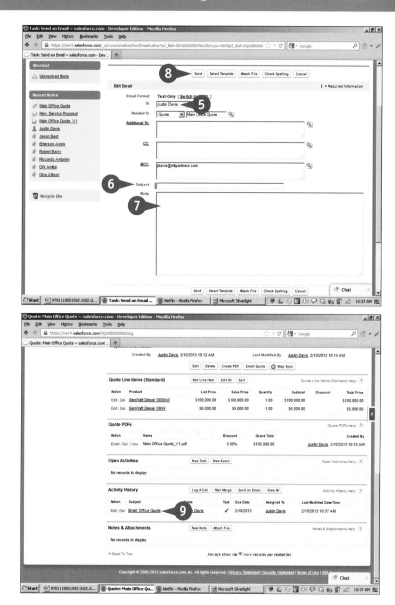

9 Salesforce adds a new activity record on the quote to let and other users know the date and time you sent the quote.

Create a Web-to-Lead Form

With a web-to-lead form, you can convert web form responses from your main website into leads in Salesforce. You can use the forms on any of your websites, and modify them to match your standard design and branding.

The web-to-lead feature generates HTML that is compatible with all web content management systems. To use the form, ask your existing web design team to replace the contact forms on your website with the new HTML generated by Salesforce.

Create a Web-to-Lead Form

1 Click your name.

2 Click **Setup**.

3 Click the **Customize** ▣.

4 Click the **Leads** ▣.

5 Click **Web-to-Lead**.

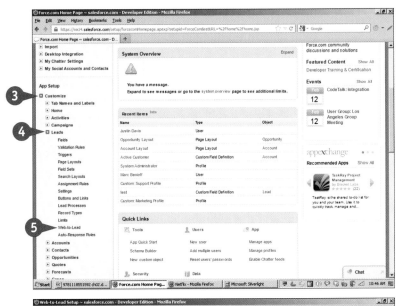

6 Click **Create Web-to-Lead Form**.

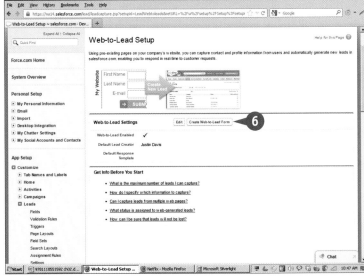

⑦ Select a field in the Available Fields list.

⑧ Click the **Add** arrow (▶) to add the field to the form.

Note: Repeat Steps **7** and **8** to add more than one field.

⑨ Type the URL for the thank-you result page.

⑩ Click **Generate**.

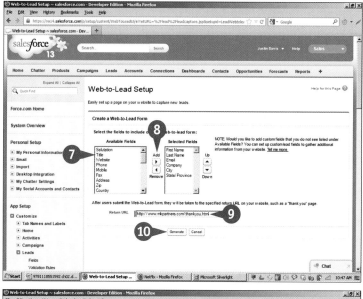

⑪ Copy the HTML generated by Salesforce.

Note: You can now paste the HTML to a separate document to save it, or paste it directly into a web editor.

⑫ Click **Finished**.

TIP

Can I include hidden fields on a web-to-lead form?

To support a hidden field, create a special field on the lead record. For example, to find which site a form arrived from, create a text field on the lead named "source web site." A web developer can then make this a hidden field and use it to hold the name of the site that generated the lead. Salesforce can read the name from the form and populate the "source web site" field automatically.

Create a Lead Assignment Rule

 ales managers can use lead assignment rules to assign new leads to sales representatives automatically. Rules are often geographically based, assigning leads from a territory to the representatives responsible for it.

Rules can also work with seniority and status. For example, you can use a rule to assign interest from an important preferred customer to your senior VP of sales instead of a sales rep.

Create a Lead Assignment Rule

1 Click your name.

2 Click **Setup**.

3 Click the **Customize** ▾.

4 Click the **Leads** ▾.

5 Click **Assignment Rules**.

6 Click **New**.

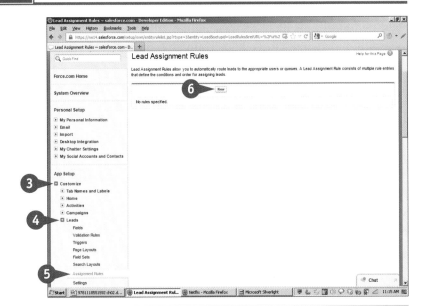

7 Click the **Set this as the active assignment rule** check box (☐ changes to ☑).

8 Type a descriptive name for the lead assignment rule.

9 Click **Save**.

⑩ Click **New**.

⑪ Select a field to use in the assignment rule.

⑫ Type a test value for the field.

Note: You can also select a logical test using the Operator lists for each rule.

Note: This example assigns a lead when the state or province value is equal to CA; in this example, the lead is from California.

⑬ Type the name of the user you are assigning the leads to.

Note: You can also click the magnifying glass icon ( ) to search for a user by name.

⑭ Click **Save**.

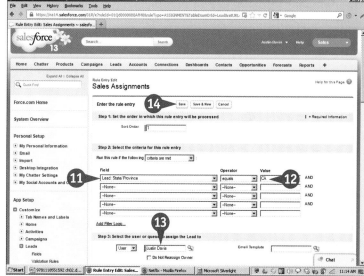

TIP

Who owns leads submitted from a web-to-lead form if they are not assigned with a rule?
Leads are owned by the default owner unless they are assigned to some other user by a rule. Your system administrator can select the default user on the Lead Settings Page in the Configuration area.

Create a Lead Queue

You can use queues to store records in Salesforce before assigning them to a user. Salesforce users often work with queues to manage leads. Typical applications include leads collected by territory, leads generated by specific websites, or leads captured from product detail pages. Queues do not count as licensed users.

Create a Lead Queue

① Click your name.

② Click **Setup**.

③ Click the **Manage Users** ▾.

④ Click **Queues**.

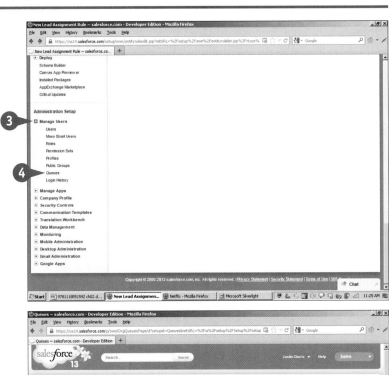

⑤ Click **New**.

6 Type a descriptive name for the lead queue.

7 Select **Lead**.

8 Click the **Add** arrow (▶).

9 Select the users you wish to add to the queue.

Note: Salesforce security and sharing rules treat queues like users, and allow or deny access according to your sharing rules. Review your sharing rules to make sure queuing works correctly. For details, see Chapter 7.

10 Click the **Add** arrow (▶).

11 Click **Save**.

TIPS

Which objects can I queue?

In addition to leads, you can create queues for cases, knowledge articles, service contracts, or any custom object. Queues for these additional record types are created in the same way lead queues are created. Remember to add queue members to the queue prior to clicking **Save**. If you miss this step, only the system administrator can access the queue.

How do I move records from a queue to a user?

Navigate to a lead and click the **Change** link next to the name of the current owner. Type the name of an active user, and then click **Save**. The user becomes the new owner.

Create an Auto-Response Rule

You can configure Salesforce to generate an e-mail from a template and send it automatically when a new lead arrives in a web-to-lead form.

E-mail templates are usually created by your marketing department and have the same branding and design elements as your website.

Create an Auto-Response Rule

1 Click your name.

2 Click **Setup**.

3 Click **Auto-Response Rules**.

4 Click **New**.

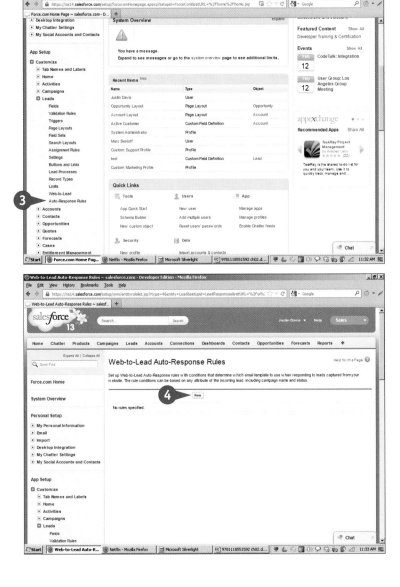

⑤ Type a descriptive name for this auto-response rule.

⑥ Check the **Set this as the active Web-to-Lead Auto-Response rule** check box (☐ changes to ☑).

⑦ Click **Save**.

⑧ Click the **Auto-Response Rule** name.

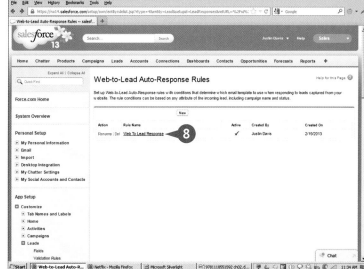

TIP

What is the difference between a workflow rule and an auto-response rule?

Auto-response rules run when a new case or lead is created manually or automatically. They send an e-mail to the person who submitted the web form that created the lead. Workflow rules are more general and typically used for internal processing rather than customer communication. They are available for most objects and can run when records are created, edited, or both.

continued ▶

You can set up auto-response e-mails so they arrive from the new owner of a lead, and not the default owner. This reduces customer frustration by creating a single reliable point of contact for customers.

To use this option, you create individual e-mail templates for each new lead owner. You can then select a new lead owner by selecting an individual template when you create your auto-response rules.

Create an Auto-Response Rule (continued)

9 Click **New**.

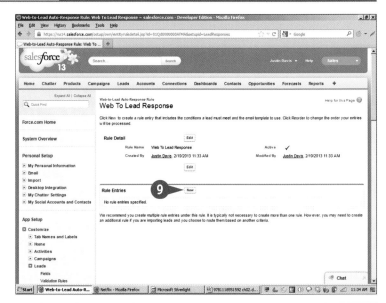

10 Select a field to use in the auto-response rule.

11 Type a test value for the field.

Note: You can also select a logical test using the Operator lists for each rule.

Note: This example auto-responds when the lead originates in Los Angeles.

12 Type the name of the sales representative or contact who appears in the From field in the e-mail.

13 Type the e-mail address of the representative or contact.

14 Type the name of an e-mail template for the auto-generated e-mail.

15 Click **Save**.

16 Salesforce adds the auto-response rule and makes it active.

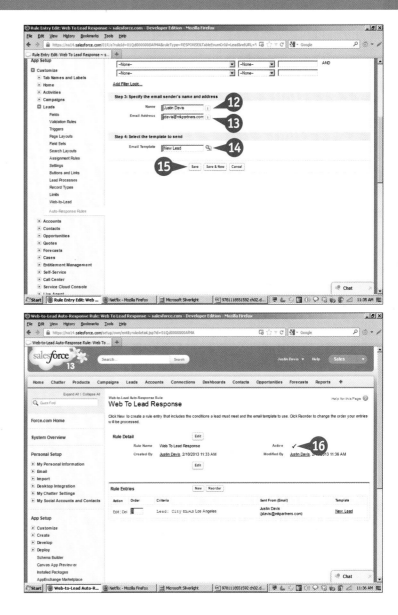

How many active auto-response rules can I have?
Auto-response rules are not available in the Personal, Group, or Contact Manager editions of Salesforce. Professional, Enterprise, and Unlimited edition customers can create up to 3,000 rules, with up to 200 actions per rule. However, only one rule can be active at a time.

Create a Campaign

arketing professionals can use campaigns to collect and process leads collected from web forms, at trade shows, or from other marketing activities.

A campaign record tracks the number of leads, contacts, and opportunities assigned to it. It can also display summary statistics, such as the total investment, the response rate, and budgeted versus actual cost. Management can use these statistics to learn from past campaigns and improve future marketing efforts.

Create a Campaign

1 Click **Campaigns**.

2 Click **New**.

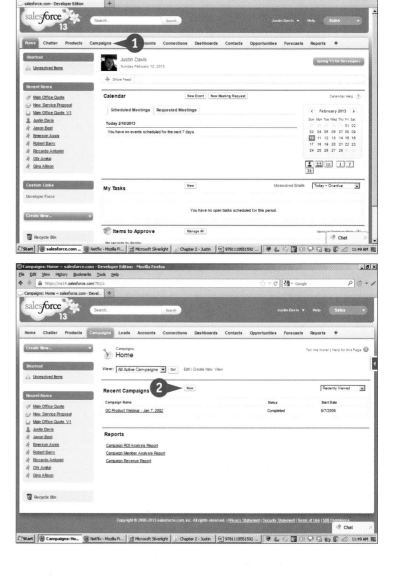

③ Type a name for the campaign.

④ Click the **Active** check box (☐ changes to ☑) to mark the campaign as a current, active project.

⑤ Click **Save**.

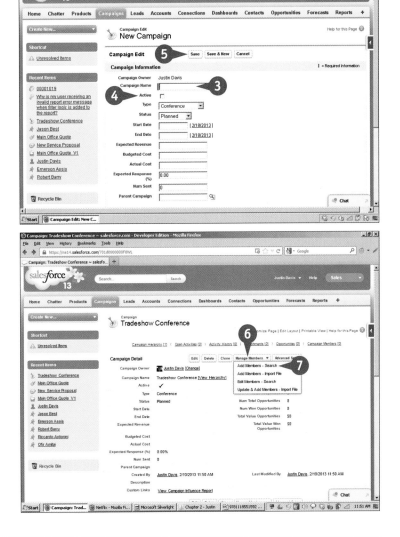

⑥ Click **Manage Members**.

⑦ Click **Add Members - Search**.

continued ▶

TIP

Can I import leads directly to a campaign?

You can import leads and contacts from a spreadsheet file exported in CSV (comma-separated values) file format. Navigate to a campaign record, click **Manage Members**, and then click **Add Members - Import File**. When the import wizard appears, click **Import Leads**. You may need to map the leads before importing them into a campaign. For details, see Chapter 6.

Create a Campaign (continued)

Y ou can use the Campaign Hierarchy feature to manage several sub-campaigns under a single master campaign. For example, you can create a parent campaign called Trade Shows to collect and manage leads from all the trade shows your organization attends. Each trade show would become a child campaign. You can have up to five levels in the campaign hierarchy. For example, you might group trade shows by territory, or by specific annual shows to discover which events give the best returns. Parent campaigns can collect and summarize statistics from all child campaigns.

Create a Campaign (continued)

⑧ Click **Go!**.

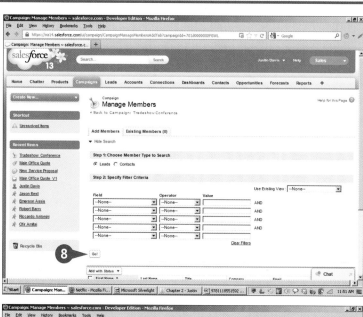

⑨ Click the check boxes of the leads you want to add to this campaign (☐ changes to ☑).

⑩ Click **Add with Status**.

⑪ Click **Responded**.

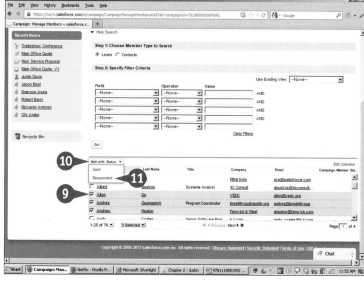

12 Salesforce displays a confirmation.

13 Click a campaign name to add the leads you selected in Step **9**.

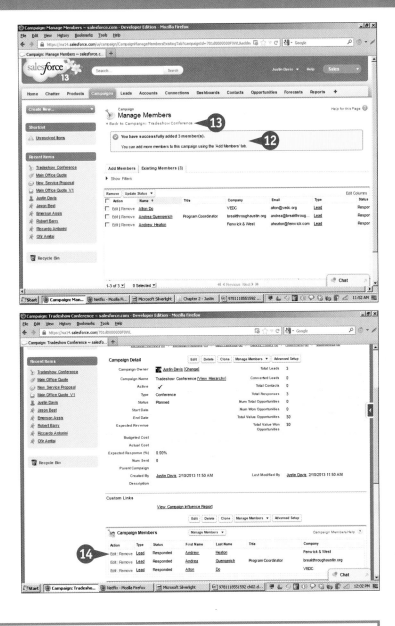

14 Salesforce adds the leads to the campaign as campaign members.

TIP

What is campaign influence?

You can enable an *influence* option in the setup area of each campaign. Influence links campaign actions so you can view all campaigns on a single contact or opportunity. For example, a prospect might receive a newsletter, an e-mail, and a cold-call as part of three separate campaigns. One campaign would be tagged the primary. The other campaigns would appear on the opportunity record under the campaign influence section.

CHAPTER 3

Using the Service Cloud

Your customer service representatives can use the Salesforce Service Cloud to manage, track, and resolve customer service issues, known as *cases*, with details stored in a special case object. Your team can create cases manually, or accept them from web forms or e-mail. You can also define assignment rules to assign cases to teams or individuals using predefined criteria.

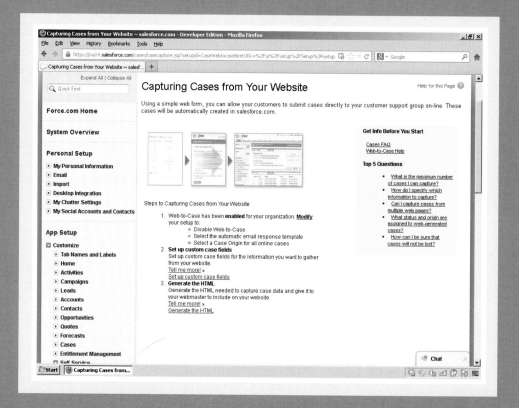

Create a New Case Record

You can create a case manually by typing details into a case record. Salesforce can also create a case record automatically when it receives an e-mail or data from a web form. Case records store information in 27 standard fields, such as status, priority, contact, subject, and description. The contact field stores contact information for the customer who logged the case. The subject and description fields hold a summary and a longer description of the problem in the customer's own words. The status field holds values such as "new," "closed," or "escalated," and the priority field describes the urgency of the case.

Create a New Case Record

1 Click the **Cases** tab.

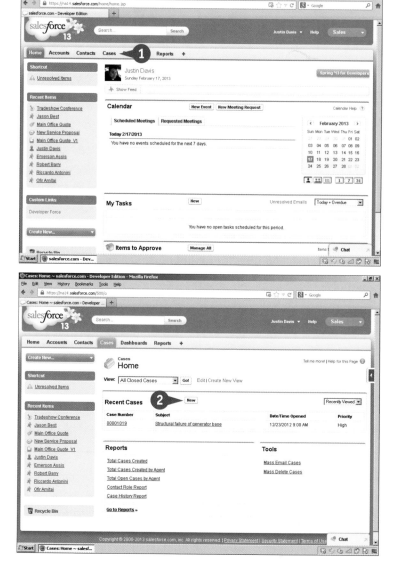

2 Click **New**.

3 Type the contact name.

4 Click **None** to open the Case Origin drop-down list.

5 Select one of the possible origins from the menu.

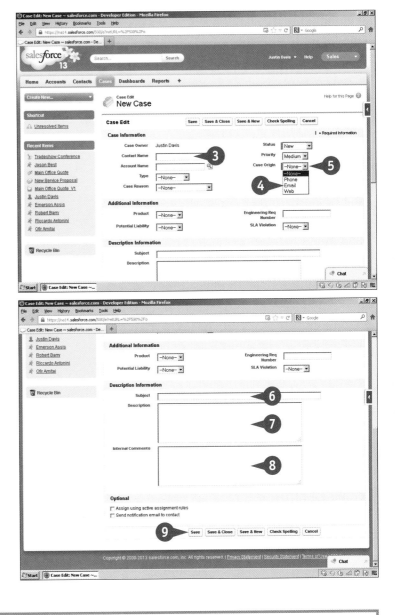

6 Type the subject of the case.

7 Type a description.

Note: Typically a customer service record uses information supplied by a customer to fill in the subject and description fields.

8 Optionally, add a comment to the **Internal Comments** field.

Note: Customer service representatives can add to the Internal Comments field as a case develops.

9 Click **Save**.

TIP

What can I do with the fields in a case record?

Salesforce generates a case number automatically. Service representatives can quote this number to a customer. The customer can quote it back during phone calls or in e-mails, and customer service staff can use it to search for the case. Note also that the staff can use the Internal Comments field to add case notes as a case progresses. Management can use the date/time opened and closed fields to generate statistics about case durations and to check the overall success rate of the service team.

Create Case Assignment Rules

Y ou can use case assignment rules to queue cases automatically or hand ownership to specific teams or representatives.

Typical applications filter cases by product, by geographical area, by time of day — assignment rules can switch between service centers automatically — or by a customer's service level agreement.

Create Case Assignment Rules

1. Click your name.

2. Click **Setup**.

3. Click the **Customize** triangle (▼).

4. Click the **Cases** ▼.

5. Click **Assignment Rules**.

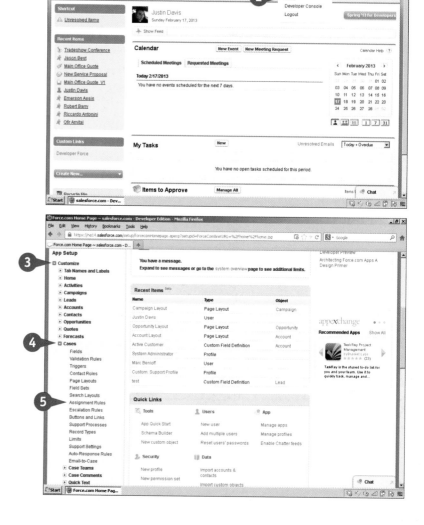

6 Click **New**.

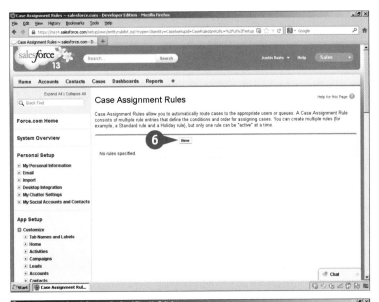

7 Type a descriptive name for the new assignment rule.

8 Check the **Set this as the active case assignment rule** check box (☐ changes to ☑).

9 Click **Save**.

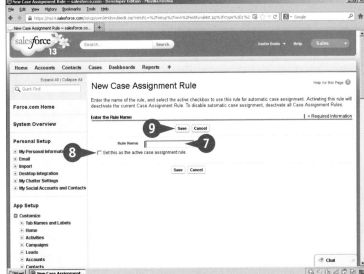

TIP

How are rule entries evaluated?
Rule entries are ordered by number, and Salesforce tries to match the criteria in order. When it finds a match, it processes that rule and stops. It does not try to evaluate rules lower down the order. So arrange rule criteria in order of importance, with the least important criteria at the bottom of the list.

continued ▶

Create Case Assignment Rules (continued)

You can use case assignment rules to dramatically improve the efficiency of your support teams. However, to get the most from this feature, organize and plan it carefully.

Before creating rules, gather requirements from at least one customer service agent, the customer service manager, and a Salesforce administrator. You can also get useful feedback by discussing possible strategies with customers. Service teams should understand the rationale behind your rule design. If possible, document your systems for customers so they understand your procedures before they log a support case.

Create Case Assignment Rules (continued)

⑩ Click the name of the rule you created.

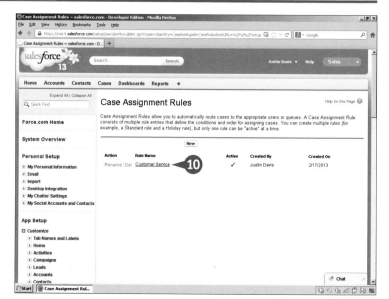

⑪ Type the number **1** in the Sort Order field.

⑫ Click **None** in the first field.

⑬ Select a field to check.

⑭ Type a value to check against.

Note: This example checks the reason for the case.

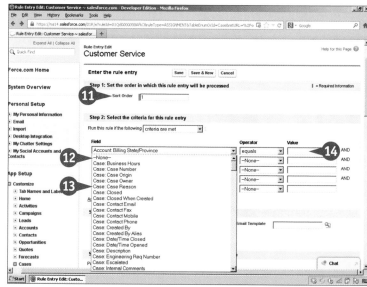

15 Type the name of a user the rule assigns the case to.

16 Type or search for the name of an e-mail template.

Note: Salesforce uses the template to send an e-mail notification to a user when it assigns a case to him or her.

17 Click **Save**.

18 Salesforce refreshes the screen and displays the new rule in the Active column.

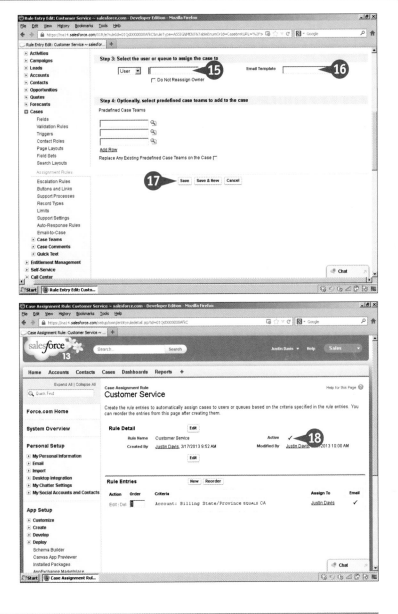

What happens if a case does not match any rule criteria?
You can force case assignment by creating a final rule with no criteria. For example, if rule entries one, two, and three check the state, product sold, and customer-service agreement, add a blank rule four that catches all other cases. Use this rule to assign the case to a default owner or queue.

How can I minimize mismatches?
Limit your staff to preset values if your rules test the content of fields such as Case Reason or Case Description. You cannot create reliable matches if you allow staff to create their own reasons and descriptions.

Create Case Escalation Rules

You can use escalation rules to prioritize cases according to severity, and to ensure that important customers get fast and effective support.

Escalation rules typically check case criticality and the time a case has been open. For example, if a customer's product fails completely, you can escalate a case automatically to prioritize support resources at the expense of minor customer issues. You can also escalate a case automatically to hand it to a customer service manager if it is not resolved within a set time.

Create Case Escalation Rules

1 Click your name.

2 Click **Setup**.

3 Click **Escalation Rules**.

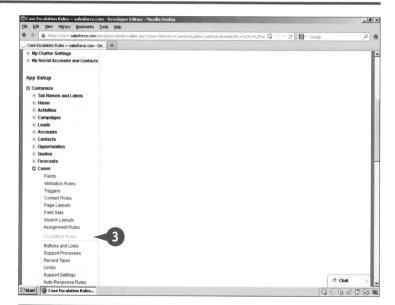

4 Type a descriptive name for the new escalation rule.

5 Click the **Set this as the active case escalation rule** check box (☐ changes to ☑).

6 Click **Save**.

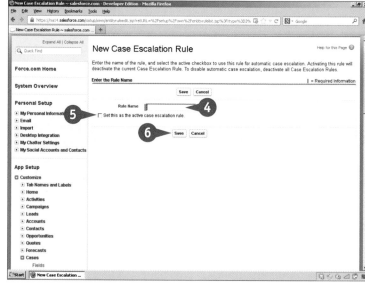

7 Click the name of the
escalation rule.

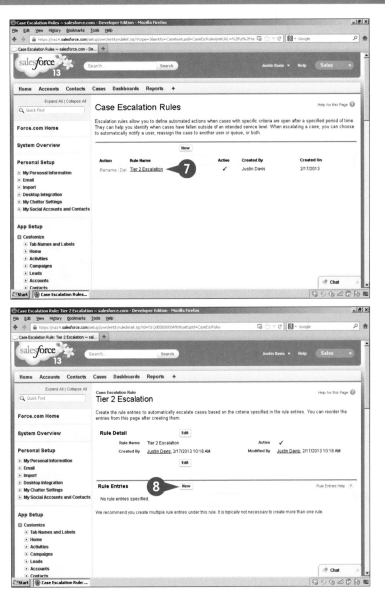

8 Click **New** in the Rule Entries
section.

TIP

What e-mail alerts are available?

For critical cases, you can use escalation rules to send an automatic e-mail alert. Options include *Notify this user*, which e-mails the person who receives the case; *Notify case owner*, which e-mails the current case owner; and *Additional Emails*, which can send a notification to a customer or to any other e-mail address inside or outside your organization.

continued ▶

Salesforce checks the escalation rules whenever your team edits a case, or when a case is assigned to a new owner. Rules are usually evaluated in order of priority.

Note that each edit counts as a separate action. If you make two related changes to a record, Salesforce evaluates each change independently.

Create Case Escalation Rules (continued)

9 Type the number **1** in the Sort Order field.

10 Click **None**.

11 Select a field to test.

12 Type a value to test against.

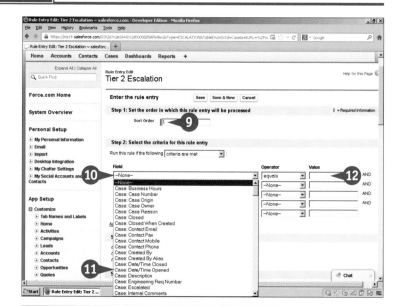

Note: This example demonstrates how to escalate a case automatically after a set period.

13 Click one of the radio buttons to select whether the rule allows escalation outside of business hours (○ changes to ⊙).

14 Click a radio button to select when Salesforce starts the clock ticking on a potential escalation (○ changes to ⊙).

15 Click **Save**.

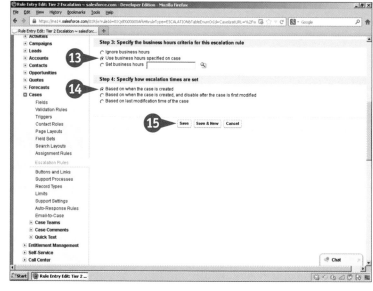

16 Click **New**.

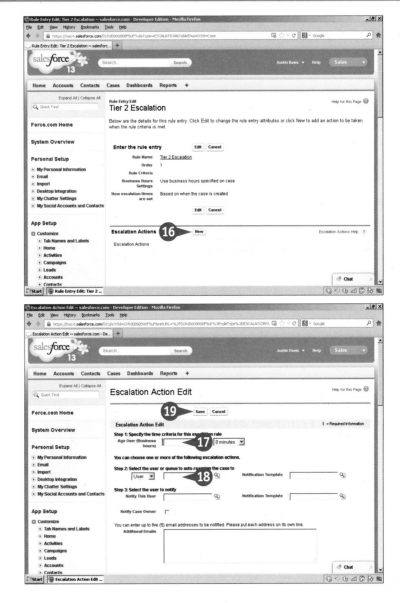

17 Enter the number of hours before Salesforce escalates the case.

18 Type the name of the user who should own this case after escalation.

19 Click **Save**.

TIP

In which order does Salesforce process rules?

Salesforce checks validation rules first, followed by assignment rules, auto-response rules, and immediate action rules. Escalation rules are checked last. You should define and create all rules together to ensure you understand the order they run in, and to check that Salesforce creates the responses you want. Note that Salesforce does not trigger escalation rules when you perform a mass transfer from a list view.

Enable Solutions

You can use solutions to give customer service agents standard fixes for common problems and issues. By default, solutions appear in plain text. You can enable an HTML option to include images and formatting information in the solution.

Enable Solutions

1 Click your name.

2 Click **Setup**.

3 Click the **Customize** ▼.

4 Click the **Solutions** ▼.

5 Click **Solution Settings**.

6 Click **Edit**.

⑦ Click the **Enable Solution Browsing** check box (☐ changes to ☑).

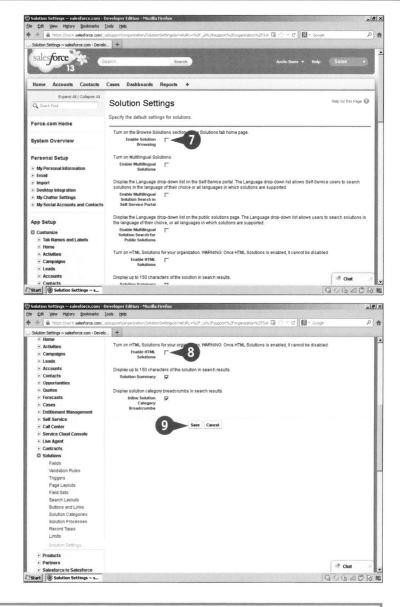

⑧ To support HTML, click the **Enable HTML Solutions** check box (☐ changes to ☑).

⑨ Click **Save**.

What is the difference between Knowledge and Solutions?
Both options include a hierarchy of records and a rich-text editor, and both can be followed in Chatter feeds. Knowledge also supports stemming and other synonyms in queries. For example, a search for "run" also returns "running" and "ran." Categories manage article access, so you can make some articles public while others remain for internal use. Knowledge also supports PDF documents, and customer service staff can e-mail them to customers. Knowledge is available as an optional feature license. Contact your salesforce.com sales executive for details.

Create a Solution

Your service managers and service staff can create solutions. However, most organizations put solutions through an approval process before making them available to others.

If you enabled HTML support in the previous section, "Enable Solutions," your staff can include links, mail to fields, FTP links, and other standard basic HTML attributes.

Create a Solution

1 Click the **Solutions** tab.

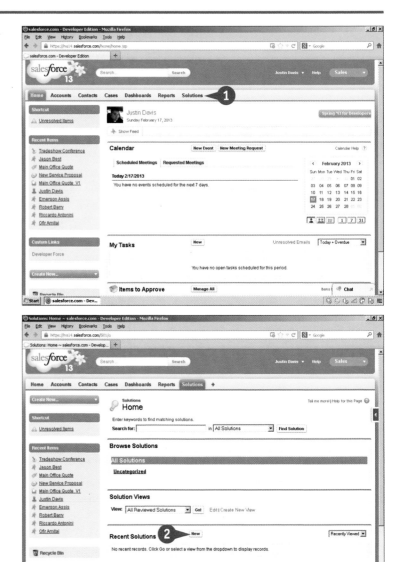

2 Click **New**.

③ Type a descriptive title for this solution.

④ Enter body text for the solution.

Note: For HTML solutions, you can use the formatting controls in the top toolbar to style text and add web links.

⑤ Click **Save**.

⑥ The solution is now active.

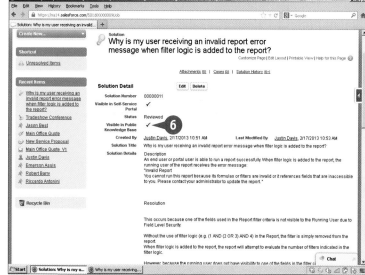

Can I support multiple languages?

Contact Salesforce support in order to have this feature enabled. Once multi-language support is enabled, you can create a translated solution by clicking **New** on the Translated Solutions list on the solution. Select a language from the list, and save the solution after you translate it.

Attach a Solution to a Case

Whenever anyone in your organization finds an effective solution to a problem, he or she can create a solution document and attach it to a case. Other users can then access the solution for similar cases. Management can also see which cases do not have solutions.

You can find a solution for a case by searching for matching terms. Solution titles that match your search terms appear higher in the search results.

Attach a Solution to a Case

1 Click the **Cases** tab.

2 Click the case number.

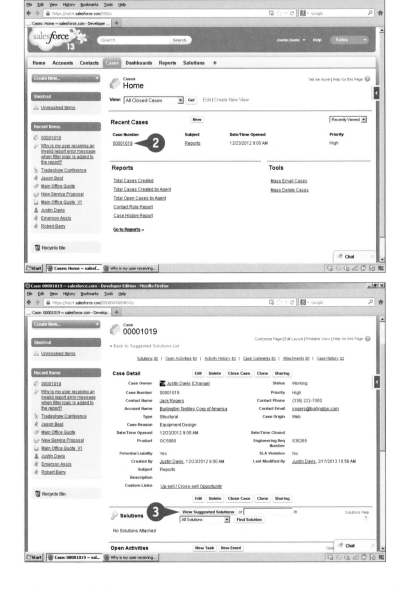

3 Click **View Suggested Solutions**.

Note: This step searches the case description and finds solutions with matching subjects and descriptions.

④ Click **Select** next to a solution to select it.

Note: This example shows one solution, but the search may return more.

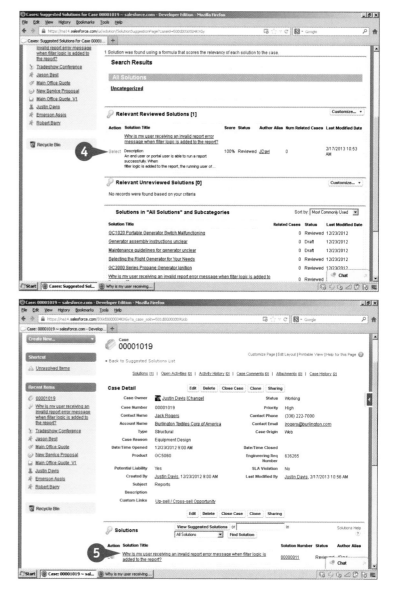

⑤ Salesforce attaches the solution to the case record.

How can I use categories to organize solutions?
To add a solution to a category, click **Select Categories** in the Solution Categories list for the solution. Your system administrator must create categories in advance. Salesforce examines categories when searching for solutions. To keep the search results relevant and focused, add solutions to no more than three categories.

Create a Web-to-Case Form

You can use a web-to-case form to automate the capture of customer issues, and to prepopulate case fields with details customers enter.

Salesforce generates web-to-case forms as HTML which you can add to any website. Optionally, you can modify the code with any HTML editor to match the styling of the web form to your usual branding.

Create a Web-to-Case Form

1 Click your name.

2 Click **Setup**.

3 Click the **Customize** ▾.

4 Click the **Self-Service** ▾.

5 Click **Web-to-Case**.

6 Click **Generate the HTML**.

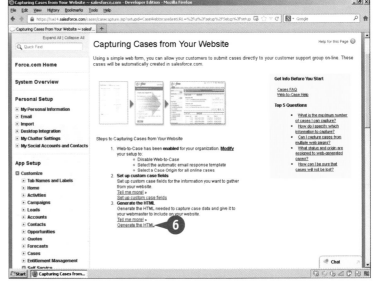

7 Select a field to include in the form.

8 Click the **Add** arrow (▶).

Note: Repeat Steps **6** and **7** to add more than one field.

9 Type the URL the user sees after he or she submits the form.

10 Click **Generate**.

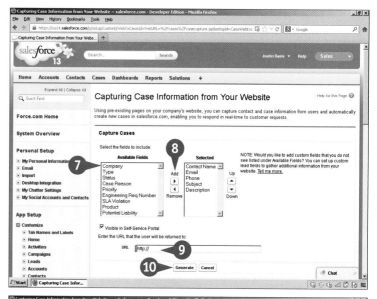

11 Copy the HTML.

Note: You can paste the code into a web editor to work on the look and feel, or you can upload it as a simple finished page on your website.

12 Click **Finished**.

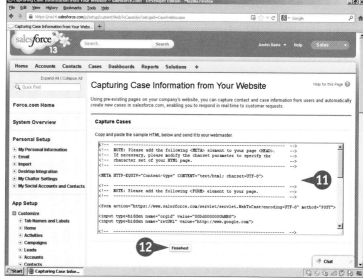

TIP

What are some important web-to-case considerations?

Web-to-case is available in the Professional, Enterprise, and Unlimited editions of Salesforce. By default, you can capture up to 5,000 cases in a 24-hour period. To increase this limit, contact Salesforce support. Cases that do not match an assignment rule remain with the default owner. When a user specifies an e-mail address, Salesforce attempts to find it in your contacts list. Note that Salesforce runs validation rules on all web submissions.

Create an Email-to-Case Address

You can use the email-to-case option to capture cases from incoming e-mails. When an e-mail is sent to a special address — you can specify more than one — Salesforce copies the e-mail subject to the case subject, and the e-mail body to the case description. Customers can use this option to submit a case with very little effort.

As with web-to-case forms, Salesforce tries to match the e-mail address of the sender the e-mail field of a contact.

Create an Email-to-Case Address

1 Click your name.

2 Click **Setup**.

3 Click the **Customize** ▣.

4 Click the **Cases** ▣.

5 Click **Email-to-Case**.

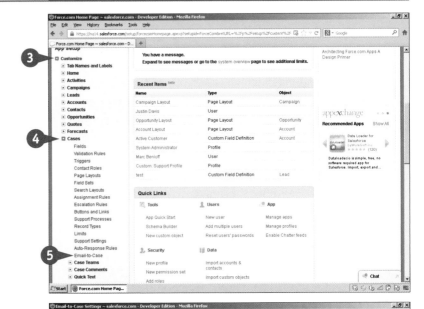

6 Click **Edit**.

Click the **Enable Email-to-Case** check box (☐ changes to ☑).

⑧ Click the **Enable HTML Email** check box (☐ changes to ☑).

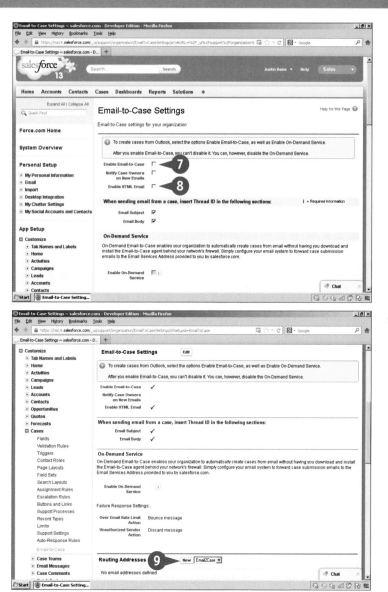

⑨ Click **New**.

TIP

Are there other ways to process inbound e-mails?
Yes. A Salesforce developer can create an Apex e-mail service in Salesforce to process any inbound e-mails. However, this option is available only to Enterprise Edition and Unlimited Edition Salesforce customers.

continued ▶

101

Create an Email-to-Case Address (continued)

Salesforce offers two types of email-to-case options. You can download and install a Java-based email-to-case agent that runs on your organization's network. The agent requires MS Exchange Server 7 or later, and supports IMAP (Internet Message Access Protocol) mailboxes. POP3 (Post Office Protocol 3) is not supported. For more information, see the email-to-case help documents by clicking the **Help & Training** link in the top right corner of your Salesforce application.

You can also set up on-demand email-to-case. This accepts e-mails at a special routing e-mail address on the Salesforce server.

Create an Email-to-Case Address (continued)

⑩ Type the routing name.

Note: The routing name is for reference only.

⑪ Type an e-mail address.

⑫ Click **Save**.

⑬ Click the **Verify** link.

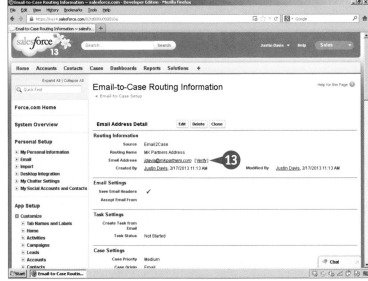

14 Click the link inside the
verification e-mail.

15 Salesforce remembers the
address you entered in Step
11 and uses it as the routing
address.

Note: When Salesforce receives
an e-mail at this address, it
creates a case automatically.

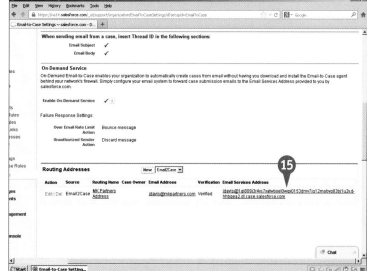

TIP

What else do I need to know about email-to-case?

On-demand email-to-case supports attachments up to 10MB. To accept larger attachments, use the email-to-case agent. On-demand email-to-case generates a verification e-mail to check that forwarding is working correctly. This option accepts up to 5,000 e-mail messages a day. If this limit is exceeded, you can set up Salesforce to bounce messages, discard them, or re-queue them.

CHAPTER 4

Using the AppExchange

Salesforce customers can install add-on applications from the AppExchange, a marketplace that has been available since 2005 and that offers more than 1,700 apps created by more than 450 partners. Any partner can publish an app and sell it, or give it away for free. Customers can also use the AppExchange to find developers and consultants for custom projects.

Introducing the AppExchange

Y ou can use the AppExchange at https://appexchange.salesforce.com to find, test-drive, and install hundreds of applications that can extend the features of your instance of Salesforce.

To help you find relevant apps, AppExchange groups them into categories: Sales, Customer Service, Marketing, IT & Administration, Human Resources, Finance, Enterprise Resource Planning, Collaboration, and Analytics.

Search on the AppExchange

By default, you use the search option to search for apps. But you can also search for consulting partners, developers, and jobs. Consulting partners can provide your business with custom solutions. They are quality certified and can provide strategic as well as technical guidance. Developers typically provide specific software solutions or specific customized features for your Salesforce instance. On the developers/consultants page, Salesforce users can browse current job listings, post a job listing, and find developers and consultants.

AppExchange Collections

The Collections area on the AppExchange groups solutions based on the size and complexity of likely buyers. The Getting Started collection displays applications designed for the initial implementation of Salesforce. Small Business apps are tailored for businesses with fewer than 20 employees. Featured Apps are selected by AppExchange staff and often include apps with good reviews and ratings. Customer Picks include those apps voted best by Salesforce customers. The Social Apps Showcase lists apps that work with social media sites such as LinkedIn and Facebook.

Collections ▲

Getting Started

Small Business

Featured Apps

Customer Picks

Social Apps Show case

AppExchange Categories

Categories on the AppExchange help identify applications by department or business processes. Sales, Customer Service, and Marketing are popular categories for their respective departments. IT & Administration, Human Resources, Finance, Enterprise Resource Planning, Collaboration, and Analytics are cross-functional applications, and are shared among departments.

Categories ▲

Sales

Customer Service

Marketing

IT & Administration

Human Resources

Finance

Enterprise Resource Planning

Collaboration

Analytics

Industry Solutions

The Industry Solutions area displays applications by industry type. For example, the Education category has apps designed for college-level institutions, and the Financial Services category includes apps geared toward insurance and securities companies. Most categories are intuitive and obvious, but a few are not. For example, apps in the Retail category are aimed more toward the e-commerce and shipping industries than brick and mortar retailers.

Industry Solutions ▲

Education

Financial Services

Government

Healthcare & Life Sciences

Manufacturing

Media

Nonprofits

Professional Services

Real Estate

Retail

Find and Select an App

You can add extra features and specialized solutions to your instance of Salesforce by installing apps from the AppExchange. To help you select apps from the hundreds that are listed on the AppExchange, use the Sort By option to sort apps by popularity, rating, release date, app name, or provider name.

Find and Select an App

1 Open a web browser and type **www.appexchange.com**.

2 Click **Popular**.

Note: You can use the other filter options that appear — rating, app name, and so on — to change the order of the apps.

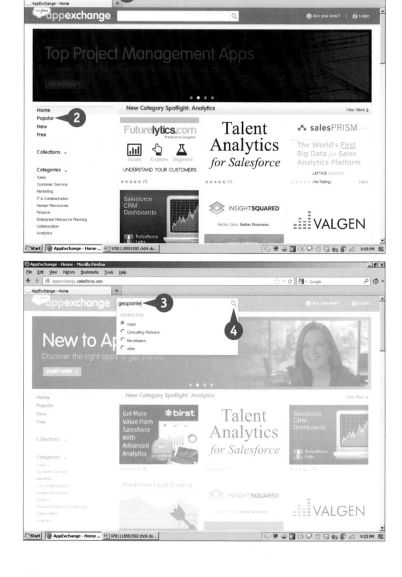

3 If you already know the name of an app, click the search box and type its name.

4 Click the magnifying glass (🔍) to search for the app.

5 To select an app for installation, click its icon.

6 Click **Get It Now** to begin installing the app.

Note: For more information, see the next section, "Install an App."

How can I find apps for my industry?

The AppExchange home page provides an Industry Solutions list in the left-hand sidebar that includes Education, Financial Services, Government, Healthcare & Life Sciences, Manufacturing, Media, Nonprofits, Professional Services, Real Estate, and Retail. Select your industry to filter the apps.

Can I install any app into my instance of Salesforce?

Each app has a Details tab on the AppExchange. Click this tab to see which Salesforce editions the app is compatible with. Always check an app's compatibility before attempting an installation.

Install an App

You can install an app in two ways. The first option is to add the app to your main Salesforce installation, and configure it to make it available to your sales team and other employees. This option is quick, but may have unwanted consequences.

If you are worried an app may break a Salesforce feature that is critical to your business, you can use the second option, known as a *sandbox installation*. In Enterprise and Unlimited editions, the Salesforce sandbox provides a safe space for testing apps, experimenting with them, and training users how to use them.

Install an App

1 Click the **Login to the AppExchange** link.

2 Type your username in the User Name field.

3 Type your password in the Password field.

4 Click **Login** to continue.

5 Click **Install in production** to make the app available to all users.

6 Click the **I have read and agree to the terms and conditions** check box (☐ changes to ☑).

7 Click **Confirm and Install!**.

How can I manage apps after installing them?

The setup area in Salesforce includes a link to *Installed Packages*. Click this link to view the apps you have installed. If your app requires licenses for individual users, a Configure Licenses link appears. Click it to set up licenses for individual users.

How easy is it to uninstall an app?

You can usually uninstall apps in less than 10 minutes. Each app has its own uninstallation instructions. Keep in mind that data created by the app will be deleted after 48 hours, and reports that use this data will display errors if the data is no longer available.

continued ▶

You can customize apps by changing their code and other elements, as long as they are *unmanaged*. This means the publisher of the app permits the Salesforce customer to potentially copy, edit, or delete the code within the app. A *managed* package, which is much more common, hides the code inside the app, making it difficult or impossible to modify or remove features. This option protects the intellectual property of the publisher and makes it difficult to steal features from the app, but it also limits the amount of customization you can perform.

You can modify any of the components of an app supplied in an unmanaged package, including labels and field names, and the code behind them. However, you may not need these options if a managed package includes all the features and elements you need.

Install an App (continued)

The Package Installation Details page appears and summarizes the product contents.

Note: You can install the Test Drive and Demo apps to try out apps before buying them. Demo versions often include a training walk-through.

8 Click **Continue**.

A dialog box appears, where you can approve third-party access requested to be used by the installed package in Salesforce.

9 Click the **Yes, grant access to these third-party web sites** check box (☐ changes to ☑).

Note: If you are concerned about security, discuss any issues with the developer or publisher before continuing.

10 Click **Continue**.

11 Click the permissions required, and then click **Next**.

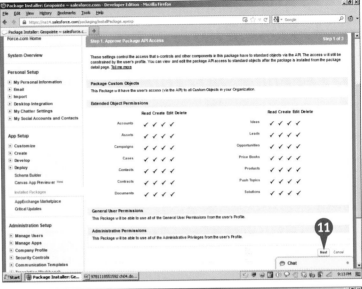

12 Click **Grant access to all users** to give all users access to the application (○ changes to ⊙).

A To limit access to administrators only, click **Grant access to admins only** (○ changes to ⊙).

13 Click **Next** to install the application.

Are free applications available?
Many apps are discounted heavily for nonprofit organizations or offered for free. Salesforce Labs is a popular publisher of free applications created by Salesforce staff. These apps are unofficial or experimental, and do not come with technical support.

Can I install more than one application?
Professional Edition has a limit of 1 installed unmanaged application, and Enterprise Edition has a limit of 25 unmanaged applications. Managed applications do not count toward your limit. Note that apps may conflict — for example, if two apps can modify opportunities, errors may appear. Contact the publisher with a list of your previously installed apps before installing the new app to ensure you will not encounter possible conflicts.

Find a Developer

You can use the AppExchange to post requests for custom development or training, or new projects that need external input.

To simplify project planning, you can specify a target budget or an hourly rate. You can also select developers by location and specify a start date. For best results, allow plenty of time before your project starts.

Find a Developer

① Open a web browser and type **www.appexchange.com**.

② Scroll to the bottom of the page and click **Find a Developer**.

③ Click **Post a Job**.

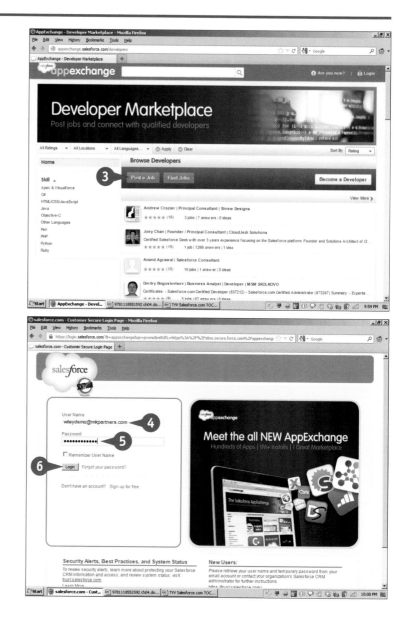

④ Type your username in the User Name field.

⑤ Type your password in the Password field.

⑥ Click **Login**.

7 In the Job Title field, type the desired name of the project.

8 In the Description field, type details of the project requirements.

Note: You can sometimes get better results by outlining the business case for your project.

9 In the Job Type drop-down list, select **Fixed Price** or **Hourly Rate**.

10 In the Budget drop-down list, select one of the available budget ranges.

11 In the Start drop-down list, select **Immediately** or define a start date.

12 In the Location drop-down list, choose **Any Location** or define a location.

13 In the Categories drop-down list, choose the category that best fits the project.

14 Click **Post Job** to post the job to the AppExchange.

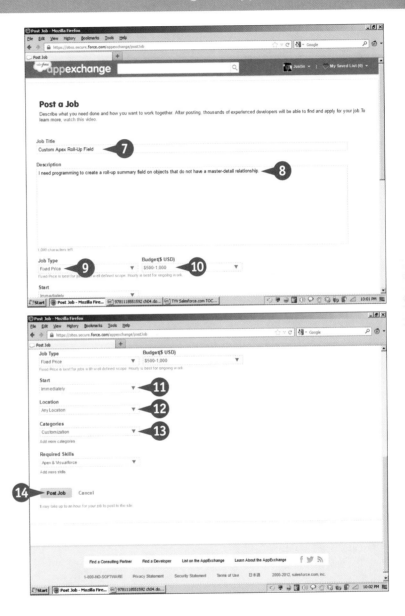

Can I work with a developer from a remote location?
Yes, some developers work remotely. Decide whether this is a possible option for your project before posting your job.

Find a Consultant

The AppExchange lists consultants who specialize in analyzing your business requirements and processes and creating a custom solution for your needs. Consultants typically provide a package that may include certified administrators, developers, sales support, and service cloud providers.

Consultants are more likely to offer full project management than smaller developers. This often costs more initially, but may save you time and money overall. Good project management is most likely to lead to a successful project with clean specifications, a tight budget, and clearly defined aims and outcomes.

Find a Consultant

1 Open a web browser and go to **www.appexchange.com**.

2 Scroll to the bottom of the page and click **Find a Consulting Partner**.

3 Select the category that most closely matches your requirements.

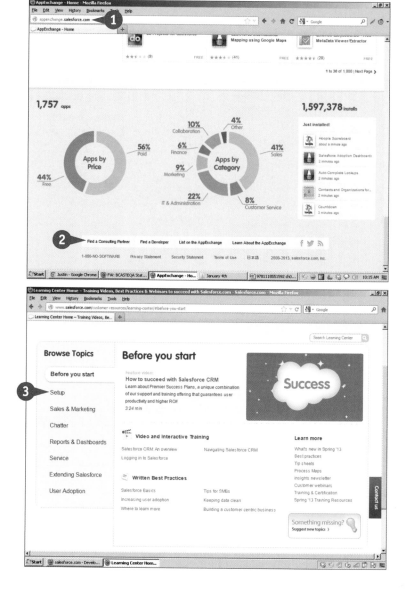

④ Select the industry that most closely matches that of your organization.

⑤ Scroll through the list of logos and select a consulting partner.

⑥ The page shows contact details for the consulting partner, including an e-mail, phone, and website.

Is the AppExchange the only way to find consulting partners?

No. Your salesforce.com account executive can also recommend a consulting partner based on your needs and location. The executive can schedule a discovery call with a consultant on your behalf after discussing your project with you. The consultant then provides a quote with a timeframe, a list of deliverables, and a cost.

How much does Salesforce consulting cost?

Consultants often supply a mix of project managers, developers, trainers, and other staff. Hourly rates vary widely, and some projects require additional costs for materials or equipment. The more detail you give your potential consultant, the more accurate the cost estimate will be.

CHAPTER 5

Configuring Reports and Dashboards

You can use reports to summarize the data in Salesforce records, and share these summaries across your organization. Dashboards display a collection of up to 20 charts, called *components*, which further summarize the data in reports.

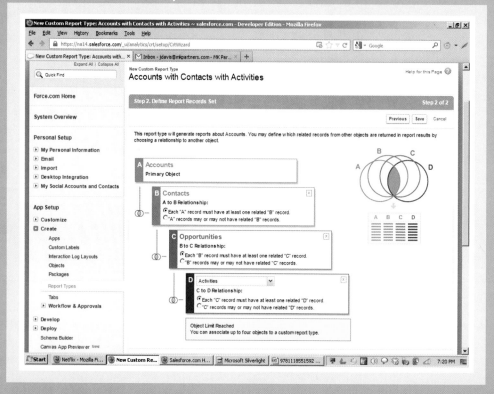

Understanding Report Formats

Y ou can view Salesforce reports in one of four formats. Users can export report data to a spreadsheet for further processing. Each format has different strengths. Select a format that displays the essential features of the data without overcomplicating it. Most of the reports created in Salesforce are summary reports; this format supports grouping and charting data, and outputting it to a dashboard, which makes it the most powerful and flexible choice.

Tabular Report

Tabular reports are the default format, and display data in a spreadsheet-like layout, with tables of numbers showing selected rows and columns of information. You cannot group the data, view it as a chart, or display it with a dashboard. However, this option displays a lot of information in a small space, and it works well for simple lists and summaries that do not require more complex graphing or analysis.

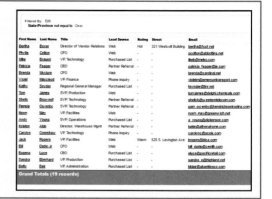

Summary Report

Summary reports are the most popular Salesforce report option. They allow charting, up to three levels of grouping on rows, and placement on dashboards. You can use summary reports to perform basic data analysis — for example, you can create subtotals for numeric and currency fields to show the total income, total possible opportunities, and conversion rate. You can also use this format to display the state of an opportunity pipeline with summaries for each opportunity owner and his or her corresponding team, or to list data from a record selected by editable criteria.

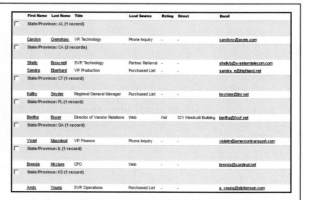

Matrix Report

Matrix reports are complex and powerful. You can group data on both rows and columns, chart fields and

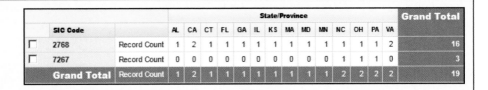

SIC Code		State/Province													Grand Total
		AL	CA	CT	FL	GA	IL	KS	MA	MD	MN	NC	OH	PA	VA	
☐ 2768	Record Count	1	2	1	1	1	1	1	1	1	1	1	1	1	2	16
☐ 7267	Record Count	0	0	0	0	0	0	0	0	0	0	1	1	1	0	3
Grand Total	Record Count	1	2	1	1	1	1	1	1	1	1	2	2	2	2	19

summaries, and display the data using dashboard components. Choose this format when you need to analyze a large collection of data and extract and summarize its key features. If you select criteria that create an empty report, a matrix report is automatically downgraded to a summary report.

Joined Report

With a *joined report* you can view two reports side by side for quick comparisons. You can also view two different summaries of the same data. The reports are independent, and there are no restrictions on which formats you select for them.

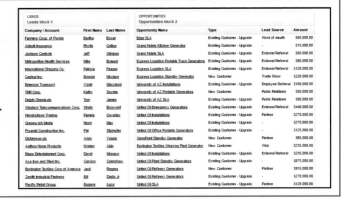

Templates and Custom Reports

Whenever you create new object relationships, Salesforce creates a set of standard *report templates* for you. You can use these templates to view useful reports with a minimum of effort. For example, you can select a template that displays parent objects but hides child records. Salesforce also supports custom report types. You can create a custom template to display records for up to four related objects.

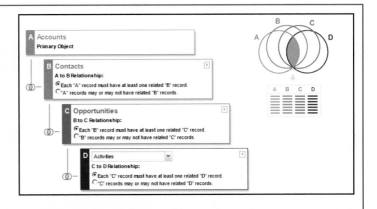

Create a Leads Report

You can use lead reports to display key information about current leads, including their number, source, status, and current owner.

Lead reports typically include some or all of the following information: the number of leads created during a given time period, the number of qualified or converted leads, the number of leads per campaign, and the number of read and unread leads assigned to each salesperson or queue.

Create a Leads Report

1 Click the **Reports** tab.

2 Click **New Report**.

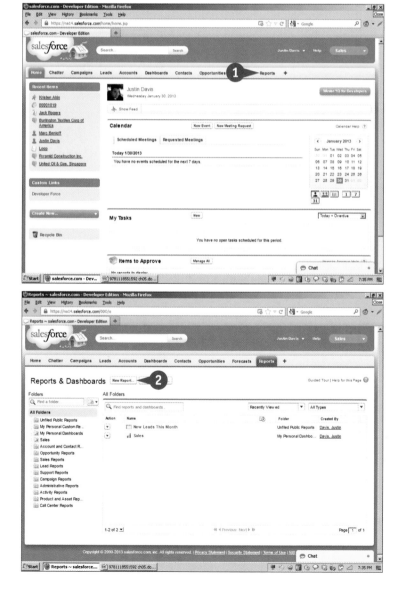

③ When you click the **Leads** +
(plus) sign (⊞), it changes
to a minus sign.

④ Click **Leads**.

⑤ Click **Create**.

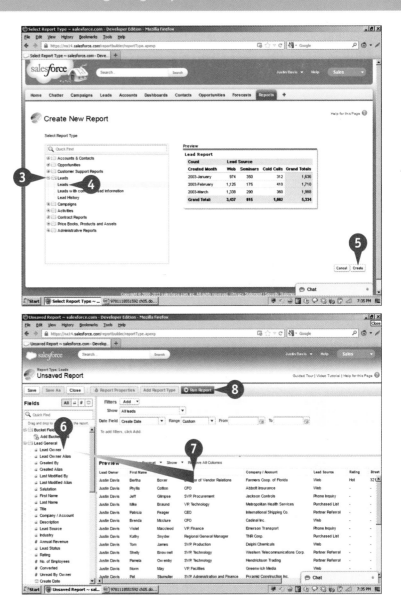

⑥ Click and hold the name of
the field you want to list in
a column in the report.

⑦ Drag the field from the
left-hand side to the Preview
area and release.

Note: You can repeat these two
steps to create more columns.

⑧ Click **Run Report**.

What is a lead history report?
If you enabled the field history option on leads, as described in Chapter 7, you can create a lead history
report. This report displays the 20 fields you selected to track. Instead of showing the current lead data, it
shows the changes made to the data, so you can see how leads have progressed through the sales pipeline.

Create a Contacts & Accounts Report

You can use a *contacts & accounts* report to view information about any account that includes a contact record. It is a quick way to view a list of contacts. You can also use this report to generate mailing list addresses, summarize active and inactive customers, view new accounts or old accounts, and summarize accounts by owner.

Create a Contacts & Accounts Report

1. Click the **Reports** tab.

2. Click **New Report**.

3. When you click the **Accounts & Contacts** + (plus) sign (⊞), it changes to a minus sign.

4. Click **Contacts & Accounts**.

5. Click **Create**.

6. Click and hold the name of the field you want to list in a column in the report.

7. Drag the field from the left-hand side to the Preview area and release.

8. Click **Run Report**.

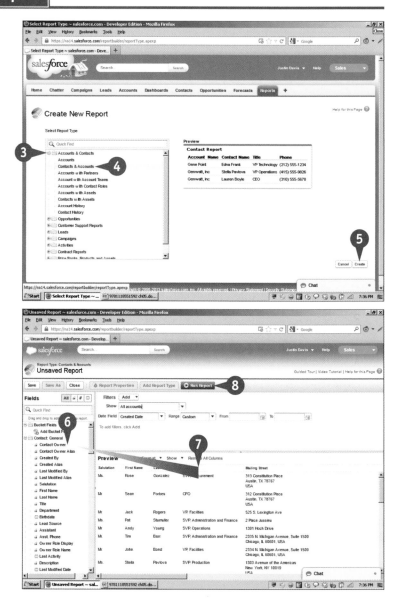

Create an Opportunity Report

You can use an *opportunity report* to display information about proposals, sales, and historical transactions. You can also view the contacts associated with each record. Opportunity reports are often used to display a sales pipeline matrix report with a list of opportunity owners and the expected close dates for their opportunities.

Create an Opportunity Report

1 Click the **Reports** tab.

2 Click **New Report**.

3 When you click the **Opportunities** + (plus) sign (⊞), it changes to a minus sign.

4 Click **Opportunities**.

5 Click **Create**.

6 Click **Current FQ** in the Range drop-down list.

7 Select a timeframe for the records from the list.

8 Click **Run Report**.

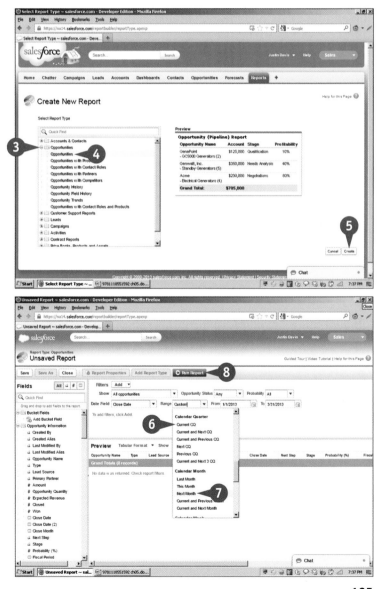

Add Leads to a Campaign

You can use reports to add leads to a campaign. This feature saves time when using bulk or imported leads. You can add up to 50,000 records to a campaign. If more than 50,000 lead records are available, the Add to Campaign button is grayed out and Salesforce alerts you that you cannot use it. You cannot add converted leads to a campaign.

The add leads feature is available for tabular, summary, and matrix reports. You cannot use it with joined reports. The feature adds leads in batches, so if you click Cancel early only some leads are added.

Add Leads to a Campaign

1 Click the **Reports** tab.

2 Click **New Report**.

3 When you click the **Leads +** (plus) sign (⊞), it changes to a minus sign.

4 Click **Leads**.

5 Click **Create**.

6 Click **Run Report**.

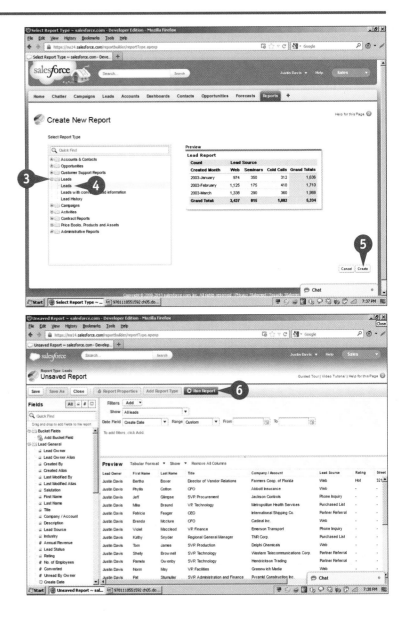

⑦ Click **Add to Campaign**.

⑧ Type the name of a campaign.

⑨ In the Member Status drop-down list, choose a default status.

⑩ Click **Add to Campaign**.

TIP

Can all users add leads to a campaign?

Only some users can work with this feature: users must be tagged as marketing users, and must have the visibility to leads marked as visible on their profile.

Create Report Charts

You can use report charts to create a graphical view of summary or matrix report data. Various standard chart options are available, including horizontal bar; horizontal bar: grouped; stacked or stacked to 100%; vertical column; vertical column: grouped; stacked or stacked to 100% line; line: grouped; cumulative or grouped cumulative; pie; donut; funnel; and scatter. Grouped charts are a good way to organize data into common categories, such as owner, territory, or product. Stacked charts are ideal for comparing chart groupings with each other. They also display a total for each group.

Create Report Charts

1. Click the **Reports** tab.
2. Click **New Report**.
3. When you click the **Leads +** (plus) sign (⊞), it changes to a minus sign.
4. Click **Leads**.
5. Click **Create**.

6. Click **Tabular Format**.
7. Click **Summary**.

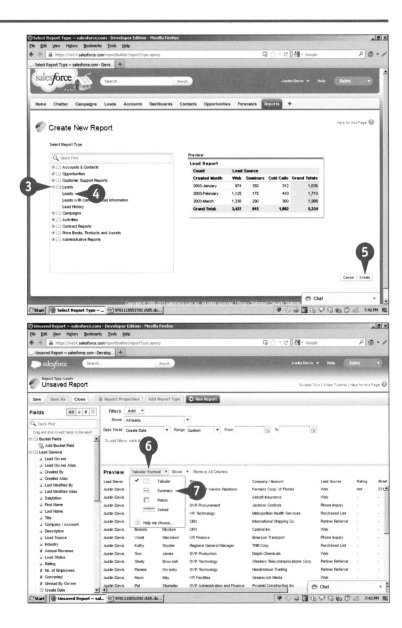

8 Click a field to select it for grouping.

9 Drag and drop this field in the Drop a field here to create a grouping area.

10 Click **Add Chart**.

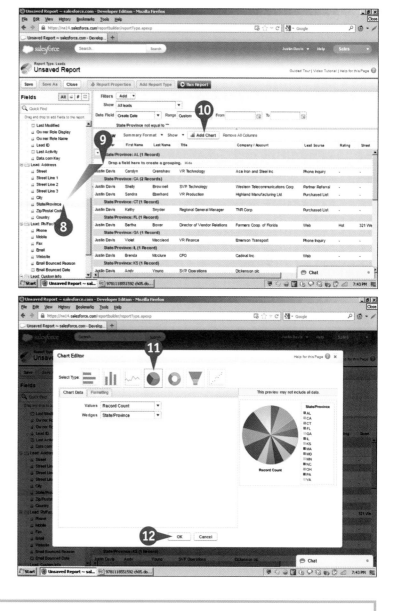

11 Select a chart type.

12 Click **OK**.

What can affect chart appearance?

You cannot display more than 250 groups or 4,000 values on a chart. Data displayed on charts depends on the numerical range of the data. One or two extreme values can completely change a chart in unexpected ways. Charts are also affected by custom summary fields and field level security settings. For example, you may lose access to a grouped field because security or project settings change. If you do, the chart displays a record count instead of the record data. For more information about field-level security, see Chapter 7.

Create a Custom Report Type

Administrators can create custom report types to customize the standard reports in Salesforce. For example, an administrator can create a new *accounts with or without contacts* report to display records with or without contact information. The administrator can set up the custom report so it always displays contact information if it is available.

Custom reports can improve productivity. You can extend and rework the standard reports and create new report types that match your internal business processes.

Create a Custom Report Type

1 Click your name.

2 Click **Setup**.

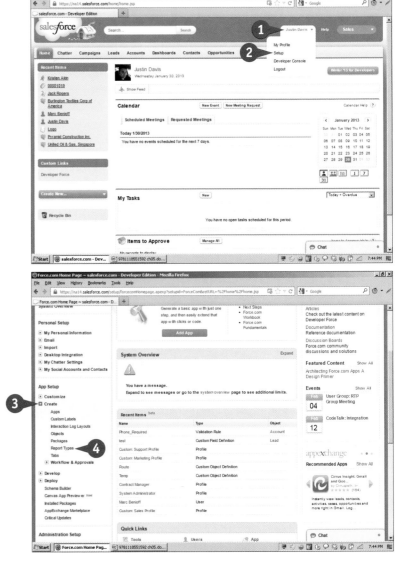

3 Click the **Create** triangle (▾).

4 Click **Report Types**.

5 Click **New Custom Report Type**.

6 In the Primary Object drop-down list, choose a primary object.

7 Type a descriptive name in the Report Type Label field.

8 Type an extended description in the Description field.

continued ▶

TIP

What happens if I delete a custom report type?
If you delete a custom report type, Salesforce deletes all reports that use it. If the custom report type appears in a dashboard, Salesforce displays an error message on the dashboard.

Create a Custom Report Type (continued)

You can select the folder in which Salesforce stores the custom report type in the Store in Category drop-down list. Typically, you select the category that matches the primary object. For example, if Accounts is the primary object, store the report in Accounts & Contacts.

Custom reports include a deployment status setting. An administrator can set the status to In Development to test a custom report type without making it available to users. If an administrator deletes the report type, users do not lose reports that rely on it. When testing is complete, an administrator can set the status to Deployed to make the report type visible to other users.

Create a Custom Report Type (continued)

9 Choose a category from the Store in Category drop-down list.

10 Select a status by clicking the **In Development** or **Deployed** option (○ changes to ◉).

11 Click **Next**.

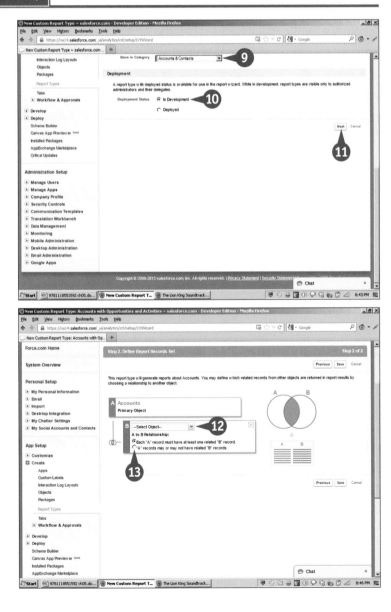

12 Choose an object from the Select Object drop-down list.

13 Click an **A to B Relationship** option (○ changes to ◉) to select whether objects must have related records.

⑭ Click the **(Click to relate another object)** box.

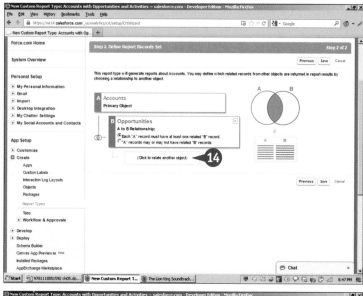

⑮ Choose another object from the Select Object drop-down list.

⑯ Click a **B to C Relationship** option (○ changes to ◉) to select whether objects must have related records.

Note: You can have up to four relationship levels in a custom report type, labeled A, B, C, and D.

⑰ Click **Save**.

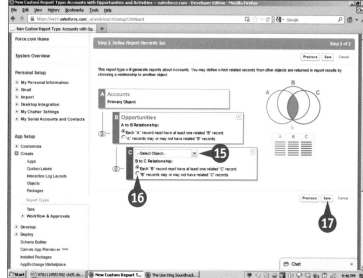

Can I create a custom report type for all objects?
Yes. Additionally, child objects must have an existing lookup field or master-detail relationship field with a parent object in order to be included in the report.

Can I create custom report types in all Salesforce editions?
Custom report types are only available in the Professional, Enterprise, and Unlimited editions of Salesforce.

Schedule Reports

In the Professional, Enterprise, and Unlimited editions of Salesforce you can schedule reports to run at set times — typically daily, weekly, or monthly. When the report runs, Salesforce sends an e-mail to the person who scheduled it, and optionally to other Salesforce users.

You can set up a total of 200 scheduled reports, and a maximum of 1 report update per hour (2 per hour for the Unlimited Edition). Report timing may not be exact; if your instance of Salesforce is very busy, reports can be delayed by up to half an hour.

Schedule Reports

1 Click the **Reports** tab.

2 Click a report to select it.

3 Click the **Run Report** drop-down arrow (▾).

4 Click **Schedule Future Runs**.

Note: You can also click **Run Report Now** to run the report immediately.

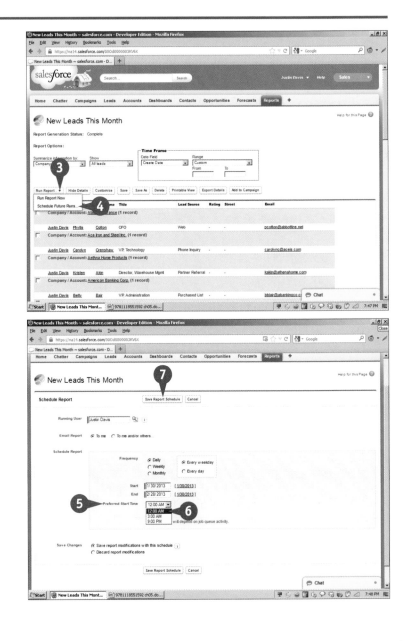

5 Click the **Preferred Start Time** drop-down list.

6 Select the desired start time.

7 Click **Save Report Schedule**.

Note: You can also use the options on this page to set a start/end date for scheduled reports, and a repeat frequency.

134

Create a Campaign Report

You can use campaign reports to summarize all your campaign data in a single report. You can include useful data such as the overall campaign ROI (return on investment); number of associated leads, contacts, or opportunities; and budgeted cost versus actual cost.

You can also use campaign reports to analyze previous campaigns, so your organization can learn from successful marketing projects.

Create a Campaign Report

1. Click the **Reports** tab.

2. Click **New Report**.

3. When you click the **Campaigns** + (plus) sign (⊞), it changes to a minus sign.

4. Click **Campaigns**.

5. Click **Create**.

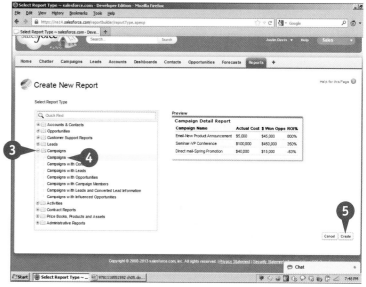

6. Type the name of the campaign in the Select campaign field.

Note: If you cannot remember the name of a campaign, click the magnifying glass (🔍) to search for it.

7. Click a field to select it.

8. Drag and drop the selected field in the Preview area.

Note: Repeat Steps 7 and 8 to add more fields.

9. Click **Run Report**.

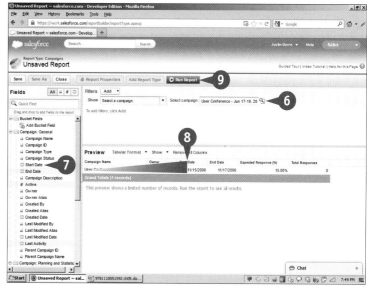

Summarize Report Data

You can use the *summarize* option to view basic statistical information in a report. Specifically, the report can calculate and display the sum and average of the numbers in a report, and the highest and lowest values.

This basic analysis is very simple, but you can use it to summarize the status of a campaign. For example, you can calculate the sum of the income amount field from all converted leads to see the total value of the campaign. Separate summaries appear for each grouping level in the report. Summary and matrix reports automatically display a grand total.

Summarize Report Data

1. Click the **Reports** tab.
2. Navigate to the desired report.
3. Click **Customize**.

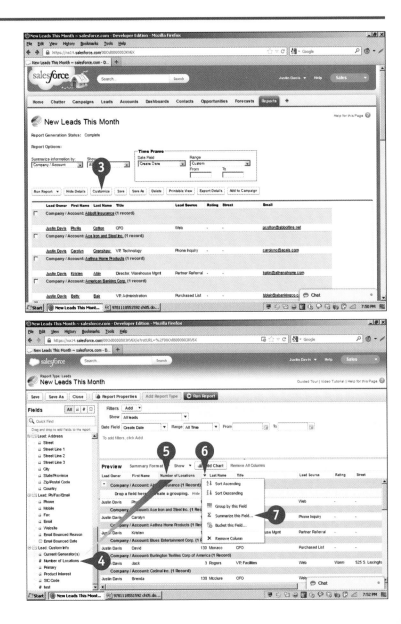

4. Click a field to select it.
5. Drag and drop the field in the Preview pane.
6. Click the field's drop-down arrow (▼).
7. Click **Summarize this Field**.

8 Click the **Sum**, **Average**, **Max**, or **Min** check box (□ changes to ☑).

9 Click **Apply**.

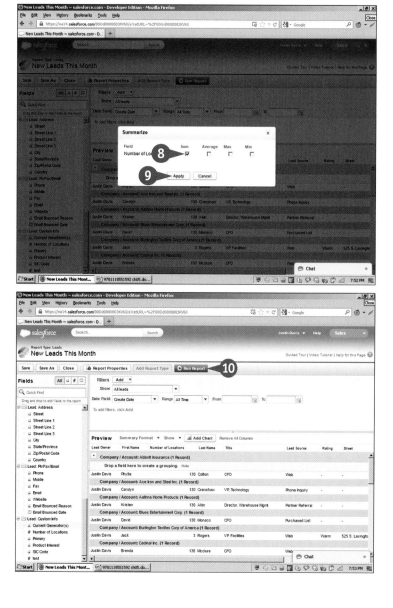

10 Click **Run Report**.

Can I use summarized fields in a dashboard?

Yes, this is a popular option. Summarized fields are ideal for a report or a dashboard chart. When you work with multiple summary fields, remember to choose the correct summary field in a dashboard chart. Otherwise a dashboard and a report may show different summary data.

Create a Joined Report

You can use a *joined report* to view data from multiple sources. You can include both standard and custom reports. Note that you can only create joined reports if Report Builder is enabled for your entire organization.

There must be a lookup field relationship between the two portions of a joined report, such as a lookup or a master-detail field. For example, if your principal report displays contacts you can also view a report that displays opportunities, because both have a relationship with accounts.

Create a Joined Report

1 Click the **Reports** tab.

2 Select a report.

3 Click **Customize**.

4 Click **Summary Format**.

5 Click **Joined**.

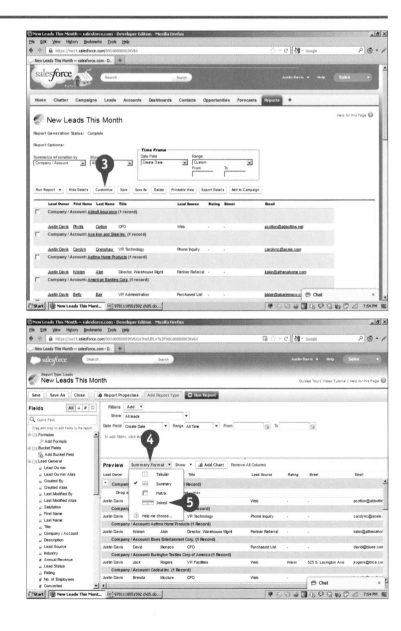

6 Click **Add Report Type**.

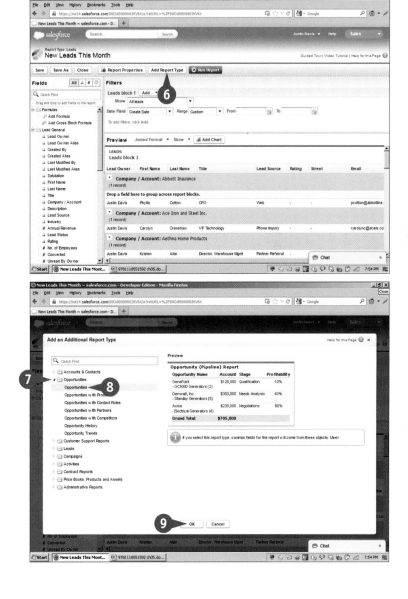

7 Click the right-pointing arrow (▷) to expand one of the main report types.

8 Click the type of report you want to add to the joined report.

9 Click **OK**.

What is a principal report?

A *principal report* is the first report you add to a joined report. For example, when you create a new opportunity report, it becomes the principal report. When a joined report has different report types, some fields may be shared by all report types. These are called *common* fields.

Export Reports to Excel

You can export any Salesforce report to a spreadsheet file, which you can then import into a spreadsheet. Two data formats are available.

The first option saves data to an XLS file with filters enabled. This format is ideal for loading the data into Excel or a compatible spreadsheet. The second option saves data to a CSV (comma-separated values) file. This format contains a simple list of values with limited formatting, and is compatible with a wider range of business software.

Export Reports to Excel

1 Click the **Reports** tab.

2 Select a report to export to Excel.

3 Click **Export Details**.

4 Click **Export**.

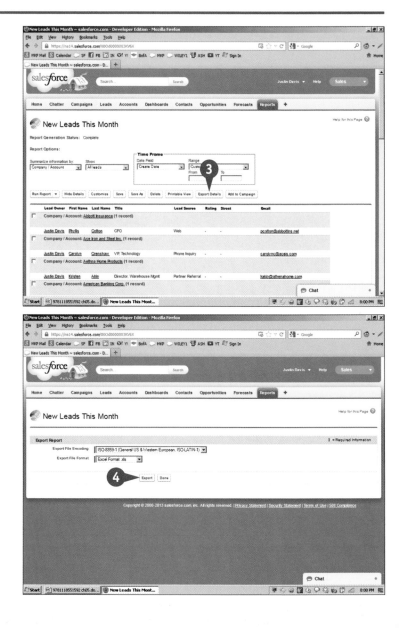

Add Grouping to Reports

When you group data, you can display related information together to communicate it more clearly. For example, when creating a new leads report, you might group the data by lead source to show the web, phone, or e-mail data for each lead. A second level of grouping might display the lead owner, and a third might display the stage of the lead. Marketing and sales teams can use a report in this format to view critical information about each lead.

Add Grouping to Reports

1 Click **Reports**.

2 Click a report to select it.

3 Click the **Summarize information by** drop-down arrow (▾).

4 Select a field for grouping.

5 Click **Run Report**.

Create a Report Formula

Y ou can add formulas to reports to perform calculations on numeric fields in an object. Create a formula by combining field formats, summary fields, basic operators, and more complex functions.

Summary fields include all available numeric fields for formulas. Operators include addition, subtraction, multiplication, division, exponentiation, and other basic mathematical operations. Functions include logical tests such as IF, AND, and OR, and numerical processing operations such as MAX and MIN.

Create a Report Formula

1. Click **Reports**.
2. Click a report to select it.
3. Click **Customize**.

4. Click **Add Formula**.
5. Drag Add Formula to the preview window.

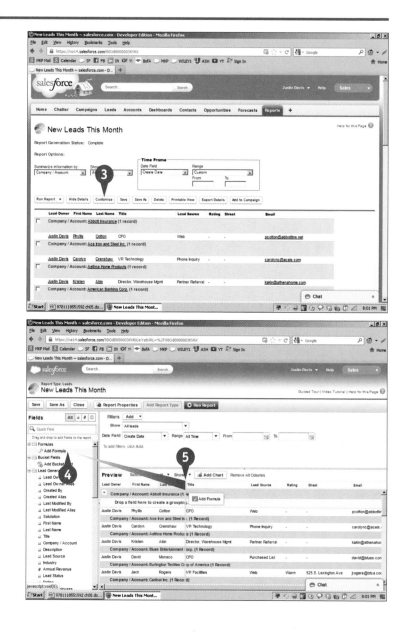

6 Type a column name for this formula.

Note: This name appears as a column header in the report.

7 Enter a formula for the column.

8 Click **OK**.

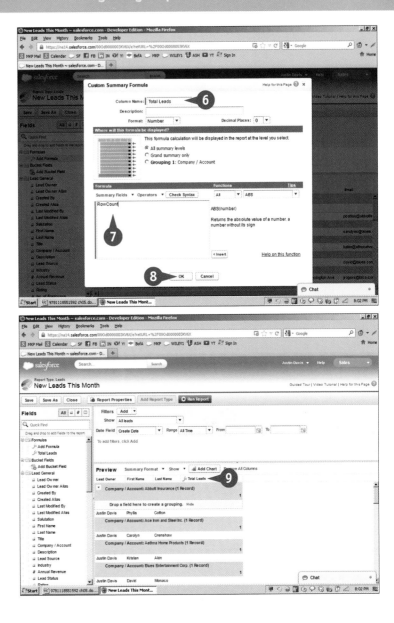

9 The formula field appears as a column on the report.

Where can I find more examples of formulas?

You can find more information in the Salesforce help documents. More advanced formula operations can perform date arithmetic, display useful percentages such as close rates, or calculate commissions automatically.

Understanding Dashboard Components

Dashboard components are charts generated from report data. You can customize the type of chart display, and control how each field appears in the chart.

Vertical Bar Components

You can use a vertical bar component to display single groupings. For example, to chart opportunities by primary campaign source, you can set up vertical bars to show the record count and graph them against campaign sources on the x-axis. Dates are another standard option; you can chart vertical bars against time on the x-axis.

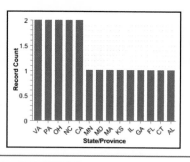

Line Components

You can use line components to show data trends. One standard option is to plot trends against time. However, you can also use line components to show a correlation between any two values in a report. Note that Salesforce does not display missing values. If a report is missing data for one point, Salesforce breaks the line.

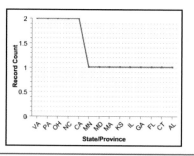

Pie Components

Use pie components to show the relationship between a proportion of pie data and a total. For example, you might create a chart showing the sources of all sales leads. The largest slice of the pie will show where the most leads come from.

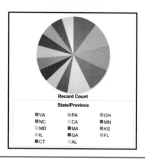

Donut Components

A donut chart is similar to a pie chart, but can also display an additional total figure in the center of the donut. Note that Salesforce donut charts cannot show multiple concentric rings.

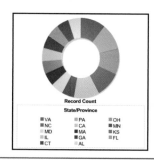

Funnel Components

You can use a funnel component to display multiple groupings and their proportions in a set of report data. For example, you might use a funnel chart to show the various opportunity stages during a campaign, in order from largest to smallest. A stage with a large area may indicate a bottleneck.

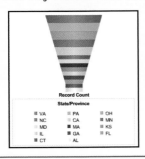

Scattered Components

Use a scatter component to show information from two groups of data, plus any related summaries. For example, you might use the scatter component to show the relationship between the average number of days to close a sale and the average number of follow-up calls logged for each opportunity.

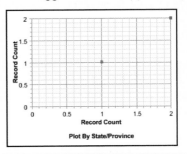

Gauge Components

Use a gauge component to display a single value on a gauge with various ranges. The *breakpoints* define the start and end of each range, and are colored different colors. Gauge components are often used to display quotas and goals, and to define acceptable and unacceptable performance for an organization, department, or individual employee.

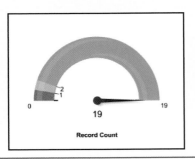

Table Component

Use a table component to show two columns of information grouped on the report. Columns can display any summary field or chart grouping, with optional second-tier groupings. For example, you can use a table to list the top ten customers based on their total purchases. This component can chart values in ascending or descending order. You can also use a metric component to display a single value.

Create a Dashboard

A *dashboard* is a collection of up to 20 components that display data from one or more reports. You can use dashboards to display report information in a clear, simple, visual format.

Each department or team in an organization can have a separate customized dashboard. For example, sales teams can have a sales dashboard showing opportunities, number of sales closed so far, and so on. A customer service dashboard can display cases and successful closure rates. And a marketing dashboard can display campaign information.

Create a Dashboard

1 Click **Reports**.

2 Click **New Dashboard**.

3 Click **Dashboard Properties**.

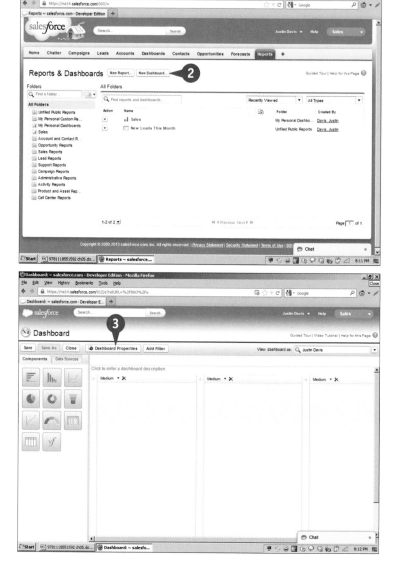

4 Type a descriptive title for
the dashboard.

5 Click **OK**.

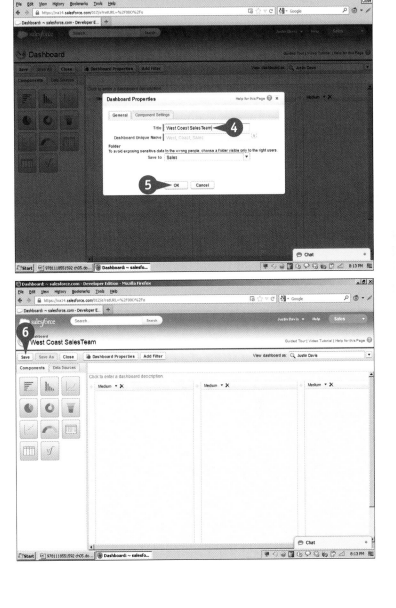

6 Click **Save**.

Refresh a Dashboard

When you create a dashboard, it displays the data that was accurate for that instant. You need to refresh a dashboard in order to view real-time information. Salesforce can refresh the dashboard automatically at a time interval you select.

Refresh a Dashboard

1. Click **Dashboards**.

2. Note the date and time it was last refreshed.

3. Click **Refresh**.

Note: A dashboard refresh can take up to a minute. If you request another refresh during this time, Salesforce ignores it.

4. The date and time are updated, and Salesforce refreshes the data on the dashboard.

Modify Columns on Dashboards

By default, dashboards have three columns. You can modify column widths and the number of columns for optimum viewing by selecting among three preset width options.

The narrow option can display all three columns on a small monitor. You can also hide the second and third column on small monitors. The medium option is the default and is a good choice for most users. The wide option stretches the charts to make them as large as possible. This option works with a large monitor. The display is too wide to fit on a smaller display.

Modify Columns on Dashboards

1 Click **Dashboards**.

2 Click **Edit**.

3 Click the drop-down arrow
(⏷) next to Medium.

4 Click either **Narrow** or **Wide**.

5 Click **Save & Close**.

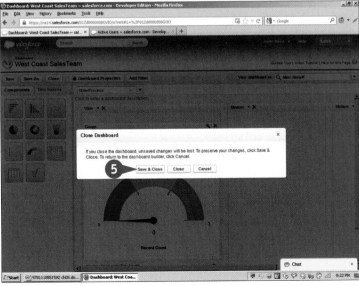

Add a Filter to a Dashboard

System administrators can add filters to dashboards for finer control over when and how data is displayed. You can use this option to customize and personalize a single dashboard across multiple teams.

For example, if your organization has four sales offices, you can create a single sales dashboard and use filters to force it to show the data relevant to each office.

Add a Filter to a Dashboard

1 Click **Dashboards**.

2 Click **Edit**.

3 Click **Add Filter**.

4 Type the name of a field to filter, or in the Field drop-down list, choose a field.

5 Choose an operator for the field.

Note: The operator controls how the filter checks each value.

6 Type a value for the operator.

Note: The value works with the operator to create a conditional test. In this example, the filter accepts records where the state is CA, and ignores records from all other states.

7 Click **OK**.

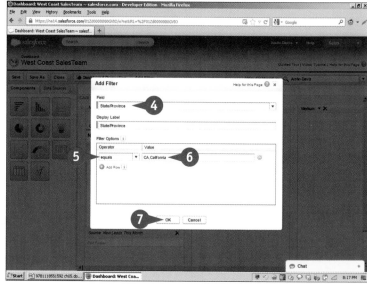

8 Click **Close**.

9 Click **Save & Close**.

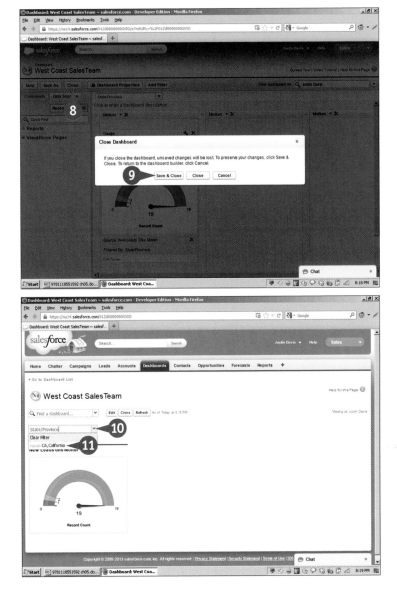

10 Click the drop-down filter (⌄).

11 Select the filter just created.

Salesforce refreshes the dashboard and displays the new filtered data.

TIP

How complex can I make filters?
You can add up to 3 filters to each dashboard. Each filter can have up to 10 options. You can increase the number of options to 50 if you request this option from Salesforce support.

Manage Access to Reports

You can control who accesses a report by saving it or moving it to a shared folder. The creator of a report can grant access to roles or public groups within Salesforce. For more information about roles and public groups, see Chapter 7.

You can make a report private by saving it to your My Personal Custom Reports folder. No other Salesforce user can view this folder. To share a report, create a special shared folder and save the report to it.

Manage Access to Reports

1. Click **Reports**.

2. Click the drop-down arrow (▼) next to the report folder you want to secure or share.

3. Click **Edit**.

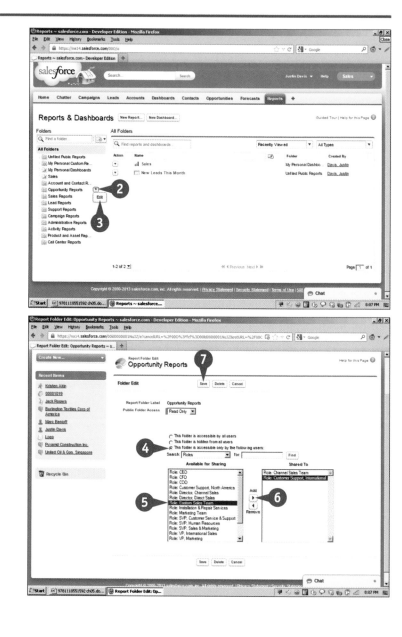

4. Click **This folder is accessible only by the following users** (○ changes to ⊙).

5. Select a role from the Available for Sharing column.

6. Click the **Add** arrow (▶) to allow that role to share the folder.

7. Click **Save**.

Schedule a Dashboard Refresh

You can schedule dashboard refreshes to keep displayed information fresh and current. After a refresh Salesforce automatically sends a formatted e-mail with a snapshot of the dashboard components. This feature can help Salesforce users who are away from the office and want to see the latest information without having to log in.

Organizations often schedule refreshes of executive dashboards at the start of each workday to give management the most recent information about customer service issue tracking and sales performance.

Schedule a Dashboard Refresh

① Click the **Dashboards** tab.

② Click the **Refresh** drop-down arrow (⏷).

③ Click **Schedule Refresh**.

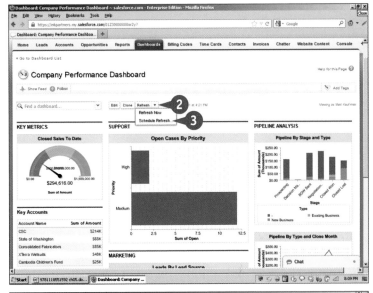

④ Choose a start time for the refresh.

⑤ Click **Save**.

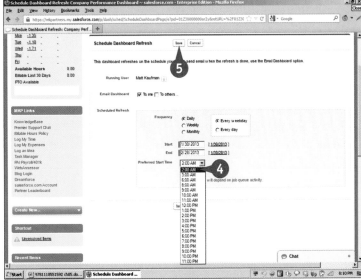

Add a Report as a Dashboard Component

You can add a summary or matrix report to a dashboard as a component. Reports can show charts. By placing these reports on a dashboard, you can show up to twenty charts on a page.

Add a Report as a Dashboard Component

1 Click the **Dashboards** tab.

2 Click **Edit**.

3 Click a chart to select it.

4 Drag and drop a report component from the sidebar.

5 Type a descriptive name into the component header area.

6 Click **Data Sources**.

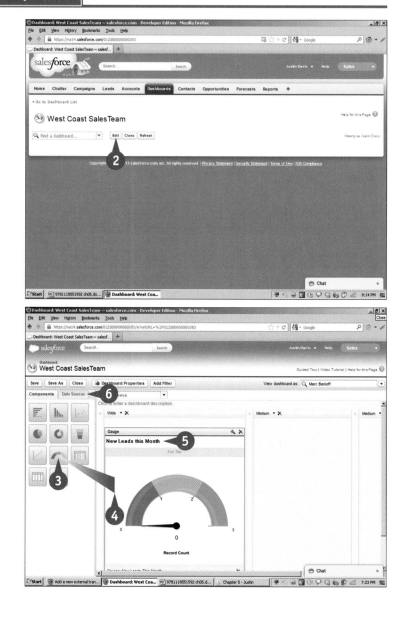

7 When you click the **Reports** + (plus) sign (⊞), it changes to a minus sign.

8 When you click the **+** (plus) sign (⊞) next to the folder with the saved report, it changes to a minus sign.

9 Drag a report from the Reports list and drop it onto the component.

10 Click **Close**.

11 Click **Save & Close**.

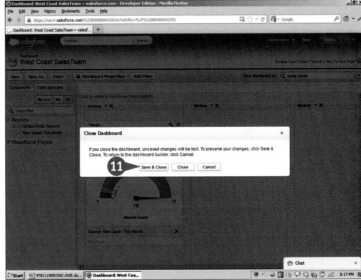

TIPS

What do the settings do?

Values select the data displayed. *Group by* determines the groupings. *Drill down* sets the page a user sees when he clicks on a component — source report is the default. *Display units* sets the value scale. *Show details on hover* shows additional data when the mouse hovers over a component. *Legend position* controls where legends and labels appear.

Are additional settings available?

Gauge charts have mandatory settings that define the value ranges displayed and their associated colors. For example, if a low numeric value represents poor performance, the low range can appear red on the gauge. If a low value suggests good performance, it can appear green or gold.

Set Up Dynamic Dashboards

Y̶ou can set up dashboards to filter data by the user's access level. For example, you can set up a manager's dashboard to show more detail than an employee's.

Only system administrators can create and configure these *dynamic dashboards*. Administrators must use the Run as specified user feature described in Chapter 7.

Set Up Dynamic Dashboards

1 Log in as an administrator and click **Dashboards**.

2 Click **Edit**.

3 Type the name of the person you are temporarily impersonating.

4 Select the name of that person from the drop-down list.

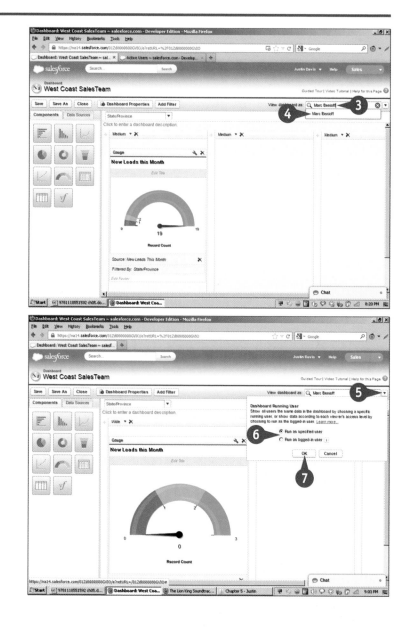

5 Click the drop-down arrow (▼) near the name.

6 Select **Run as specified user** or **Run as logged-in user** (○ changes to ◉).

7 Click **OK**.

⑧ Click **Save & Close**.

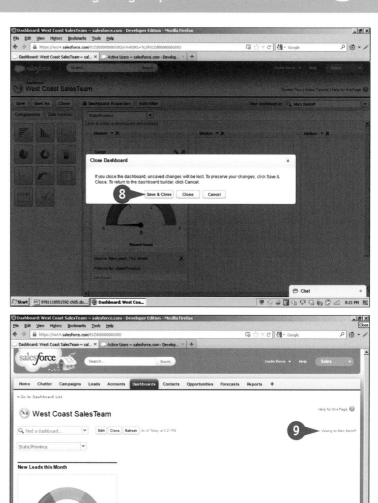

⑨ Salesforce displays the correct Viewing-as-name on the Dashboard.

TIP

What are the limitations of dynamic dashboards?

Enterprise Edition customers can have up to 5 dynamic dashboards, and Unlimited Edition customers can have up to 10. Dynamic dashboard components cannot be followed on Chatter, saved to personal folders, or scheduled for an automatic refresh.

Enable Dashboards for the iPad

By default, users cannot view dashboards on an iPad. Salesforce includes an iPad option, but you must enable it manually before it becomes active.

This option may not be available to you. If you cannot see a Mobile Dashboards option on your Setup page, contact Salesforce support to activate this feature.

Enable Dashboards for the iPad

1 Click your **Name**.

2 Click **Setup**.

3 Click the **Mobile Administration** ▼.

4 Click the **Mobile Dashboards** ▼.

5 Click **Settings**.

6 Click the **Enable the Mobile Dashboards** check box (□ changes to ☑).

7 Click **Save**.

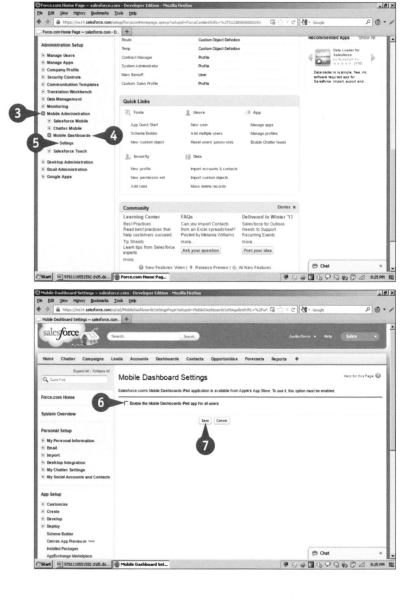

Modify Report and Dashboard Features

You can enable optional features on dashboards and reports to make them more useful. For example, you can allow users to create dashboard component snapshots they can post to Chatter.

Other options include a dashboard finder that can help users find specific dashboards; a report timeout warning that appears when a report is too large; and floating report headers that keep the headers of a report fixed near the top of a web page as you scroll down to view report data.

Modify Report and Dashboard User Features

1 Click your **Name**.

2 Click **Setup**.

3 Click the **Customize** .

4 Click the **Reports & Dashboards** .

5 Click **User Interface Settings**.

6 Click the **Enable Floating Report Headers** check box (changes to).

7 Click the **Enable Dashboard Finder** check box (changes to).

8 Click the **Enable Report Timeout Warning** check box (changes to).

Note: You can also click the **Enable Dashboard Component Snapshots** check box on this page.

Note: All options work independently. You can enable some, all, or none.

9 Click **Save**.

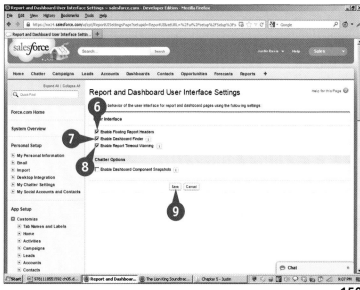

Activate the Report Builder on Profiles

You can use the Report Builder to create and edit reports more quickly. The two key features are simplified column and filter editing, and a live preview pane.

With Report Builder, you can group reports and filter them into columns. This is faster than using the usual report selection and display options. The preview pane displays changes to a report as you make them. You can preview and test changes instantly without having to wait while the report runs.

Activate the Report Builder on Profiles

1 Click your **Name**.

2 Click **Setup**.

3 Click the **Manage Users** ▾.

4 Click **Profiles**.

5 Click a profile to select it.

Note: You must enable report builder separately for each profile.

6 Click **System Permissions**.

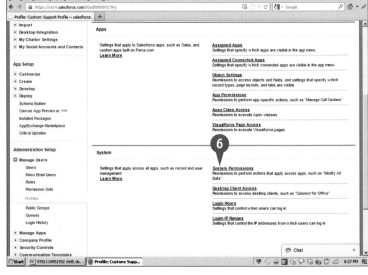

7 Click **Edit**.

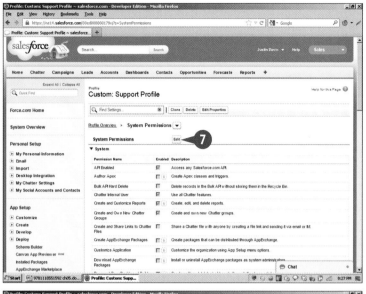

8 Click the **Report Builder** check box (☐ changes to ☑).

9 Scroll to the top of the page and click **Save**.

TIP

What if I don't see my records in the preview pane?
Report builder can select records from three areas. The *fields page* shows all available fields in a sidebar. You can drag and drop fields into a report. The *filters pane* allows you to create filters and select data by logical tests and conditions, such as value and date. The *preview pane* shows a selection of records. The preview updates when you edit your filters.

CHAPTER 6

Collaborating

Salesforce includes powerful communication tools to enhance the productivity of your organization. *Chatter* provides internal messaging and data sharing. *Libraries* store your digital documents, with optional comments, likes, and other feedback. *Salesforce-to-Salesforce* shares your data with customers and business partners who also use Salesforce. *Salesforce Mobile* supports mobile access for BlackBerry, iPhone, and Android users.

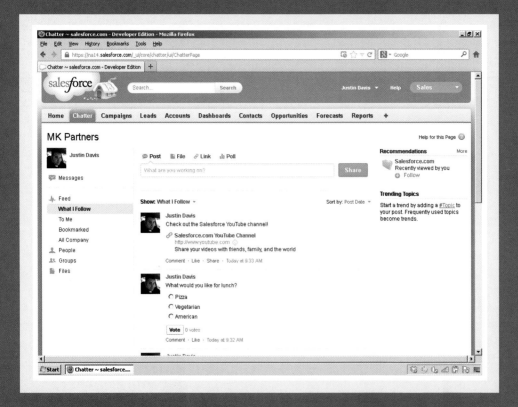

Understanding Chatter

Chatter is fundamental to collaboration in Salesforce. You can use it to exchange messages, follow records and users, share files and reports, and communicate with customers. Each Salesforce instance includes up to 5,000 free Chatter licenses.

Sidebar

The sidebar gives you quick access to the most useful features in Chatter. *Feed* displays posts, files, links, and polls. *To Me* displays posts or messages that mention you or are sent to you. *Bookmarked* displays Chatter content you have bookmarked. *All Company* displays the company Chatter feed. *People* displays other Chatter users, including other employees and customers. *Groups* help teams and projects communicate. *Files* are documents shared on Chatter. *What I Follow* displays the records and people you follow in Salesforce.

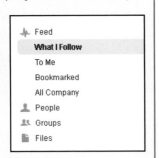

Chat

Chatter has an optional instant messaging feature called *Chat*. Conversations appear in a special chat window. Chat can display whether users are online, offline, or idle.

Messages

You can use the *Messages* feature to send private messages to other users. Messages provides many of the features e-mail does, but also supports the file- and report-sharing features built into Chatter.

Feed and Posts

The *Feed*, also known as What I Follow, provides a running list of posts, files, links, or polls in your organization. Other users can make comments on a feed, like items, or share items from a feed with other employees in your organization.

Trending Topics

Trending Topics supports Twitter-like hash tags. Users can add hash tags to feeds and posts simply by putting a hash (#) in front of any word. Salesforce automatically lists the most the popular hash tags in the Trending Topics area.

Trending Topics

Start a trend by adding a #Topic to your post. Frequently used topics become trends.

Upload a Chatter File

Chatter supports collaborative file sharing. Any user can upload a file of 2GB or less to Chatter from his or her computer or from another file area in Salesforce. Other users can then download it to view it, comment on it, or edit it.

Justin Davis
Here's the new company logo - please use this in your email signatures!
Image 005
⬇ Download png (63 KB) · More Actions ▼

Create a Chatter Poll

Chatter users can create polls for other chatter users and post them on a Chatter feed or to a specific group. One Chatter user posts a question and provides up to ten possible answers. Other Chatter users can then choose an option and click Vote on the poll. Salesforce counts the votes and displays the results.

Justin Davis
What would you like for lunch?

○ Pizza
○ Vegetarian
○ American

Vote | 0 votes

Comment · Like · Today at 9:32 AM

Create a Chatter Link

With Chatter links, users can post links to external videos, documents, or other external resources. Links can be included in a feed or shared in messages. Users can click a link to view the external resource.

Justin Davis
Check out the Salesforce YouTube channel!

🔗 **Salesforce.com YouTube Channel**
http://www.youtube.com
Share your videos with friends, family, and the world

Comment · Like · Share · Today at 9:33 AM

Enable Chatter

You can use Chatter to provide instant chat, messaging, and record-sharing capabilities across your organization. In addition to providing basic chat and messaging features, Chatter supports *following*. When users follow a record, Chatter sends a message whenever the record changes. Users can also follow other users to receive messages and other updates from them.

If your organization uses Chatter, you must enable it for all users. You cannot enable it selectively for some users but not others.

Enable Chatter

1 Click your name.

2 Click **Setup** to show the configuration area.

3 Click the **Customize** triangle (▼).

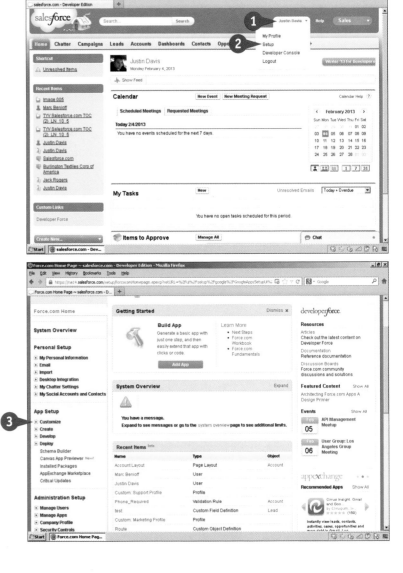

④ Click the **Chatter** ▾.

⑤ Click **Settings**.

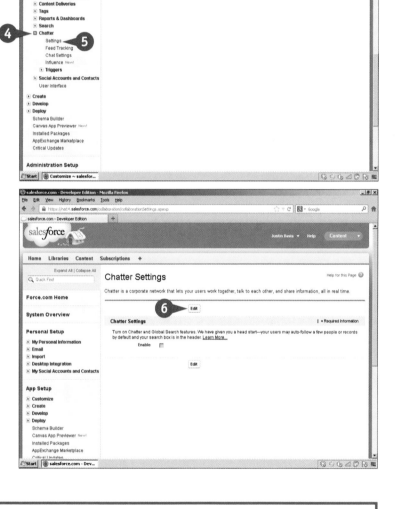

⑥ Click **Edit**.

continued ▶

Enable Chatter (continued)

I f your organization has purchased Chatter Plus licenses, you cannot downgrade those licenses to Chatter Free licenses. As a workaround, you can deactivate a Chatter Plus user and create a Chatter Free user with a different username. Note, however, that this loses the old Chatter Plus account's history.

Enable Chatter (continued)

7 Click the **Enable** check box (☐ changes to ☑).

8 Click **Save**.

9 Click **Chat Settings**.

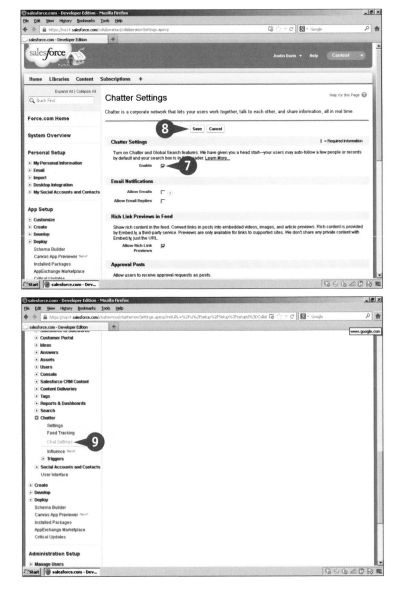

10 Click **Edit**.

11 Click the **Enable Chat** check box (☐ changes to ☑).

12 Click **Save**.

TIP

How does Chatter manage security?

Chatter respects all the security and sharing rules users create to limit access to records, files, reports, and dashboards. For example, if a user is not allowed to see leads, Chatter does not show the user lead information in his or her feed. For more information about security, see Chapter 7.

Enable Chatter Feeds on Accounts

You can include changes to account records in a Chatter feed. This is called *enabling a feed on accounts*. Users can choose the fields and edits they want to see. Chatter automatically updates a feed whenever this information changes. Chatter can also generate updates when contact and opportunity records change.

For example, you can set up Chatter to insert a message in a feed whenever the status of an account changes from inactive to active.

Enable Chatter Feeds on Accounts

1 Click your name.

2 Click **Setup** to show the configuration area.

3 Click the **Chatter** ▼.

4 Click **Feed Tracking**.

5 Click **Account**.

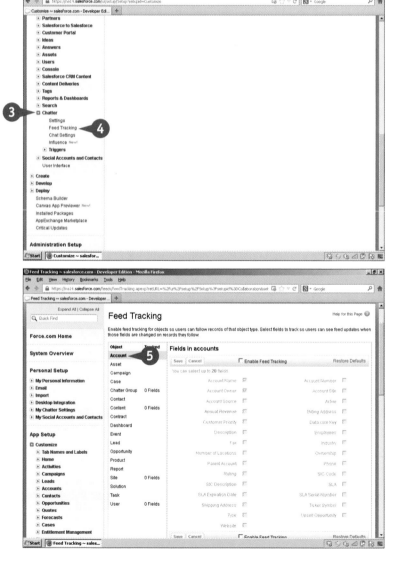

⑥ Click the **Enable Feed Tracking** check box (☐ changes to ☑).

⑦ Select fields for tracking by clicking their check boxes (☐ changes to ☑).

Note: When feed tracking is enabled and one of the selected fields changes, Salesforce posts an update to the company Chatter feed.

⑧ Click **Save**.

⑨ Salesforce displays a confirmation message.

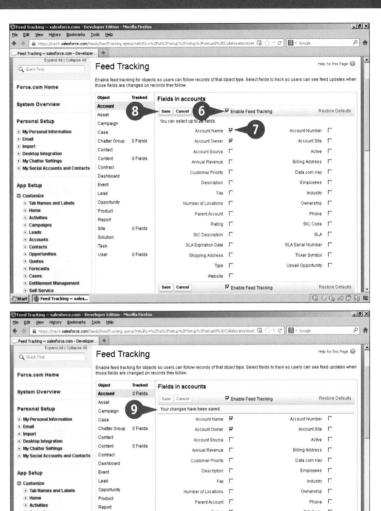

TIP

How many fields can I include in the Chatter feed?

By default, you can select up to 20 fields for tracking. You may be able to increase this limit. Contact Salesforce support for more information.

Configure Chatter Groups

You can control access to certain Chatter traffic by creating public and private groups. Public group traffic is visible to all Salesforce users in your organization. Private group traffic can only be viewed and changed by group members. To create a private group, give the group a name and choose the users who belong to it.

Configure Chatter Groups

1 Click the **Chatter** tab.

2 Click **Groups**.

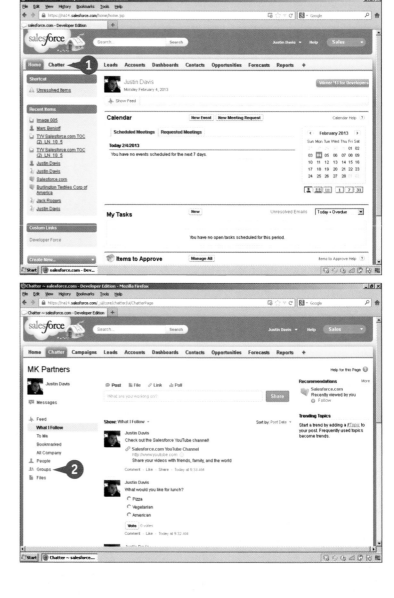

3 Click **New Group**.

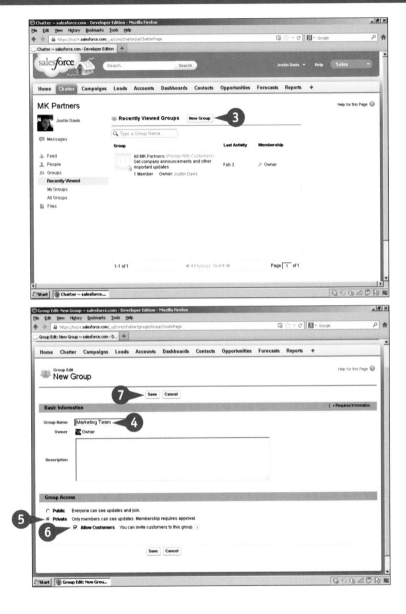

4 Type a descriptive name into the **Group Name** field.

5 Select either the **Public** or **Private** option (◌ changes to ◉) to set accessibility.

6 For a private group, click the **Allow Customers** check box (☐ changes to ☑) if you want to allow customers to join this group.

7 Click **Save**.

TIP

Can I change these settings after the group is created?
Yes. After a group is created, you become the moderator of that group. You can change the group settings at any time to manage privacy, add or remove members, and set a group photo or image.

Create a Chatter Free User

You can give your customers, resellers, distributors, and other business partners access to Chatter. Salesforce provides up to 5,000 Chatter Free licenses for customers and partners. External users can contribute to conversations, view feeds, and access the same features as employees in your organization.

External users do not have to pay for Salesforce access. When you create an account for an external user, Salesforce generates an e-mail with registration details. External users can only access Chatter if they register.

Create a Chatter Free User

1 Click the **Chatter** tab.

2 Click **Groups**.

3 Select a group to hold customers and external users.

4 Click **Invite People**.

5 Type the e-mail address of an external user in the To box.

6 Optionally, type a message in the Message box.

7 Click **Send**.

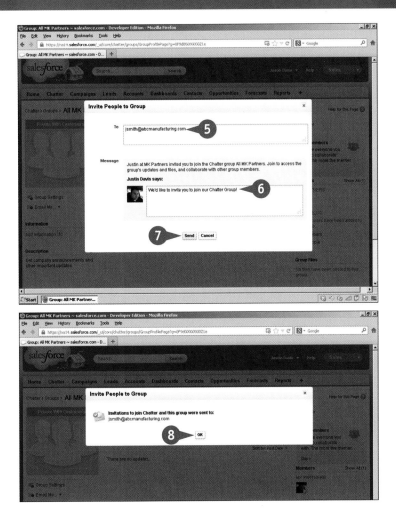

Salesforce displays a confirmation message.

8 Click **OK**.

TIPS

Can a customer see all posts and files in the group?

Yes, if a customer is invited and participates in the group, all posts and files will be accessible to that customer. It is a best practice not to create private groups for internal purposes with customers, but rather private groups specifically intended for customers, such as product feedback or a suggestions forum.

Is it possible to create more than one user at a time?

You can create multiple Chatter Free users at a time using the *data loader,* which performs a variety of mass record modifications. Create a CSV (comma-separated values) spreadsheet of user information, including first and last name, e-mail, profile, and role. Then use the *insert* function in the data loader to load the file and create the users. Afterward, return to the users area and mass reset the password for these users to force Salesforce to send them a password e-mail.

Set Up E-mail Notifications

Chatter can send an e-mail notification when you receive a private message, content appears on your feed, or a record changes. You can use this feature to receive updates from Chatter about important updates or other news.

Notifications are optional and are turned off by default. As an administrator, you must enable them before Salesforce begins generating notifications.

Set Up E-mail Notifications

1 Click your name.

2 Click **Setup**.

3 Click the **Customize** ⬜.

4 Click the **Chatter** ⬜.

5 Click **Settings**.

6 Click **Edit**.

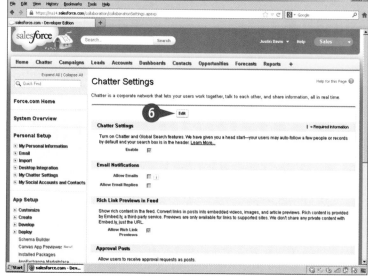

7 Click the **Allow Emails** check box
(☐ changes to ☑).

Note: This option enables notifications generated by Salesforce.

8 Click the **Allow Email Replies** check box (☐ changes to ☑).

Note: This option allows users to reply to automatic e-mails.

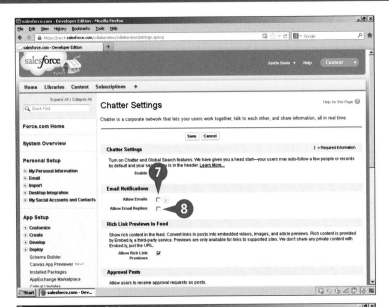

9 Click the **Allow Coworker Invitations** check box
(☐ changes to ☑).

Note: This option enables employees who do not have full Salesforce access to use Chatter.

10 Type your company domain name in the Company Email Domains field.

Note: A company domain name is usually the company e-mail address after the @.

Ⓐ If your company uses multiple domains, add them all here.

11 Click **Save**.

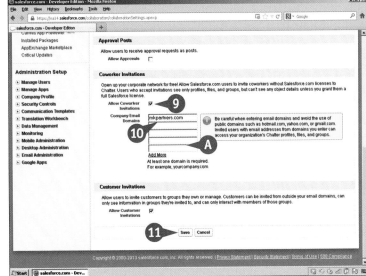

TIP

What are Chatter digest e-mails?
Digest e-mails collect updates into a single e-mail and send them together. Some users find digests more convenient than single e-mails because they appear to take less space in a user's incoming e-mail list. You can enable or disable digests, select topics, and set the digest frequency in your e-mail settings. Go to My Settings, click **Email Settings**, and then click **Chatter Email Settings** to set up digests.

Install Chatter Desktop

With Chatter Desktop, users can install Chatter directly onto their computers and use Chatter even if they do not have their web browsers open.

Chatter Desktop supports updates, comments, chat, messages, group updates, and record following. To make a post, click the **Comment** button. You can add a separate comment or simply like an item.

Install Chatter Desktop

1 Click your name.

2 Click **Setup**.

3 Click the **Desktop Integration** ▼.

4 Click **Chatter Desktop**.

5 Click **Download Now**.

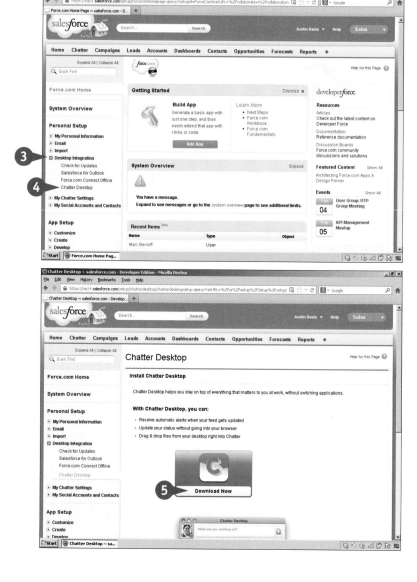

6 Click **Install** to install Chatter Desktop.

7 Click **Yes** to install Adobe Air.

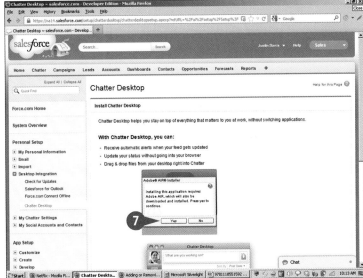

TIP

What are the minimum system requirements?

Chatter Desktop uses Adobe AIR, which runs on Windows, Mac, and 32-bit Linux. Windows computers require a 2.33GHz x86-compatible processor, or an Intel Atom 1.6GHz processor. Macs require at least an Intel Core Duo 1.83GHz, Mac OS X v 10.5, 10.6, or 10.7. Both systems require 512MB of RAM; however, 1GB is recommended.

continued ▶

To install Chatter Desktop, a user requires administrator rights on his or her machine, but not administrator rights in Salesforce. Installation includes the most recent version of Adobe Integrated Runtime (AIR). Periodically, Chatter Desktop checks for updates from Salesforce. Users must accept Adobe's end user license agreement the first time Chatter Desktop launches.

Install Chatter Desktop (continued)

8 Click **Continue**.

9 Click **I Agree**.

10 Click **Accept**.

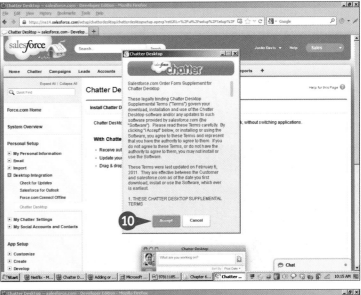

11 Type your username.

12 Type your password.

13 Click **Login**.

Note: Click the **Remember User Name** check box (☐ changes to ☑) to save your name so you do not have to retype it.

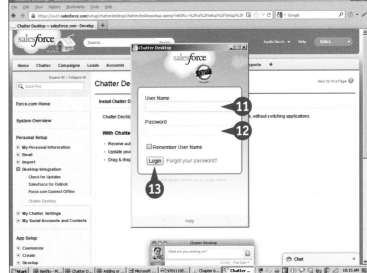

TIP

Is there a managed version of Chatter Desktop?
Salesforce does provide a one-point installer for enterprise deployment. However, computers must have Adobe Air installed. See the Salesforce help documents for more information. One-point installation does not check for updates, and does not post automatically to Chatter.

Enable Salesforce-to-Salesforce

With Salesforce-to-Salesforce, your organization can share records with other Salesforce users — typically your customers, resellers, or distributors.

Shared records can include leads, contacts, accounts, cases, and opportunities. Note that only system administrators can enable and manage Salesforce-to-Salesforce.

Enable Salesforce-to-Salesforce

1 Click your name.

2 Click **Setup**.

3 Click the **Customize** ▢.

4 Click the **Salesforce to Salesforce** ▢.

5 Click **Settings**.

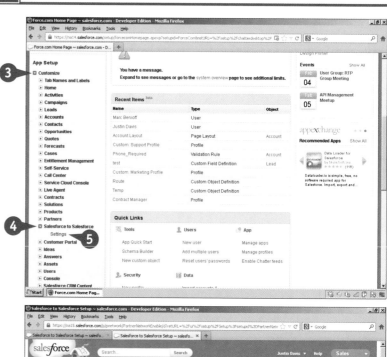

6 Click **Edit**.

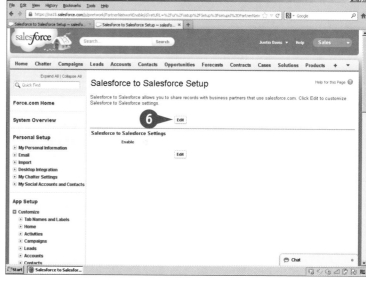

⑦ Click the **Enable** check box
(☐ changes to ☑).

⑧ Click **Save**.

⑨ Type the name of the desired
Invitation Template.

Note: The Invitation Template
and other templates on this page
define the messages that
Salesforce-to-Salesforce users
send to each other to accept or
reject sharing requests.

⑩ Click **Save**.

TIP

What are some common uses of Salesforce-to-Salesforce?
Organizations can access records from a single location; integrate business processes; view a sales pipeline across all channels; extend workflow, monitoring, and approval processes across organizations; and find out more about the performance and status of partner programs.

Configure Salesforce-to-Salesforce

After enabling Salesforce-to-Salesforce, you must configure it. You can change the e-mail addresses and message templates that define what Salesforce sends to other Salesforce customers when you create an invitation, accept or refuse an invitation, or update your Salesforce-to-Salesforce profile.

Configure Salesforce-to-Salesforce

1 Click the + (plus) sign (**+**).

2 Click **Customize My Tabs**.

③ Click **Connections** in the Available Tabs column.

④ Click the **Add** arrow ().

⑤ Click **Save**.

⑥ Click the **Connections** tab.

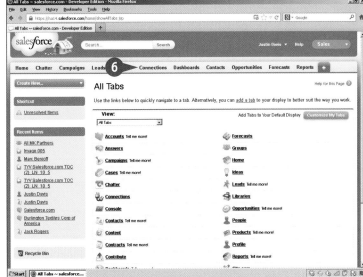

TIP

What are templates?

Templates are standard form e-mails. To view and edit templates, click **Personal Setup**, click **Email**, and then click **My Templates**. You can customize templates to change the text and links embedded in them. You can also create styled HTML (Hypertext Markup Language) templates, with images and other extra content. Most e-mail readers display HTML correctly. But for the best possible compatibility and to minimize wasted bandwidth, use text templates when you can.

continued ▶

Y ou can control which objects your partner organizations can access. In Salesforce, shared objects are *published*. You can select which objects are published for each external connection. Recipients must *subscribe* to a record before they can access it.

Configure Salesforce-to-Salesforce (continued)

7 Click **New**.

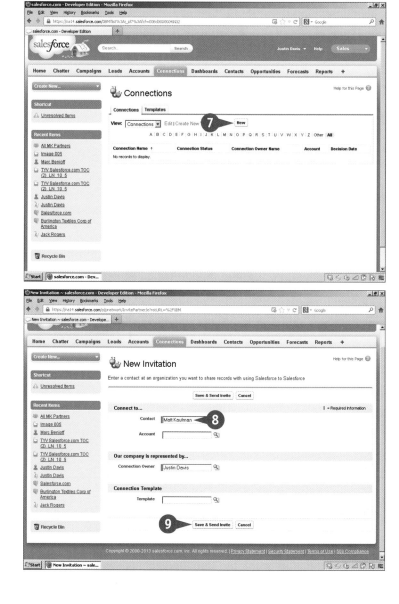

8 Type the name of a contact you wish to invite.

9 Click **Save & Send Invite**.

⑩ Click **Publish/Unpublish**.

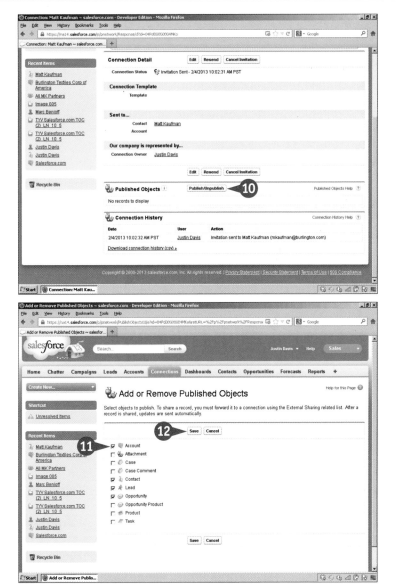

⑪ Click the check boxes next to the objects you want to share with this partner (☐ changes to ☑).

⑫ Click **Save**.

TIP

Should I publish all objects?

You should publish as few objects as possible, but enough to give partner organizations the information they need to run their business processes. For example, if you are sharing information with a reseller, you may want to publish leads and opportunities. If you are communicating with an outsourced call center, publish contacts and support cases, but not sales or marketing records.

Share an Account

After you enable and configure Salesforce-to-Salesforce, users can share records manually by selecting them from an external sharing list. An administrator must add the list to the user page layouts before users can share the records.

Shared records include a header that displays the status of the record and whether it is active, pending, or inactive. This information shows local users whether external users can access the information.

Share an Account

1 Click the **Accounts** tab.

2 Click the name of an account you wish to share.

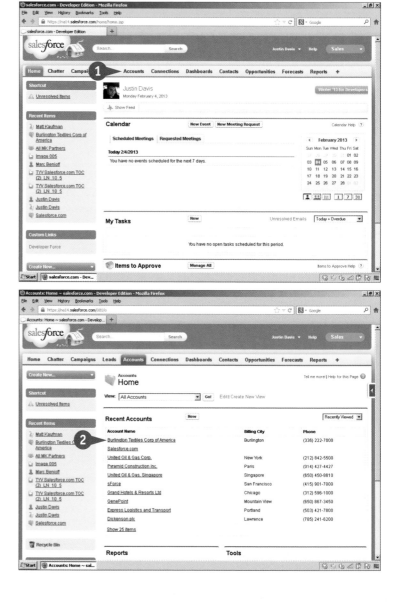

3 Click **Edit Layout**.

4 Click **Related Lists**.

5 Click **External Sharing**.

6 Drag and drop **External Sharing** down to the list area.

Note: You can add the External Sharing list above or below Contacts, Opportunities, and the other lists in this area.

Note: Most users drop External Sharing below the other items.

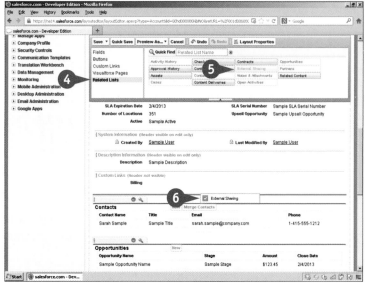

TIP

Can I see the changes a connection makes to a shared record?
Yes. When a connection changes a record, the change is sent immediately to your instance of Salesforce. To view a list of changes, enable field history for that record. You can then view a list of changes at the bottom of the record. You can also generate a field history report that shows the original and modified values for each change.

continued ▶

If your Salesforce-to-Salesforce connection is used for customer service applications, you can set up Salesforce to automatically assign a case to a connected partner. The partner must subscribe to the relevant records and set up a case queue for them. You can also share cases, escalations, and case assignment rules.

Share an Account (continued)

7 Click **Save**.

8 In the Overwrite Users'
Related List Customizations?
dialog box that appears,
click **Yes**.

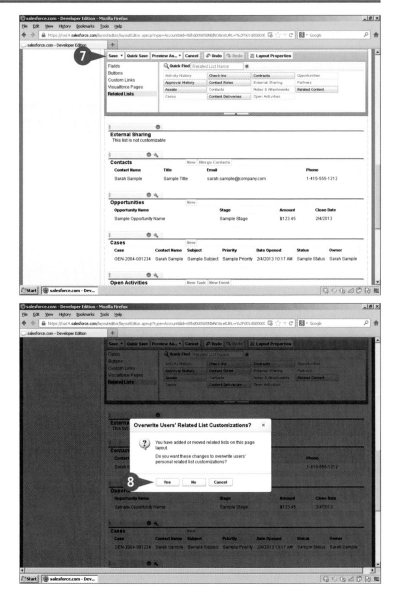

9 Click **Forward this Account**.

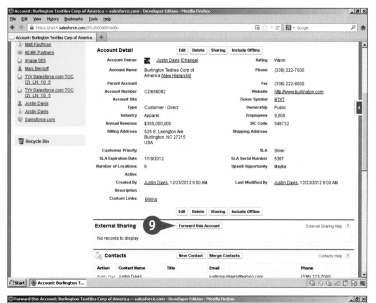

10 Click an available connection to select it.

11 Click the **Add** arrow (▶).

12 Click **Save**.

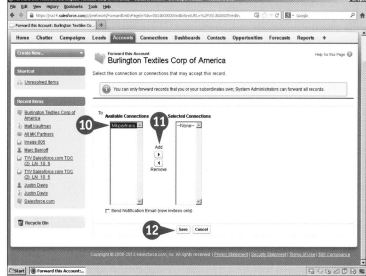

TIP

Can I share more than one record at a time?
No. You can only share one record at a time. However, you can share that record with more than one external organization. Any other organization that subscribes to an object can receive records if you share them manually or automatically.

Accept a Connection

When you enable Salesforce-to-Salesforce, you can create and receive connections from your partners. Whenever either party tries to create a connection, Salesforce sends an invitation message to the other party using an invitation template.

The other party must accept the invitation to complete the connection. Both parties can then publish and subscribe to records to share them.

Accept a Connection

① Click the link in the invitation e-mail.

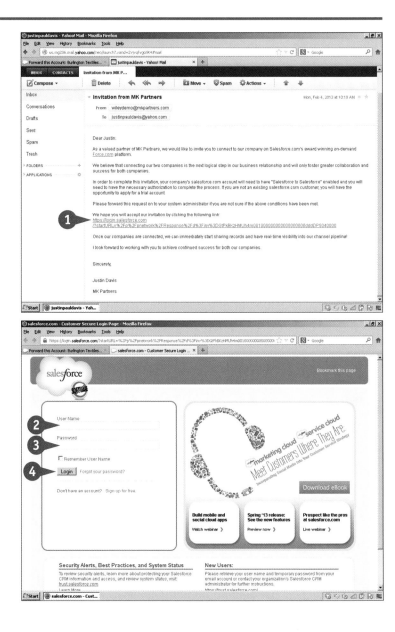

Salesforce displays a login page.

② Type your username.

③ Type your password.

④ Click **Login**.

5 Click **Accept** to accept the connection.

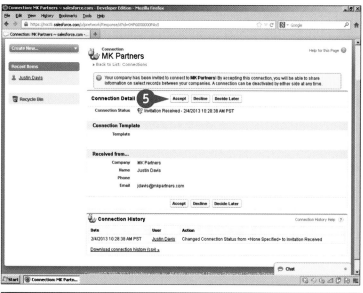

6 Salesforce displays a confirmation message.

7 Click **Subscribe/Unsubscribe** to begin sharing objects.

TIPS

How are workflow rules affected by connections?

Workflow rules can be triggered on shared records. Your organization must subscribe to all fields that trigger a rule, and the owner of the received record must be its parent.

How are validation rules affected by shared records?

If you accept shared records that do not meet the criteria defined in your current validation rules, you can exclude them from validation by adding an extra rule. Test if the Received Connection Name is null. This option enforces the rest of a validation rule only if there is no connection on that record.

continued ▶

Accept a Connection (continued)

You can share records you subscribe to with further instances of Salesforce to create a multilevel network. This feature is especially useful in supply-chain management. Information can propagate through the entire network automatically, keeping all levels updated.

For example, if a retailer purchases a computer from a reseller, both organizations can receive a shared order record from the manufacturer of the computer. Meanwhile the manufacturer can keep track of sales from all resellers automatically.

Accept a Connection (continued)

8 Click the **Account** drop-down arrow (⏷) and choose **None**.

9 Select an object to share.

10 Click **Save**.

11 Click **Publish/Unpublish**.

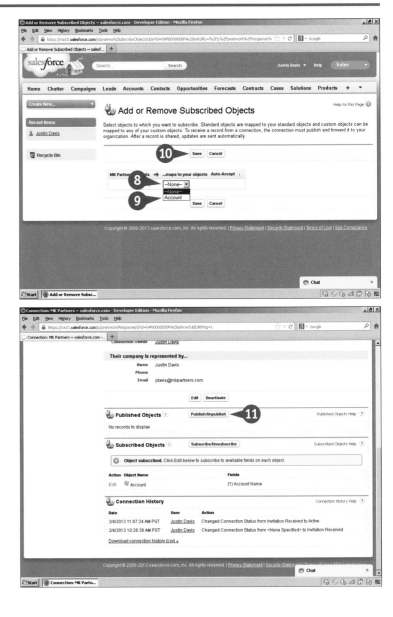

⑫ To create a two-way sync, click the check boxes for the object or objects you selected in Step **9** (☐ changes to ☑).

⑬ Click **Save**.

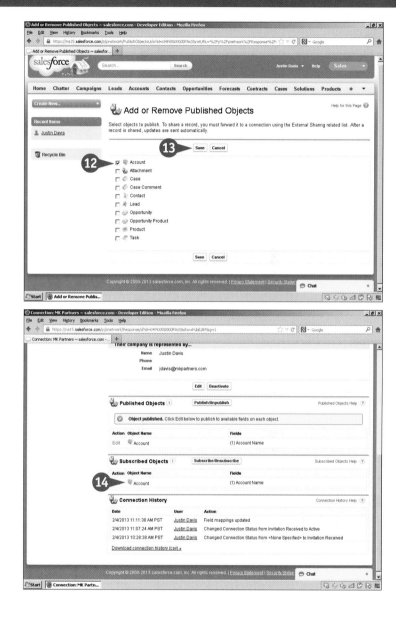

⑭ Salesforce displays the shared objects in both the Published Objects and Subscribed Objects lists.

TIP

How are attachments handled on shared records?

Attachments on records are automatically shared. If you do not want to share attachments — for example, if they contain sensitive information or are very large files — you can disable this option by deselecting the **Share With Connections** check box on any record (☑ changes to ☐).

Enable Ideas

Salesforce *Ideas* provide an internal forum for posting suggestions for product ideas and improvements, or for holding more open-ended conversations about business processes and strategy. The Ideas forums are ideal for discussing long-term projects, suggesting new projects, or managing internal company issues such as vacation times. For short-term conversations and debates, use Chatter polls.

Enable Ideas

1 Click your name.

2 Click **Setup**.

3 Click the **Customize** ▾.

4 Click the **Ideas** ▾.

5 Click **Settings**.

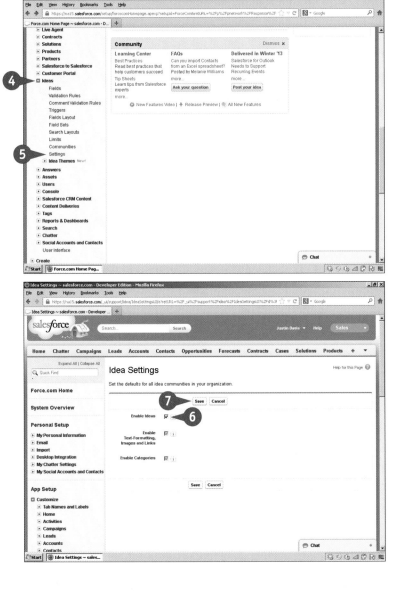

6 Click the **Enable Ideas** check box (☐ changes to ☑).

7 Click **Save**.

8 Click **Communities**.

9 Click **New**.

continued ▶

TIP

How can I work with duplicate Ideas?

Salesforce provides a merge option to manage duplicate Ideas. Click the title of the idea you wish to merge. Click the **Find Duplicates** button to search for similar or duplicate ideas. Select the ideas you want to merge. Click **Merge with Current Idea**. You can only merge ideas within the same community.

Salesforce *communities* are available to users of Professional, Enterprise, and Unlimited editions. In communities, questions are organized into logical groups to provide a focus for conversations.

By default, you can have up to 50 communities within Salesforce. (Professional Edition users are limited to one community.) You can increase this limit by contacting Salesforce support.

Enable Ideas (continued)

10 Type a descriptive name for the community.

11 Click **Save**.

12 Click **Fields**.

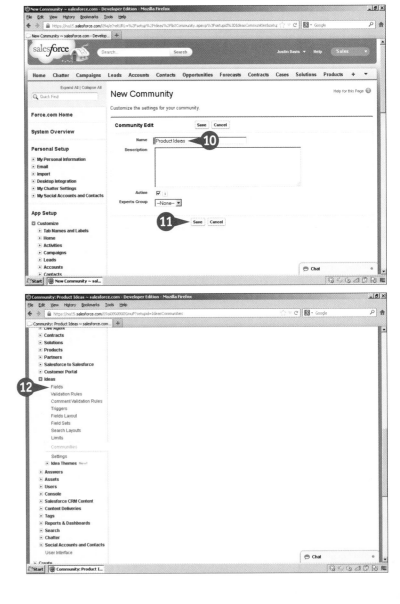

13 Click **Status**.

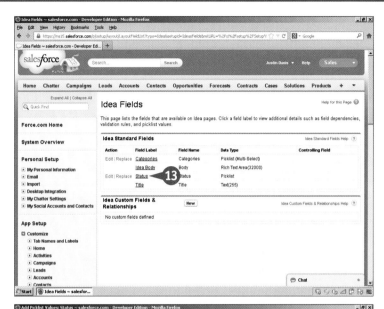

14 Type a list of possible statuses for each community.

15 Click the check box next to each community to add the new status options to it (☐ changes to ☑).

16 Click **Save**.

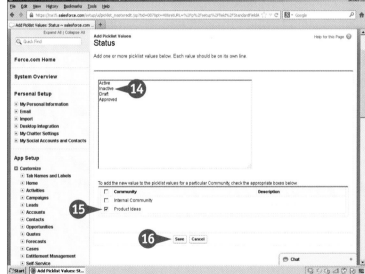

TIP

Can my customers or partners participate in Ideas?
Yes. You can include Ideas in your customer and partner portals. Your administrator must add the Ideas tab to these portals. Customers and partners can then view and comment on ideas. You can use this option to obtain feedback from partners and customers about new products or services.

Configure Ideas Themes

You can use *themes* in Ideas to organize discussions into topics, such as new product names, new office design choices, or technical purchasing decisions.

Themes make discussions more productive and focused. Posts made to themes can include pictures and videos.

Configure Idea Themes

1 Click your name.

2 Click **Setup**.

3 Click the **Ideas** 🔽.

4 Click the **Ideas Themes** 🔽.

5 Click **Settings**.

6 Click **Edit**.

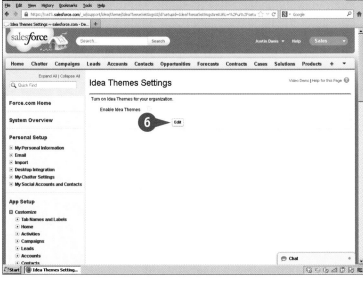

7 Click the **Enable Idea Themes** check box (☐ changes to ☑).

8 Click **Save**.

9 Click **OK** to enable themes.

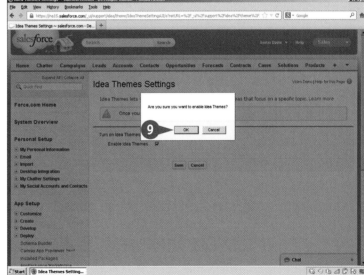

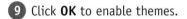

TIP

How do I manage themes?

When a theme is active, you can edit, delete, filter, and otherwise moderate any idea within the theme. You can also create custom list views based on themes for faster access to specific ideas and communities. Users need to have Read permission for idea themes and Create permission for ideas in order to manage them.

Enable Social Contacts

You can use the Social Accounts and Contacts feature in Salesforce to track social media posts from your leads, accounts, and contacts. Salesforce reads information from LinkedIn, Twitter, Facebook, YouTube, and Klout and displays posts as a *combined feed*.

Social Accounts and Contacts is enabled automatically for all new Salesforce customers as of Spring 2012. Customers with earlier versions of Salesforce can enable this feature by following the steps in this section.

Enable Social Contacts

1 Click your name.

2 Click **Setup**.

3 Click the **My Social Accounts and Contacts** ▼.

4 Click **Settings**.

5 Click the **Use Social Accounts and Contacts** check box (☐ changes to ☑).

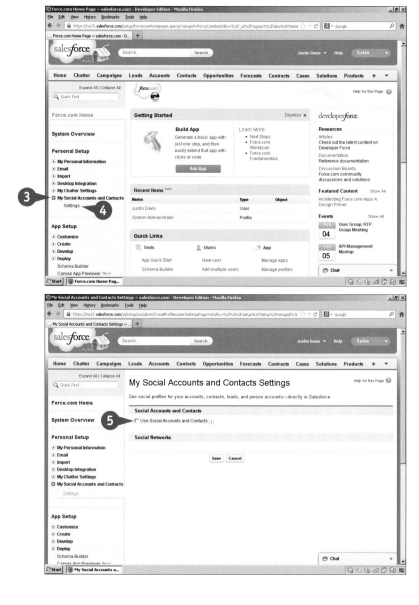

6 Select or deselect boxes to choose the social media feeds you want to see (□ changes to ☑ or vice versa).

7 Click **Save**.

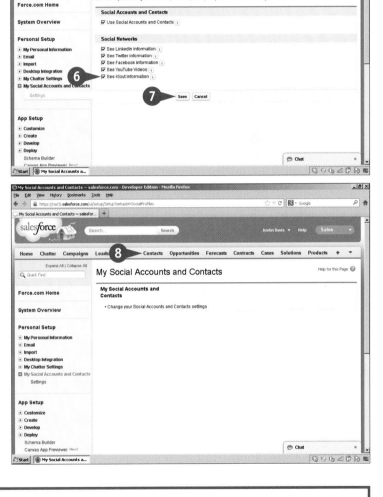

8 Click the **Contacts** tab.

continued ▶

TIP

Do I need social media accounts to use Social Contacts?
Yes, you must have an account on each of the services you want to use. After you log in to your accounts, Salesforce asks for permission to access your profile. Salesforce then pulls information from your accounts into the the Social Contacts feature. You must stay logged in to your social media accounts while you use this feature.

Enable Social Contacts (continued)

Social Contacts displays different information from different services. LinkedIn displays current title, profile photos, and location. Twitter displays bios, recent tweets, and the people following your contact. Facebook data includes your business customers' company profile and wall posts. YouTube displays related videos. Klout displays your contacts' influence on social media, such as who they influence and the topics they discuss.

Enable Social Contacts (continued)

9 Click the name of a contact.

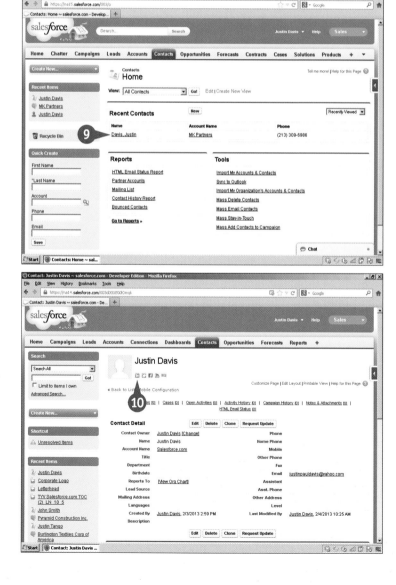

10 Click a social media icon to set up login details.

Note: This example sets up a feed from LinkedIn.

11 Click **Sign in to LinkedIn**.

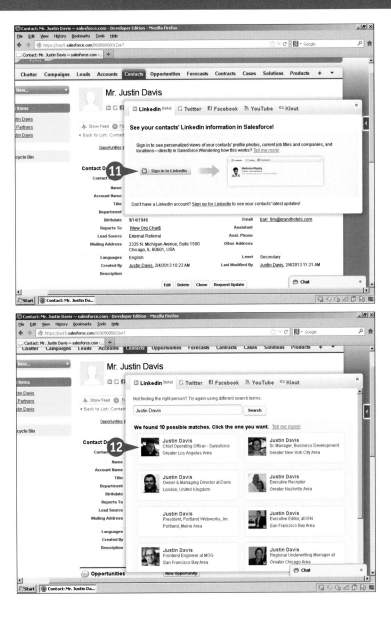

12 If more than one contact appears, click one to select his or her feed.

TIP

Which editions of Salesforce include Social Accounts and Contacts?

Social leads are available in every edition except Contact Manager. All Salesforce customers with business accounts have access, except for users of database.com. Salesforce customers using personal accounts have access in the Enterprise and Unlimited editions of Salesforce.

Enable Libraries and Content

You can use Salesforce Content to organize, share, and search digital content. Salesforce Content uses *libraries* to collect documents into useful categories, such as marketing, sales, or customer service. You can search libraries to find content. Salesforce searches inside documents to give you more useful search results. Content is available in all editions of Salesforce.

Enable Libraries and Content

1 Click your name.

2 Click **Setup**.

3 Click the **Customize** 🔽.

4 Click the **Salesforce CRM Content** 🔽.

5 Click **Settings**.

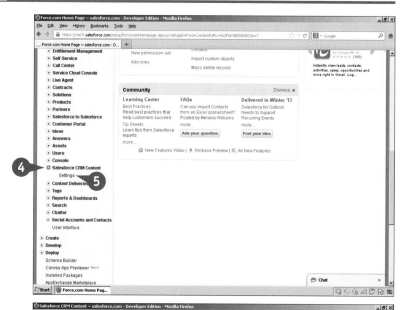

6 Click **Edit**.

7 Click the **Enable Salesforce CRM Content** check box (☐ changes to ☑).

8 Click the check boxes to set options for Salesforce CRM Content (☐ changes to ☑).

9 Click **Save**.

TIP

Can Google docs be uploaded to Salesforce Content?
Yes. You can associate Google docs with Content to maintain them in one repository. Your users can then add feedback to Google docs. Click the **Add Google Doc** button in the Libraries tab to create a new Google document. Share the document with other Google Apps users via the Google Apps security options.

continued ▶

Like standard and custom objects, Content records can have custom fields and validation rules. You can use custom fields to create relationships between Content objects and other objects. For example, you can create a lookup field in Content to link a document with a campaign record. To manage custom fields, choose **Setup**, **Customize**, **Salesforce**, **CRM Content**, and **Fields**.

Enable Libraries and Content (continued)

⑩ Click the **Sales** drop-down list.

⑪ Click **Content**.

⑫ Click the **Libraries** tab.

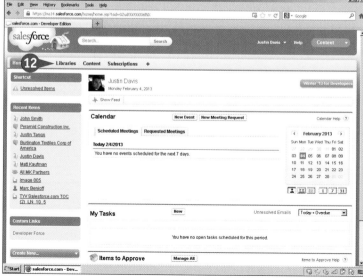

13 Click **New**.

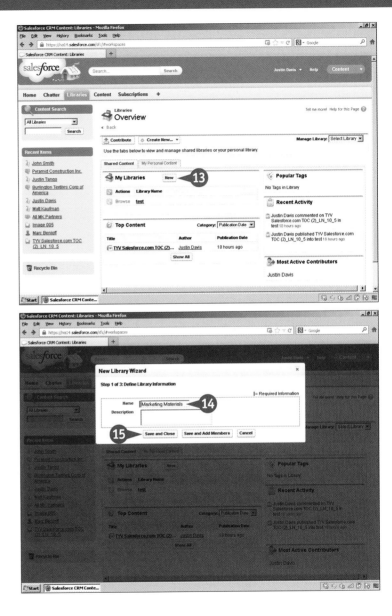

14 Type a descriptive name for the library in the Name field.

15 Click **Save and Close**.

TIP

Is Salesforce Content available in Salesforce Mobile?
Salesforce users can view and share content from a mobile device. This feature is not enabled by default. An administrator can enable it on the Setup and Mobile Configuration page.

Customize Libraries and Content

Libraries have their own settings, and are assigned to one or more users who administer the content. Before users can store documents in a library, a system administrator must configure these settings.

Administrators can also control how content is *tagged* in the library. Tags help library administrators keep the content organized, and help library users find it more easily.

Customize Libraries and Content

① Click the **Libraries** tab.

② Click a library to select it.

③ Click **Add Members**.

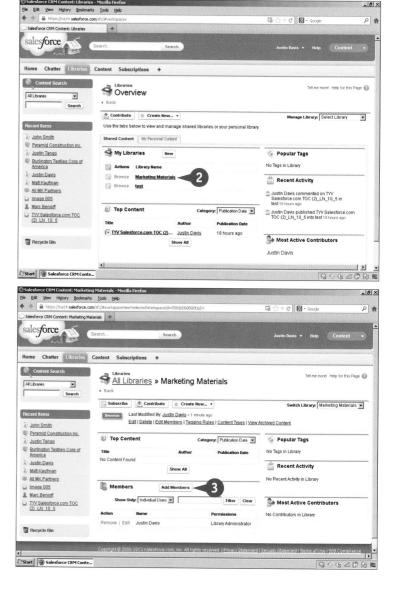

④ Click the name of the User you want to add to this library.

⑤ Click **add**.

⑥ Click **Next**.

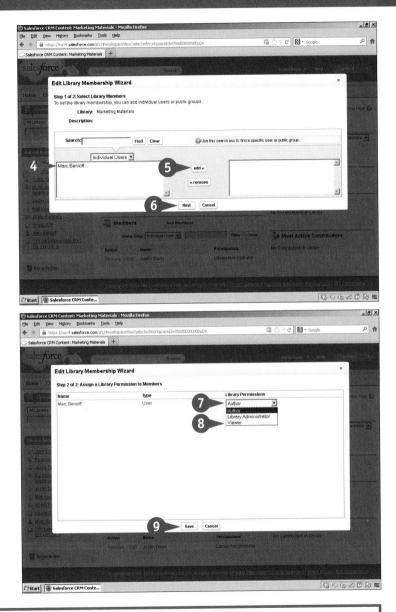

⑦ Click **Author** to open the drop-down list.

⑧ Select the desired level of access for the user.

⑨ Click **Save**.

continued ▶

TIP

How can I deliver content from a lead or opportunity?
Your system administrator can add the Deliver Content button to leads and opportunities so users can link documents to them. To add a document, users click the button and either upload the document or select it from elsewhere in Salesforce. Salesforce creates a new entry for the lead or opportunity with the name of the file and the date of delivery.

Customize Libraries and Content (continued)

Content tags allow users and administrators to add descriptive labels to uploaded documents. With open tagging, users can add any custom tags to a document. Guided tagging allows custom tags but also supports predefined and recommended tags. Restricted tagging forces contributors to select tags defined by a system administrator.

Customize Libraries and Content (continued)

10 Click **Tagging Rules**.

11 Click **Guided Tagging**
(○ changes to ⊙).

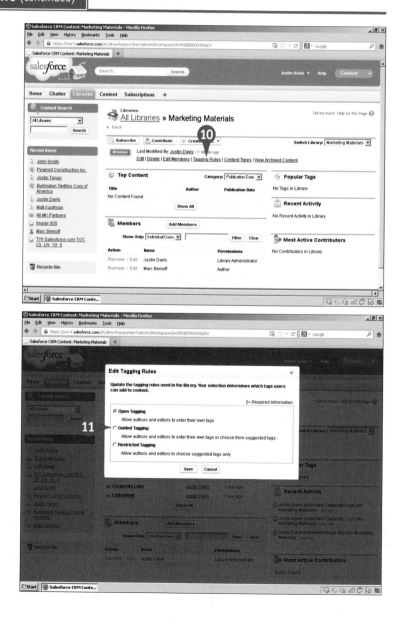

12 Type in the suggested tags for this library.

13 Click **Save**.

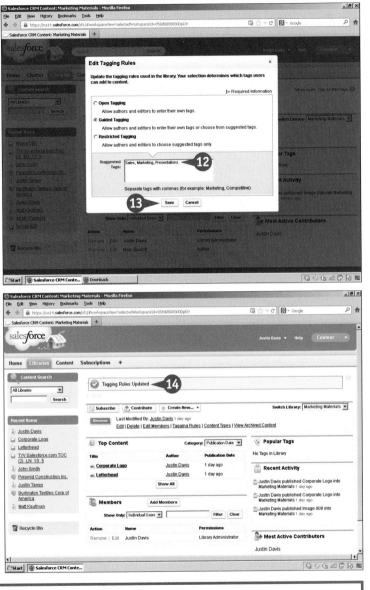

14 Salesforce displays a message showing that the tagging rules have been updated.

TIPS

Are there other library options?
After you create a library, you can edit its contents, delete it, set permitted content types, and view archived content. You can also search for documents using filters or tags.

How does archiving work?
Salesforce provides two options in Content for removing documents when they are no longer needed. The first option is deleting content, which removes the document from content to the recycle bin. The second option is archiving, which removes documents from search results and they cannot be downloaded. If desired, an author can return to the document in Content and click the **Restore Content** button to return the document to an active status.

Upload Documents to Content

You can upload documents to your library, but note there are three levels of library access — *viewer*, *author*, and *library administrator*.

A viewer can see and comment on documents. This level is ideal for sales representatives. An author can view, comment on, upload, edit, and delete documents. This level is ideal for individuals working on campaign strategies in a marketing department. A library administrator has complete control over documents and user access. This level is usually reserved for system administrators.

Upload Documents to Content

1 Click the **Libraries** tab.

2 Click **Contribute**.

3 Click **Browse**.

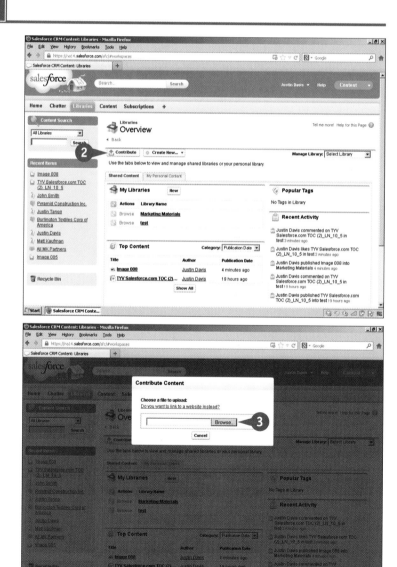

4 Select a file to upload.

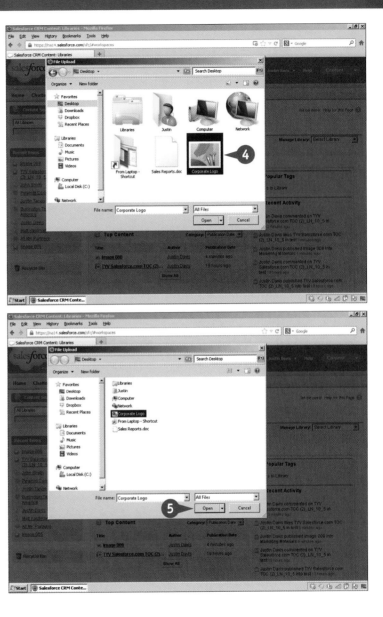

5 Click **Open**.

Does Salesforce support content-only user licenses?

Content-only licenses are available, but you must purchase them separately. Content-only users can see the Home, Libraries, Content, and Subscriptions tabs. They can also generate reports, but only for documents and records in the content library.

continued ▶

Upload Documents to Content (continued)

When uploading content, you can publish to a shared library or a personal library. A shared library makes its documents available to all users of that library. Documents in your personal library are not shared. You can use this option to work with drafts and confidential documents.

You can publish a document from your personal library in a shared library by clicking the **My Personal Content** tab, clicking the check box next to the document, and clicking **Publish Selected**. You can then choose a shared library.

Upload Documents to Content (continued)

⑥ Type a descriptive title for the document into the Title box.

⑦ Click **Publish to a shared library** (○ changes to ◉).

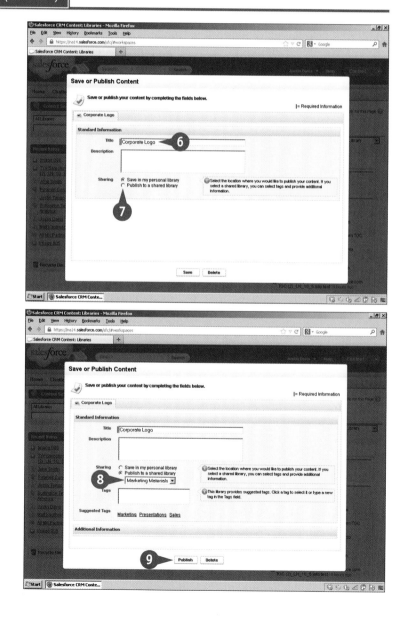

⑧ Select the desired library to publish to.

⑨ Click **Publish**.

10 Click **Done Publishing**.

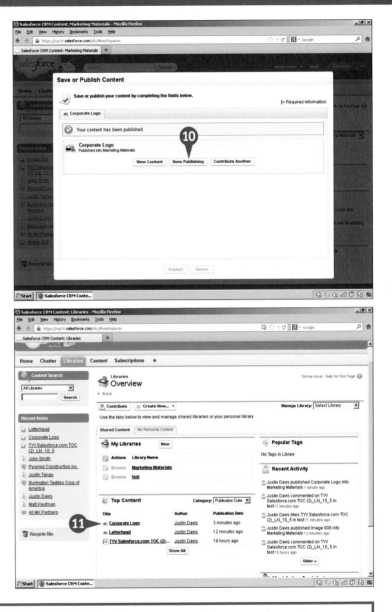

11 The document is now displayed in the selected library for others to view.

Leave Feedback on Documents in Content

U sers can leave feedback on documents uploaded to Content. They can subscribe to documents to be notified of changes, add comments, and mark documents with a thumbs up or thumbs down.

For example, a marketing department might create a slide deck for a sales division. The sales team can use feedback to suggest how the deck can be improved, or to tell the marketing team how it is used, and how leads respond to it.

Leave Feedback on Documents in Content

1 Click the **Libraries** tab.

2 Click the document you want to access.

3 Click the **Comments** tab.

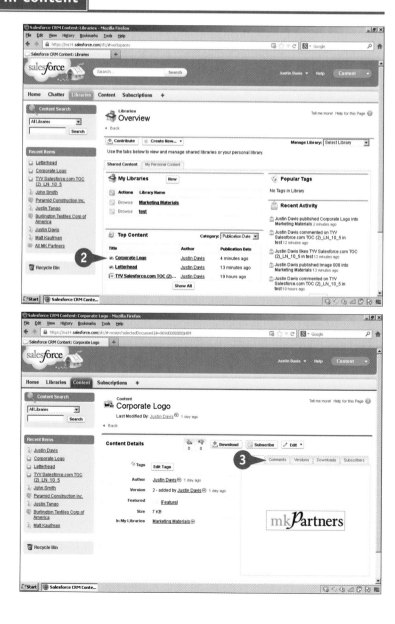

④ Click **Write Comment**.

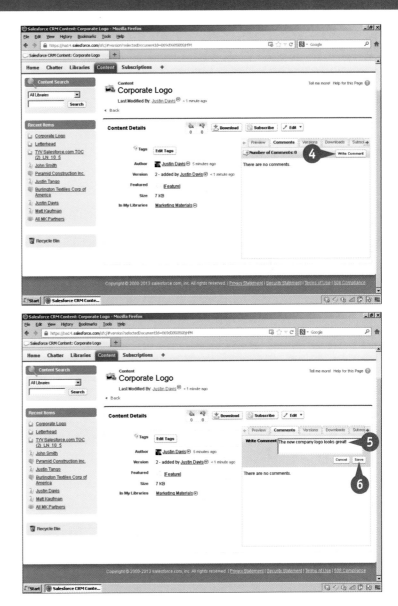

⑤ Type a comment for the document.

⑥ Click **Save**.

Note: Other users can view the comment by clicking the **Comments** tab.

TIP

When would I subscribe to a document?

Some documents go through regular revisions. Content tracks revisions automatically with a version number. When you subscribe to a document, Salesforce notifies you by e-mail whenever a new version is available. You can use this feature to reduce confusion and avoid duplicated effort; users can always be sure they are reading and commenting on the most recent version of a document.

Enable Salesforce Mobile

You can use Salesforce Mobile to access records from an Android, BlackBerry, or iPhone. The free version of Salesforce Mobile provides limited access to records. The paid version provides more comprehensive access.

Salesforce Mobile is not enabled by default. A system administrator must enable it before mobile users can work with it.

Enable Salesforce Mobile

1. Click your name.
2. Click **Setup**.
3. Click the **Mobile Administration** ▼.
4. Click the **Salesforce Mobile** ▼.
5. Click **Settings**.

6. Click **Edit**.

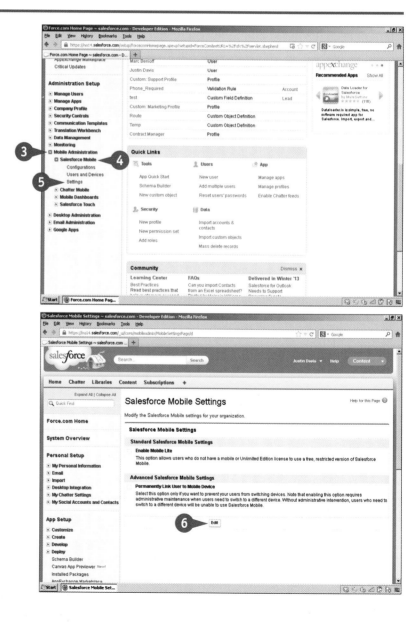

7 Click the **Enable Mobile Lite**
check box (☐ changes to ☑).

8 Click **Save**.

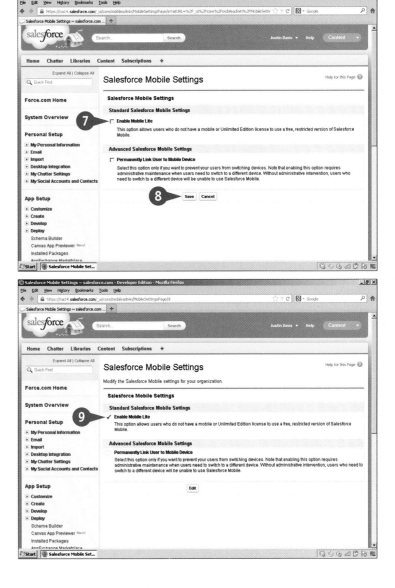

9 Mobile Lite is now active.

What is the difference between the paid and free versions of Salesforce Mobile?
The free version can sync recently viewed records. You can also search for other records before syncing, but
the free version excludes them by default to keep syncing fast. You can use the free version to manage most
records, events, and tasks, and to view dashboards. With the paid version, you can select specific records
for syncing. You can also create reports and view custom object records.

CHAPTER 7

Configuring Security

Salesforce security exceeds industry standards. Applications and data use 128-bit encryption for user data to protect sensitive information. Salesforce.com data centers are physically secured in concrete vaults, with redundant power supplies, video surveillance, foot patrols, environmental controls, fire detection and suppression, and robust backups. Users should configure local security policies to further enhance the security offered by Salesforce.

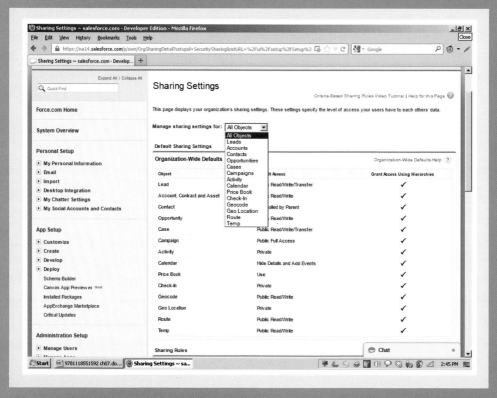

View Object Security

Objects (*tables* in database terminology) are the basic data containers in Salesforce. You can control security by configuring access to objects, allowing users to read, edit, create, or delete objects on a per-object, per-profile basis. You can also hide or display object tabs for different user profiles.

However, it is important to pay attention to child/parent object relationships. Users can typically see all the child objects of a parent object in a master-detail relationship they are allowed to view. But users may also be able to see the parent record of a child object, even if you set up security rules to prevent this. To avoid this, use a standard lookup field rather than a master-detail lookup field in the record.

View Object Security

1 Click your name.

2 Click **Setup** to show the configuration area.

3 Click the **Security Controls** triangle (▼).

4 Click **Sharing Settings**.

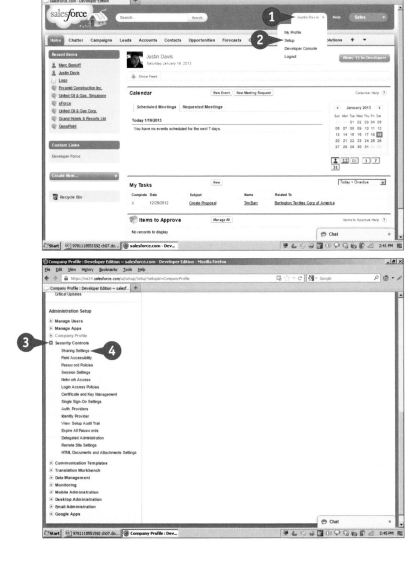

5 In the Manage sharing settings for drop-down list, choose **All Objects**.

6 Select an object to view it.

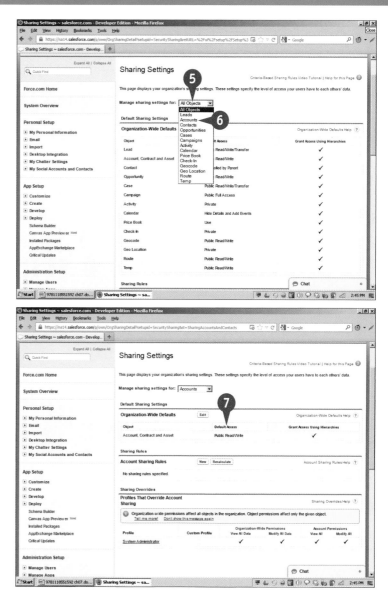

7 The Sharing Settings page displays security information about the object.

Are there exceptions to these settings?

You can override the default settings in two ways. Users can share objects manually. Administrators can also create custom sharing rules that override these settings.

Change Default Record Access

By default, Salesforce allows public read/write access for all objects. You can improve security by changing the default setting. The access options are private, public read only, public read/write, public read/write/transfer, public full access, and controlled by parent. *Private* means record owners and users with a superior role in the hierarchy can view or edit a record. *Public read only* permits all users to view but not edit records. *Public read/write* permits users to view and edit records. *Public read/write/transfer* and *Public full access* allow users to view, edit, and transfer records to another user.

Change Default Record Access

① Click your name.

② Click **Setup** to show the configuration area.

③ Click the **Security Controls** ▼.

④ Click **Sharing Settings**.

⑤ Click **Edit**.

6 Click the **Default Access** drop-down arrow (▾) next to the object whose settings you want to change.

7 Select a default security level from the drop-down list.

Note: You can repeat Step **7** for some or all the objects listed in the Default Access column.

8 Click **Save**.

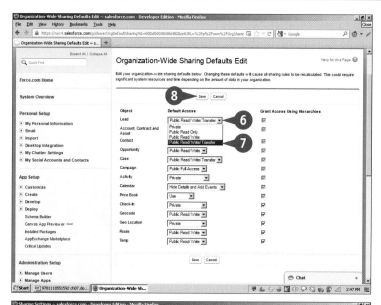

9 Salesforce shows the new security setting for the object or objects you changed.

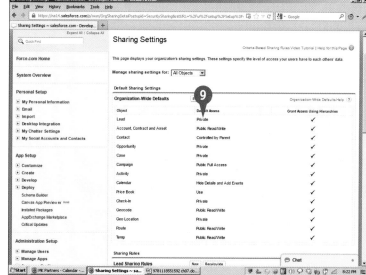

How soon do my security changes take effect?
The moment you click **Save**, Salesforce starts to process your changes. It can take a few minutes for changes to propagate through the system. Salesforce notifies you via e-mail when the process is complete.

How do I create a consistent security policy?
Create a spreadsheet listing all the roles in your organization and decide a suitable access level for each role. Depending on the structure and size of your organization, you may need to submit the spreadsheet for executive review before implementing it.

View the Role Hierarchy

Y ou can use the role hierarchy to determine which users will have access to certain object data. Think of the hierarchy as an organizational chart that defines the security relationships between the employees, managers, and executives within your organization.

You can use this chart as a starting point for assigning roles. However, you typically create roles for every level in the hierarchy, not for every position. For example, all vice-presidents can share the same role.

View the Role Hierarchy

1. Click your name in the top-right corner.

2. Click **Setup** to show the configuration area.

3. Click the **Manage Users** ▾.

4. Click **Roles**.

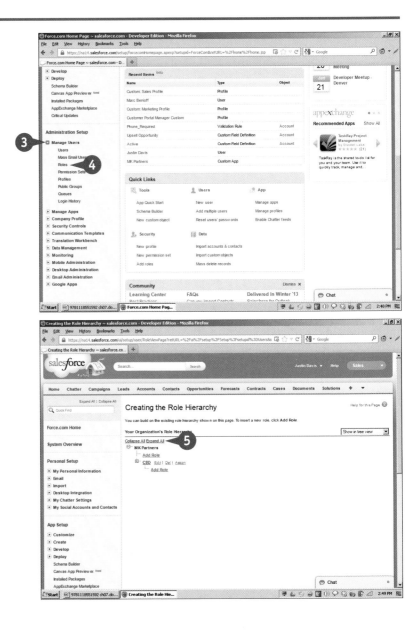

5. Click **Expand All**.

Configure Session Settings

You can use session settings to control when and how users can access your instance of Salesforce. For example, you can set a time-out duration for a session and force a user to log out after the time-out. When Salesforce is configured for the first time, your administrator should review and change the default settings to enhance your security and minimize the risk of unauthorized access. This example demonstrates how to change the session time-out. You can find and change the other session settings in a similar way.

Configure Session Settings

1 Click your name.

2 Click **Setup** to navigate to the configuration area.

3 Click the **Security Controls** ▣.

4 Click **Session Settings**.

5 Click **2 hours** in the Timeout value drop-down list.

Note: This logs out a user after 2 hours of inactivity. Shorter times are more secure, but may be less convenient for users.

Note: To change the other settings, select or deselect the check boxes on this page.

6 Click **Save**.

Create a New Role

A role represents a title or position a user has within Salesforce or within your organization itself. You can use roles to define how users view and share records.

Role design is an important task because it directly affects communications, efficiency, and security. For example, you can create separate East and West Coast sales manager roles to keep territory data separate and private. Or you can create a single sales manager role to allow all managers to see sales data from all territories. The correct option depends on your organization's culture.

Create a New Role

1. Click your name to display a submenu.

2. Click **Setup** to show the configuration area.

3. Click the **Manage Users** ▾.

4. Click **Roles**.

5. Click **Expand All**.

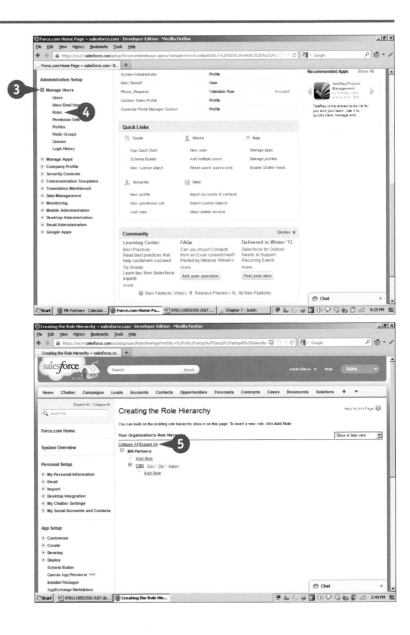

6 Click **Add Role**.

Note: When you add a role, you automatically assign a supervisor. In this example, the supervisor is the CFO.

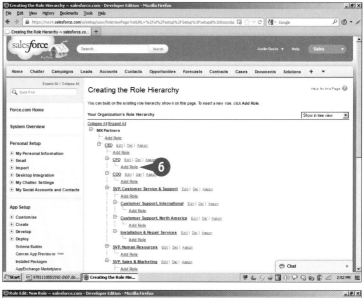

7 Type the role label in the Label field.

8 Optionally, type a descriptive name in the Role Name field as displayed on report.

Note: This version of the role name appears on reports only.

9 Click **Save**.

TIP

How are users outside the organization affected by roles?

The portal feature in Salesforce gives external users, resellers, and customers limited access to your instance of Salesforce. For example, external users may need to file support tickets and register possible sales leads. You must create roles for these portal users manually to make sure they cannot access your internal records without explicit authorization.

Enable Field History

You can use the field history feature in Salesforce to log changes to account records. When you enable the history feature, field history keeps a record of updates and changes showing the time and date of a change, the nature of the change, and the name of the user who made the change.

You can enable history separately for different kinds of data. For example, you can enable logging for changes to the Upsell Opportunity field in a record, but leave it disabled for changes to the ticker symbol.

Enable Field History

1 Click your name.

2 Click **Setup** to navigate to the configuration area.

3 Click the **Customize** ▼.

4 Click the **Accounts** ▼.

5 Click **Fields**.

6 Click **Set History Tracking**.

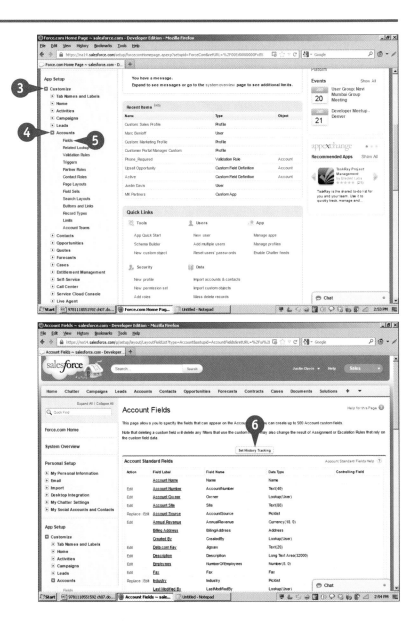

7 Click the **Enable Account History** check box (□ changes to ☑).

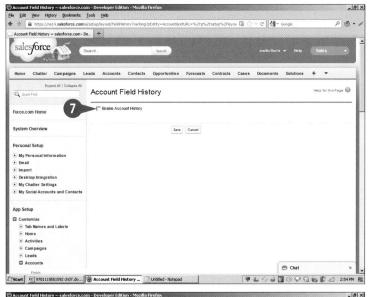

8 Click the check boxes next to the names of the fields you wish to track (□ changes to ☑).

9 Click **Save**.

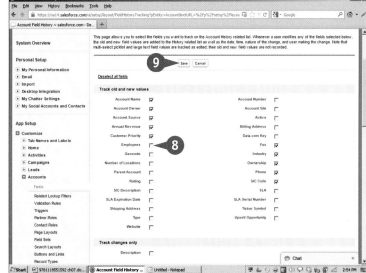

TIPS

How do I view field history?

You must edit the page layout to include account history logs. To view an account record, click the **Edit Layout** link in the top-right corner of the page and add the related list to the layout. If you do not do this, the history remains invisible.

Which fields and objects support field history?

Salesforce supports up to 20 fields per eligible object. Eligible objects include accounts, cases, contacts, entitlements, service contracts, contract line items, contracts, leads, opportunities, and solutions.

Configure the Password Policy

The Salesforce password policy sets minimum requirements for password security. By default, Salesforce requires a password with at least eight characters, which is not the same as the three preceding passwords the user used. Other settings include a 90-day expiration time-out, and support for alphanumeric characters.

The default settings are fairly secure. However, you can make them even more secure by customizing them and selecting options such as a shorter expiration time or a longer minimum password length.

Configure the Password Policy

1 Click your name.

2 Click **Setup** to navigate to the configuration area.

3 Click the **Security Controls** ▼.

4 Click **Password Policies**.

5 Select one of the preset time-outs in the User passwords expire in drop-down list.

Note: When users log in with an expired password, Salesforce prompts them to change it.

6 Select one of the options in the Enforce password history drop-down list.

Note: In this example, users cannot re-use any of their previous three passwords.

7 Select one of the options from the Minimum password length drop-down list to set the shortest allowed password length.

8 Select one of the options from the Password complexity requirement drop-down list to select the required mix of letters, numbers, and symbols.

9 Select **Cannot contain password** in the Password question requirement drop-down list to make sure the user's password hints do not contain the password.

10 Select a number from the Maximum invalid login attempts drop-down list to set the number of time users can try to log in before being locked out.

11 Select the lockout period from the Lockout effective period drop-down list.

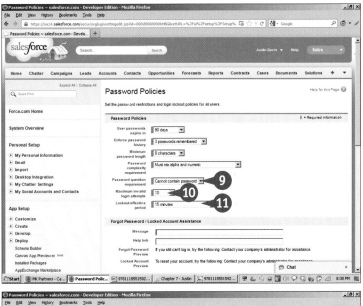

12 Type the message that appears to locked-out users.

13 Click **Save**.

TIPS

How quickly does Salesforce respond to policy changes?	Can I expire all passwords at once?
The new policies become active as soon as you click **Save**.	You can expire all passwords using an expire option on the Security Controls page. Users can log in with their current passwords, but must create a new password for subsequent logins.

Configure Network Access

You can use the network access feature to control which IP address ranges users can log in from. Users with an address in a trusted range can log in as usual. Users accessing Salesforce from some other address must use an activation code, which Salesforce e-mails them automatically.

You can specify ranges or single addresses. Note that a user working from home may have a dynamic IP address assigned by his ISP. White-listing the entire address range used by the ISP is not secure, and e-mail verification is preferred.

Configure Network Access

1 Click your name.

2 Click **Setup** to navigate to the configuration area.

3 Click the **Security Controls** ▢.

4 Click **Network Access**.

5 Click **New**.

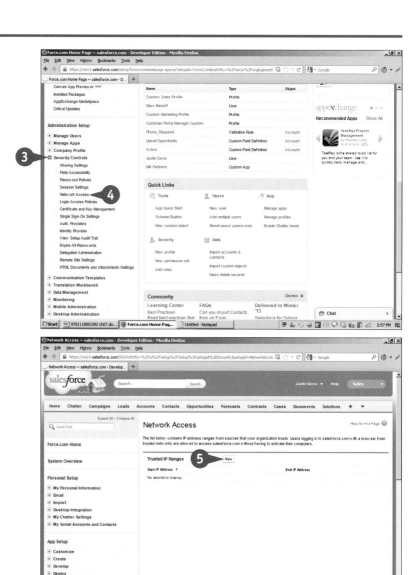

6 In the Start IP Address field, type the beginning range of the IP address.

7 In the End IP Address field, type the ending range of the IP address.

8 Click **Save**.

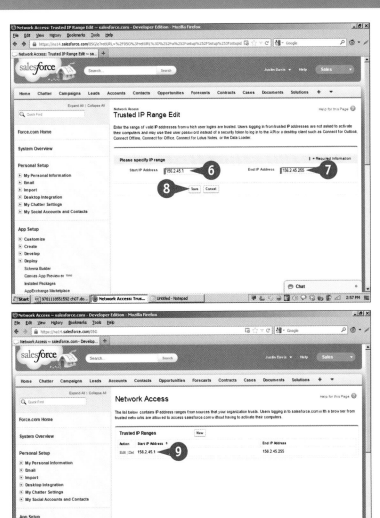

9 Salesforce displays the new trusted IP range.

TIPS

Can I use IPv6 addresses?
Yes. You can specify IPv4 or IPv6 address ranges, as long as the starting and ending IP address of a range are in the same format. Salesforce does not accept mixed ranges.

What permissions are needed to change network access settings?
Network access settings are typically configured by system administrators. However, any user with the Manage Users permission enabled on their profile can also configure them.

Configure Remote Site Settings

You can use the Remote Site Settings options to control which external websites and resources users can access from within your instance of Salesforce.

Note that you must specify ports and protocol settings for each site. For example, sites that use HTTPS (Hypertext Transport Protocol Secure) connections must allow a connection to port 443.

Configure Remote Site Settings

1. Click your name.

2. Click **Setup**.

3. Click the **Security Controls** .

4. Click **Remote Site Settings**.

5. Click **New Remote Site**.

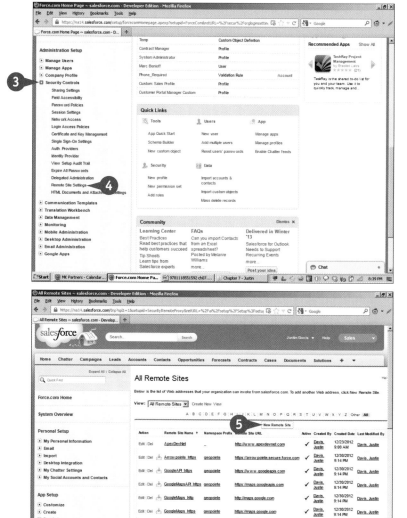

⑥ Type the site name in the Remote Site Name field.

⑦ Type the URL provided by the external web service in the Remote Site URL field.

⑧ Click the **Active** check box (☐ changes to ☑).

⑨ Click **Save**.

⑩ You see the new remote site displayed.

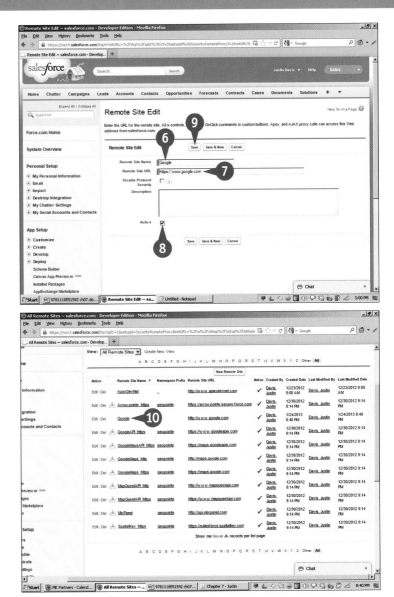

TIP

What if the connection is HTTP and HTTPS?

If a connection requires both HTTP (port 80) and HTTPS (port 443) access, click the Disable Protocol Security check box. This allows Salesforce to send data from a secured (HTTPS) session to an unsecured (HTTP) session. However, this option can affect your network security, so confirm it with an Internet security expert before enabling it.

Reset a Security Token

Users logging in over an untrusted connection can confirm their identity with a security token, which they type immediately after typing their passwords. Tokens are sent by unencrypted e-mail. You can reset a token and resend it if a user loses the original, or if you suspect its security has been compromised.

Reset a Security Token

1 Click your name.

2 Click **Setup**.

3 Click the **My Personal Information** ⯆.

4 Click **Reset My Security Token**.

5 Click **Reset Security Token**.

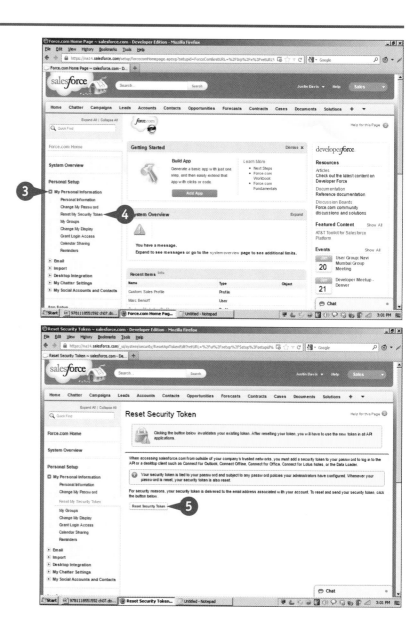

Grant Login Access

You can grant an administrator or technical support agent temporary access to your Salesforce account. This gives the administrator or agent the power to make changes to records and settings on your behalf, and to deal with support requests.

As an administrator, you can use this option to check a user's settings, troubleshoot problems, and make corrections. The login access time is limited to various preset periods between a day and a year.

Grant Login Access

1 Click your name.

2 Click **Setup**.

3 Click the **My Personal Information** 🔽.

4 Click **Grant Login Access**.

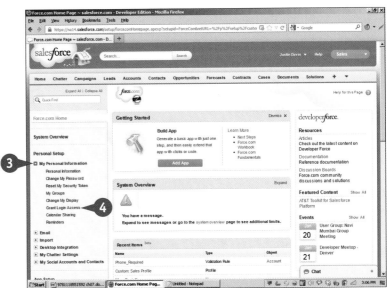

5 In the top Access Duration drop-down list, choose an administrator access period.

6 In the Salesforce.com Access Duration drop-down list, choose a support agent access period.

7 Click **Save**.

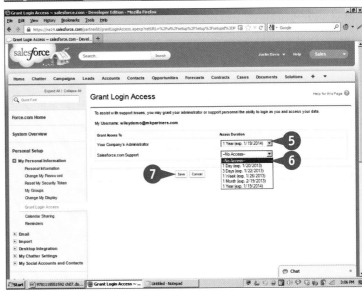

Create a Validation Rule

You can use validation rules to check that data entered into a record is logically consistent and makes sense. For example, you can confirm that a zip code is correct, an account number contains digits and no letters, or a phone number is in a valid format.

Rules evaluate as "true" when there is a problem or error. Salesforce displays a red error message below the field with a problem or at the top of the page. Rules that evaluate as "false" are valid and allow the user to continue editing or entering data. When creating validation rules, it is important to remember the rule itself is looking for an outcome of "true" in order to display the error message.

Create a Validation Rule

① Click your name.

② Click **Setup**.

③ Click the **Customize** ▾.

④ Click the **Accounts** ▾.

⑤ Click **Validation Rules**.

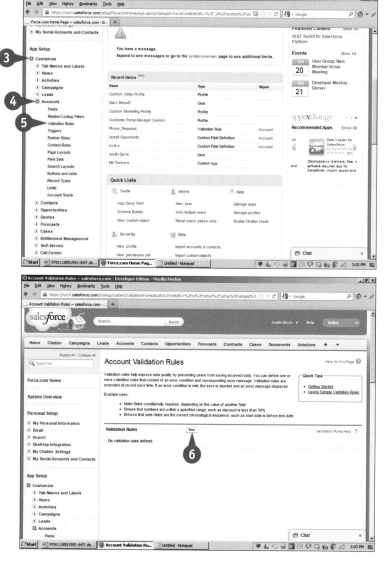

⑥ Click **New**.

7 Type the rule name in the Rule Name field.

Note: Use a descriptive name, and use underscores to avoid spaces.

8 Type the name of a field to check.

9 Click **Insert Operator**.

10 Type the value you are checking against after the operator symbol.

Note: This example returns "true" if the Phone field is empty, triggering an error.

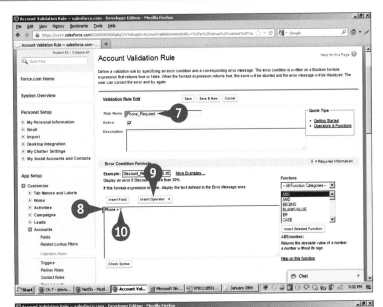

11 Type an error message.

Note: This message appears when the rule fails because the user made an error.

12 Click **Save**.

Note: For more information and examples, click the **Help for this Page** link at the top right of the page.

TIPS

Are there any restrictions on validation rules?

Validation rules cannot test compound fields, such as addresses, and combined first and last name fields. Dependent fields that are generated "live" are also excluded, including campaign statistics; auto-number fields; picklists, which are drop-down lists of options; and lookups, which associate records together.

Are validation rules always enforced?

Validation rules are not enforced when you use Quick Create, a one-click record creation on the home page, or when you are working with campaign hierarchies. You can enable or disable them when converting leads to accounts. For details, see the next section, "Disable a Validation Rule."

Disable a Validation Rule

You can selectively disable validation rules for testing and debugging. For example, if your organization uses more than one page layout per object, you should test all relevant validation rules to make sure there are no conflicts and no potential user disruption.

You should also test validation rules carefully when integrating your data with outside systems. Thorough and consistent testing guarantees there should be no errors during record creation or editing.

Disable a Validation Rule

1 Click your name.

2 Click **Setup**.

3 Click the **Customize** ▾.

4 Click the **Accounts** ▾.

5 Click **Validation Rules**.

6 Click **Edit**.

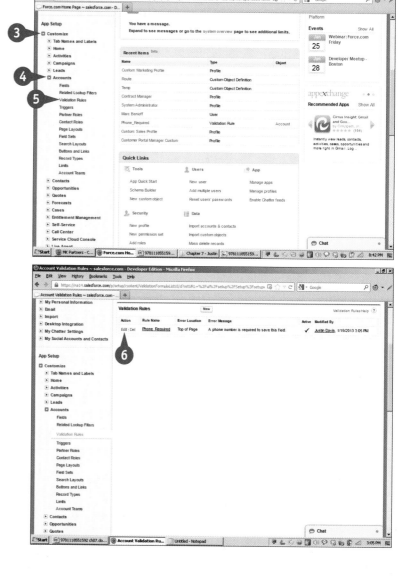

7 Deselect the **Active** check box (☑ changes to ☐).

8 Click **Save**.

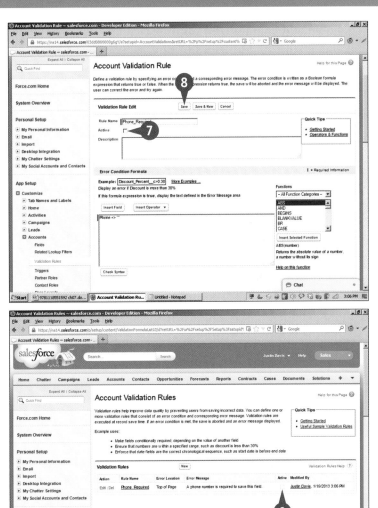

9 Salesforce disables the validation rule.

Create an Account Sharing Rule

As an administrator, you can use sharing rules to give roles, groups, or individual users access to data they would otherwise be excluded from. You cannot restrict data access with sharing rules — you can only use rules to override existing restrictions.

If record ownership changes, the rules automatically determine the correct level of security. Sharing rules are only available in the Professional, Enterprise, and Unlimited editions of Salesforce.

Create an Account Sharing Rule

1 Click your name.

2 Click **Setup**.

3 Click the **Security Controls** .

4 Click **Sharing Settings**.

5 Click **New** in the Account Sharing Rules section of the Object Security page.

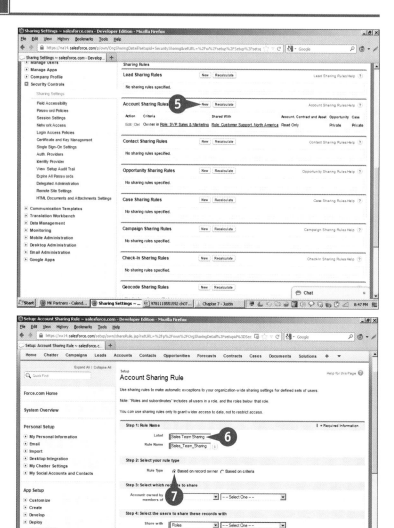

6 Type a label for this sharing rule.

7 In the Rule Type area, select **Based on record owner** or **Based on criteria** (changes to).

Note: The first option checks the record owner when evaluating the account. The second option checks the criteria you specify.

8 Click the drop-down arrow
(▼) in the second Share
with drop-down list.

9 Choose the role or group
desired.

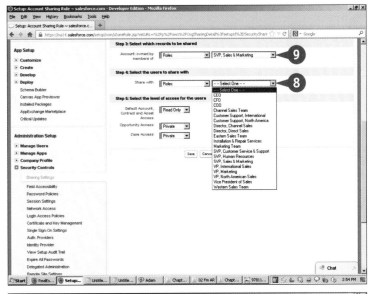

10 Choose the desired level of
access in the Default
Account, Contract and Asset
Access drop-down list.

11 Choose the desired level of
access in the Opportunity
Access drop-down list.

12 Choose the default level of
access in the Case Access
drop-down list.

13 Click **Save**.

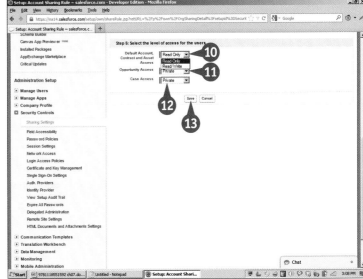

Can sharing rules be used to restrict access?
Sharing rules can only grant access; they cannot restrict
access. To restrict viewing, you need to change record
access as described in "Change Default Record Access,"
earlier in this chapter. Typically, you use sharing settings
to make records private, and then use sharing rules to
define which groups and roles can access them.

How do I define default access options?
The default account settings set the default
security for an account. Opportunities and
cases have a related setting. Combining
these settings with sharing rules gives you
very fine control over access security.

Create a Public Group

You can create groups in Salesforce to simplify sharing and security. Groups can include individual users, users with specific roles and their subordinates, or members of other public groups. You can define unique security and sharing options for all members in a group. This is often quicker and simpler than using the more detailed security options in Salesforce.

Create a Public Group

1 Click your name.

2 Click **Setup**.

3 Click the **Manage Users** ▼.

4 Click **Public Groups**.

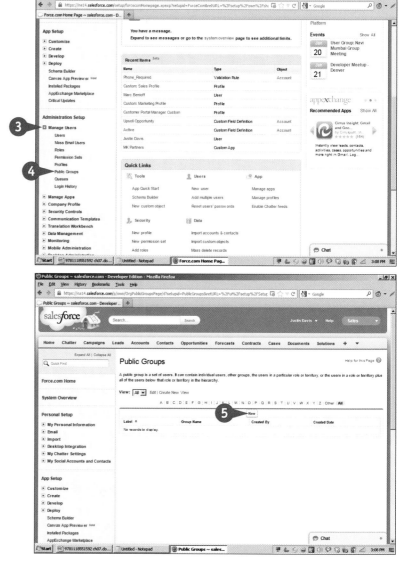

5 Click **New**.

6 Type a new label for this group.

7 Click the **Search** drop-down arrow (▼).

8 Choose roles you wish to add to this public group.

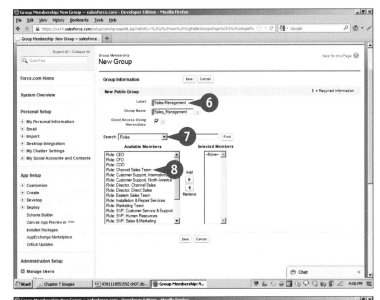

9 Choose the desired roles in the Available Members column.

10 Click the **Add** arrow (▶) to move a role or user from the Available Members column to the Selected Members column.

11 Click **Save**.

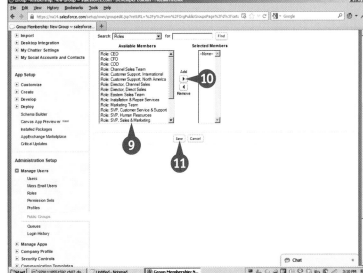

How can I use groups in Salesforce?
Groups are used in sharing rules to manually share records with others, to designate which contacts should be synced and owned by other users, and to add multiple users to Salesforce content. You can assign sharing rules or standard Salesforce content to groups.

Modify Object Settings for Profiles

You can use profiles to set configuration and data permissions and restrictions in Salesforce. When you assign a profile to a user, you can control which records that person can view and edit, and define how the user can change his or her configuration options. Profiles are available in the Enterprise and Unlimited editions of Salesforce.

Modify Object Settings for Profiles

1 Click your name.

2 Click **Setup**.

3 Click the **Manage Users** ⏷.

4 Click **Profiles**.

5 Click the profile name you wish to edit.

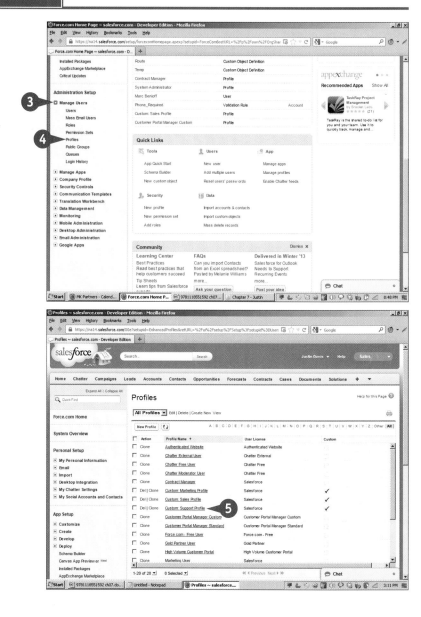

6 Click the **Object Settings** link.

7 Click the **Accounts** link.

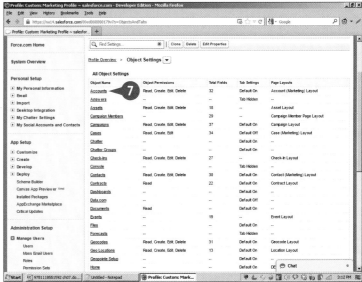

TIP

What other situations require adjusting profile security?
When creating custom objects, access is given to the system administrator by default for testing purposes. The administrator needs to modify each profile in use in order for those users to see the newly created custom object. This is most easily performed using enhanced profile list views.

continued ▶

Modify Object Settings for Profiles (continued)

You can assign the following permissions to objects: *read*, *create*, *edit*, *delete*, *view all*, and *modify all*. Create, edit, and delete give users permission to perform the corresponding action on an action. Read allows users to read objects, subject to any security rules. View all is a privileged option that allows users to view all object records. Modify all is even more powerful: It allows users to view and make changes to all object records.

Modify Object Settings for Profiles (continued)

8 Click **Edit**.

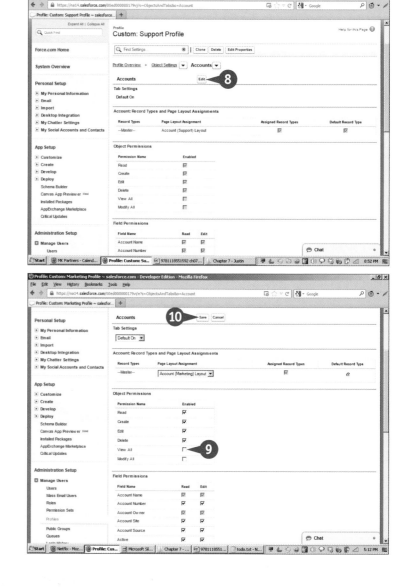

9 Select or deselect the object and field permissions to set them for this profile.

Note: This example enables the View All object permission for the profile.

10 Click **Save**.

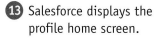

11) The View All permission is selected.

12) Click the **Profile Overview** link.

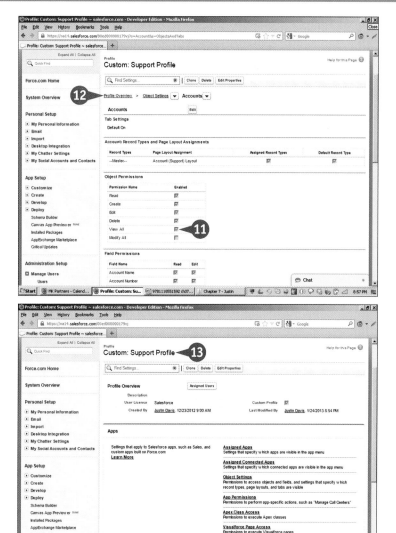

13) Salesforce displays the profile home screen.

What can I do with profiles?

Profiles control many security features. You can control access to the following settings: page layout assignments, field-level security, custom app settings, tab settings, record type settings, administrative permissions, general user permissions, standard object permissions, custom object permissions, desktop integration client selection, login hours, login IP ranges, enabled Apex classes, enabled Visualforce page access, and enabled external data source access.

Reset a Password

Users often forget their passwords. As an administrator, you can reset a password manually. When you do this, Salesforce sends an e-mail to the user with a link to a page that gives the user an opportunity to create a new password.

Optionally, the user may also have to answer a security question. If he or she fails to answer it, the password remains unchanged.

Reset a Password

1 Click your name.

2 Click **Setup**.

3 Click the **Manage Users** ▼.

4 Click **Reset users' passwords**.

5 Click the check box next to the forgetful user's name (☐ changes to ☑).

6 Click **Reset Password(s)**.

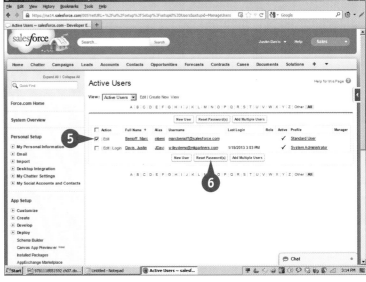

Download the Setup Audit History

You can check the setup audit trail to review the changes made to your instance of Salesforce over the last six months. If your organization has multiple administrators, the audit shows the date and description of each change, and the name of the administrator who made it.

Administrators should perform regular audits to check for unauthorized changes. Monthly checks are acceptable; weekly or even daily checks are better.

Download the Setup Audit History

1 Click your name.

2 Click **Setup**.

3 Click the **Security Controls** ▼.

4 Click **View Setup Audit Trail**.

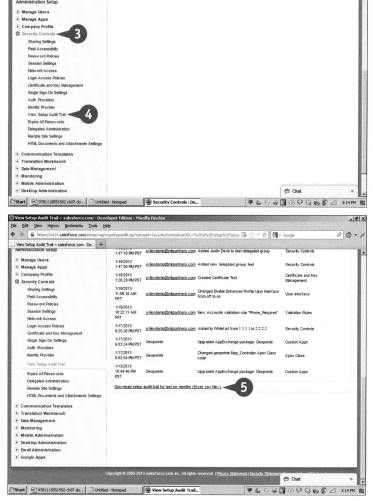

5 Click **Download setup audit trail for last six months**.

Note: Salesforce saves the data as a CSV (comma-separated values) file at your browser's usual download location.

Configure Account Field-Level Security

You can use field-level security to restrict view and edit access to critical fields in Salesforce records. Field-level security is managed on a per-profile basis. You can keep certain profiles out of some records altogether, while giving other profiles full access.

Removing edit access restricts access to field edits. Removing view access prevents a user from running a report or creating a list view to see the information in a field. This gives you greater control over access than removing a field from a page layout.

Configure Account Field-Level Security

1. Click your name.
2. Click **Setup**.
3. Click the **Customize** ▼.
4. Click the **Accounts** ▼.
5. Click **Fields**.

6. Click the name of the field whose security you wish to edit.

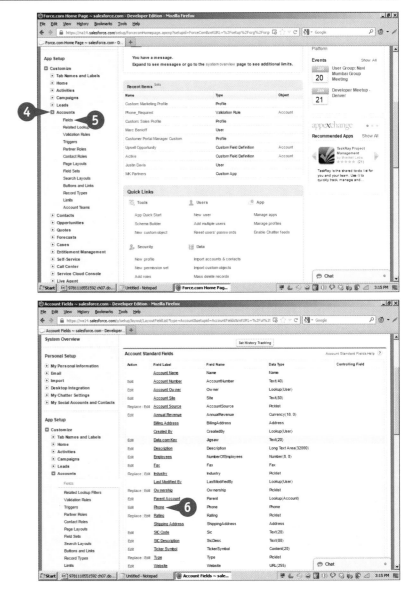

7 Click **Set Field-Level Security**.

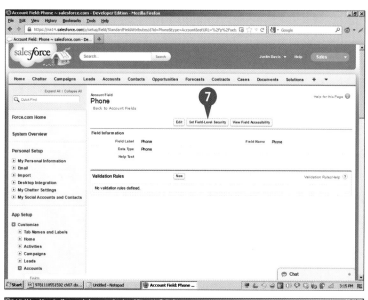

8 Select or deselect the check boxes in the Visible column next to each profile to control view access.

Note: A profile can view a field when Visible is selected.

9 Select or deselect the check boxes in the Read-Only column next to each profile to control edit access.

Note: A profile can edit a field when Read-Only is left unchecked.

10 Click **Save**.

TIPS

In which editions of Salesforce can I edit field-level security?
Field-level security is only available in the Enterprise and Unlimited editions of Salesforce.

Does field-level security affect searches?
Search results may show field values even though field-level security should keep those fields invisible. There is currently no way to work around this issue.

Restrict Login IP Ranges

You can add a login IP range to a profile to restrict access to a certain set of IP addresses and exclude access from unauthorized addresses. You can specify any valid IP address range. Attempts to log in from an excluded address are not permitted, even if the user has a valid activation code.

This feature is only available in the Enterprise and Professional editions of Salesforce.

Restrict Login IP Ranges

1. Click your name.
2. Click **Setup**.
3. Click the **Manage Users** ⬛.
4. Click **Profiles**.
5. Click a profile.

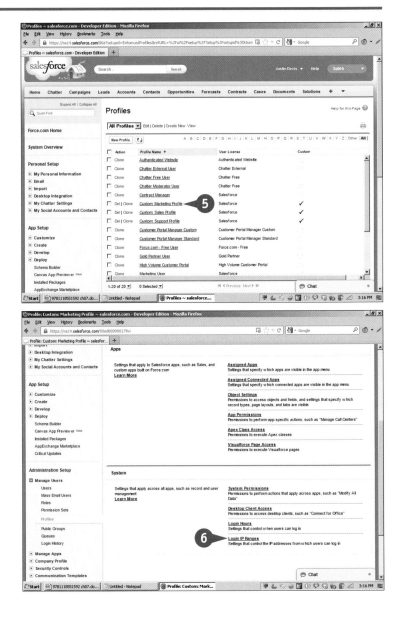

6. Click **Login IP Ranges**.

7 Click **Add IP Ranges**.

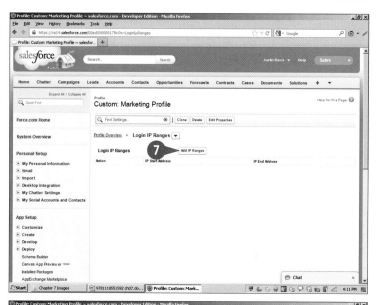

8 Type the IP start address.

9 Type the IP end address.

10 Click **Save**.

Salesforce restricts logins for that profile to addresses within the range you defined.

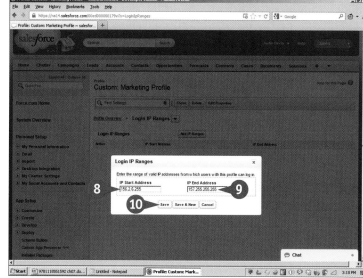

Does this option affect users who are already logged in?

Users who are logged in are not logged out. Once users log out, they cannot login again if their IP address is in a restricted range.

How do IP ranges affect Salesforce Mobile and Mobile Lite users?

Users can bypass IP security through the Salesforce mobile app. To deny users mobile access, disable mobile access for a given profile or for individual users.

Download a Secure Certificate

You can use a secure certificate to confirm the identity of your organization when you use Salesforce to communicate with an external resource or website. A certificate is essential for secure web traffic. If you do not plan to use external websites, you do not need to install a certificate.

Download a Secure Certificate

1 Click your name.

2 Click **Setup**.

3 Click the **Security Controls** ⬛.

4 Click **Certificate and Key Management**.

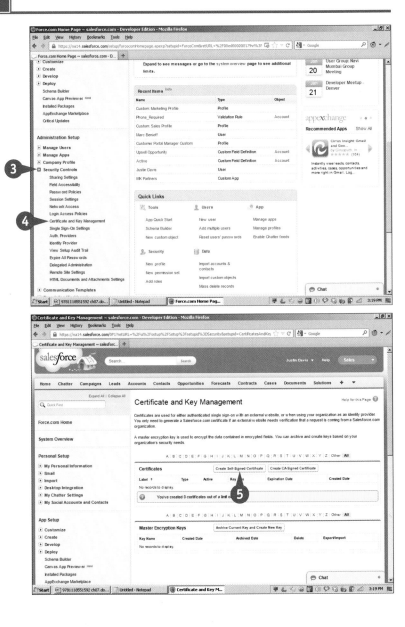

5 Click **Create Self-Signed Certificate**.

6 Type a descriptive label for this certificate.

7 Adjust the key size if necessary.

Note: 2048 is a standard default size.

8 Click **Save**.

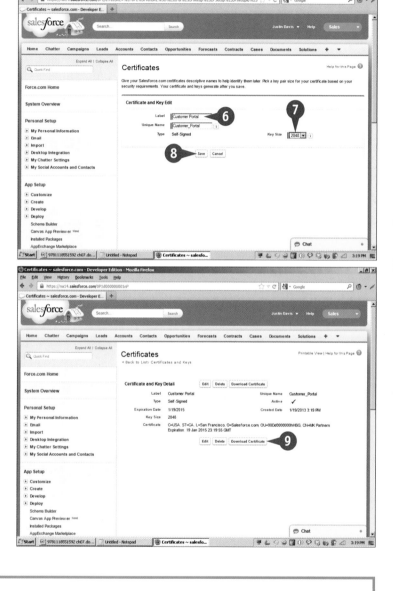

9 Click **Download Certificate** to download the certificate to your computer.

TIP

How do I install a certificate?

A certificate is not active and cannot be used until it has been signed by a certificate authority and uploaded to Salesforce. After the certificate has been uploaded, its status changes to Active and it is ready for use. To upload and install a certificate, choose **Setup**, then **Security Controls**, and **Certificate and Key Management**. Click the name of the certificate. Click **Upload Signed Certificate** and select the certificate file on your computer. Click **Save** to finish.

Set Up Delegated Administration

You can use delegated administration to nominate some users for limited and routine administrative tasks, such as creating new users, resetting passwords, and creating fields in records. Use this option to give groups and departments some administrative autonomy, and to give official administrators more time to deal with technical tasks such as troubleshooting, integration, and software development.

You can assign a user to more than one delegate administration group. The user can assign any profile he or she has access to, to any user.

Set Up Delegated Administration

1 Click your name.

2 Click **Setup**.

3 Click the **Security Controls** 🔽.

4 Click **Delegated Administration**.

5 Click **New**.

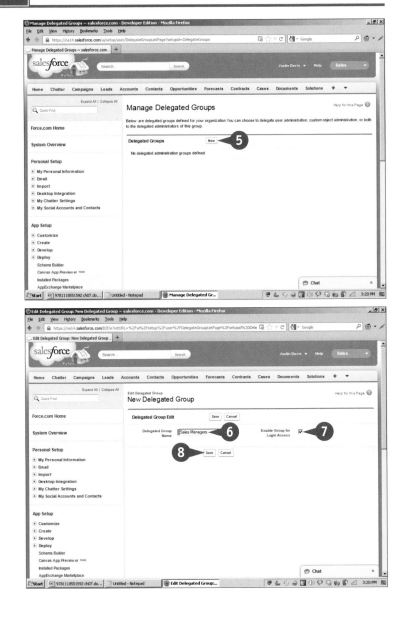

6 Type the delegated group name.

7 Click the **Enable Group for Login Access** check box (☐ changes to ☑).

8 Click **Save**.

9 Click **Add**.

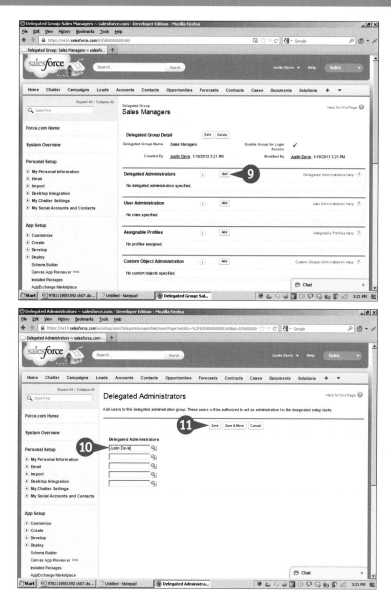

10 Type the name of a user in the Delegated Administrators box.

11 Click **Save**.

Note: You can also search for users if you cannot remember their names.

TIP

What can delegated administrators do?

It is up to you to define the role of delegated administrators. Commonly, delegated administrators manage users in their department or administrative unit and deal with routine tasks such as password resets.

Modify User Roles and Profiles

When you create a role or profile you must amend the related user record. You can perform this edit on an active user who is logged in. Users will see a change when they next reload a Salesforce page.

Note that administrators cannot change their own profiles, but can change their roles.

Modify User Roles and Profiles

1 Click your name.

2 Click **Setup**.

3 Click the **Manage Users** ▾.

4 Click **Users**.

5 Click **Edit** next to the user you wish to modify.

6 Click the **Role** drop-down arrow (▾) and select a role for this user.

7 Click the **Profile** drop-down arrow (▾) and select a profile.

8 Click **Save**.

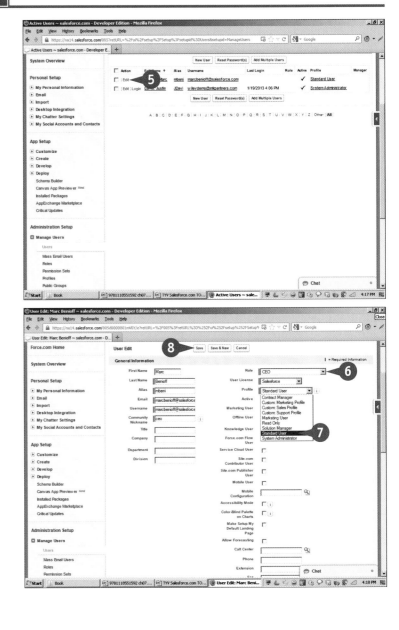

Modify Login Access Policies

By default, users can grant login access to administrators or to technical support staff. As an administrator, you can restrict login access. This limits the possibility of an unauthorized access incident before a user logs in.

You can allow or exclude login access for certain administrators, technical support staff, or applications installed from the App Exchange.

Modify Login Access Policies

① Click your name.

② Click **Setup**.

③ Click the **Security Controls** ▼.

④ Click **Login Access Policies**.

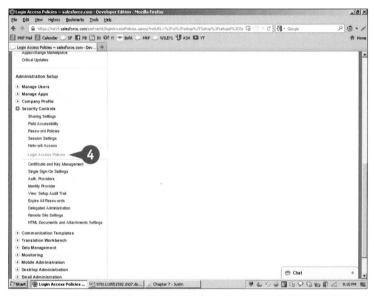

⑤ Click the radio buttons to enable or disable access for each support organization.

Note: Other support options may appear in your instance of Salesforce.

⑥ Click **Save**.

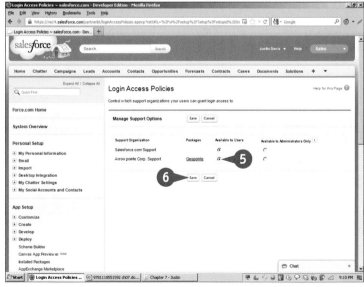

Set Up an Authentication Provider

You can give users the option to log in to Salesforce using an external username and password. Note that this is a nonstandard feature, and it is not built into standard versions of Salesforce. Your instance must include a suitable Apex registration-handler class, which must be created by a Salesforce developer and customized for your organization.

Set Up an Authentication Provider

1. Click your name.
2. Click **Setup**.
3. Click the **Security Controls** ▼.
4. Click **Auth. Providers**.

5. Click **New**.

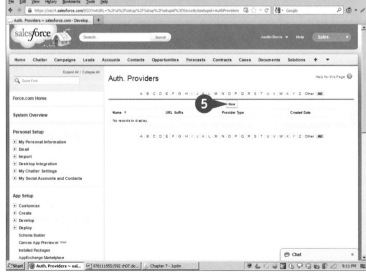

6 Choose a provider type.

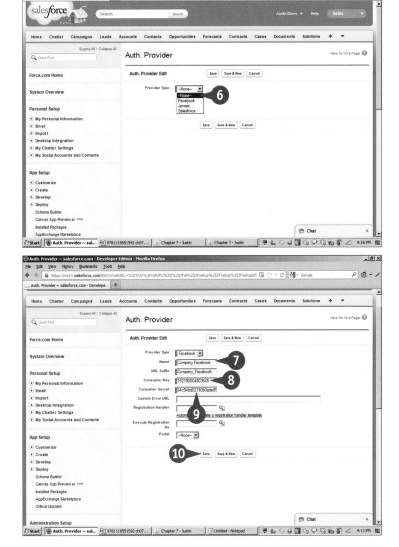

7 Type the name.

8 Type the consumer key.

9 Type the consumer secret.

10 Click **Save**.

Which providers can I use for authentication?

Salesforce currently supports Janrain, Facebook, and Salesforce native applications.

How do I obtain a consumer secret and key from Facebook?

Go to https://developers.facebook.com/apps, log in with your Facebook username and password, and then click **+ Create New App**. Choose a name for an application — use any text — and enter the CAPTCHA text. Click **Continue**. Facebook generates an app ID and an app secret code. You can copy them from this page and use them to set up Facebook authentication.

CHAPTER 8

Managing Your Data

Salesforce provides two main tools for importing, updating, transferring, and deleting data. The *Import Wizard* takes you through data management step by step. The *Data Loader* runs as a separate application on Windows machines. Both tools work with CSV (comma-separated values) files, which should begin with a row of column headers, and include one record per row in the rest of the file.

Import Leads

You can use the Import Wizard to import leads into Salesforce. Leads must be in a CSV file — a standard data-interchange format used by spreadsheet and database applications.

With the Import Wizard, you can import up to 50,000 leads. You can also associate them with a campaign. Any user with "import leads" or "create leads" permissions in his or her user profile can use the Import Wizard to import leads.

Import Leads

① Click your name.

② Click **Setup**.

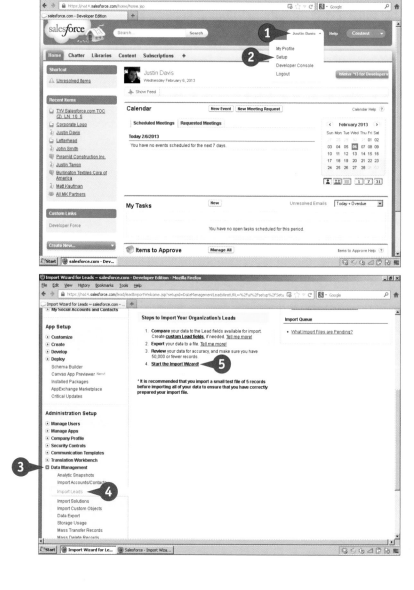

③ Click the **Data Management** triangle (▼).

④ Click **Import Leads**.

⑤ Click **Start the Import Wizard!**.

6 Click **Browse**.

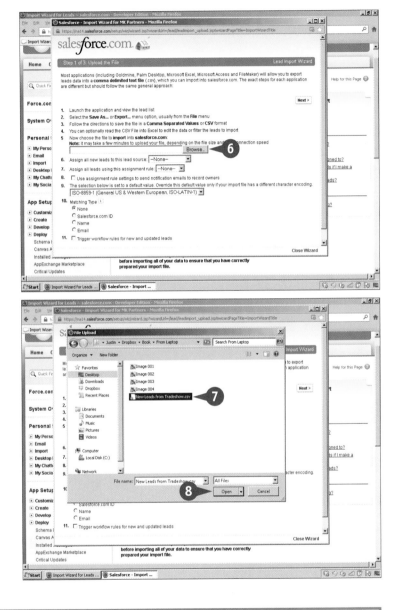

7 Select a CSV file of leads to import from your hard disk.

8 Click **Open**.

Who owns the leads imported by the Import Wizard?

By default, imported leads are owned by the person importing them. If you have lead assignment rules enabled for your Salesforce instance, you can use a rule to assign ownership automatically. Click the **Assign all leads using this assignment rule** drop-down list and select a rule for the data.

continued ▶

Import Leads (continued)

When importing leads from a spreadsheet, you must perform an action called *mapping*. This links Salesforce lead fields with columns of data from the imported spreadsheet.

For example, if one of the columns in your spreadsheet is a business name, you can link this to the Company field in Salesforce. Salesforce attempts to auto-map fields to minimize the amount of work you have to do. However, you should always check the mappings before an import.

Import Leads (continued)

9 Click **Next**.

10 Use the drop-down lists to map the imported fields in the CSV file to the corresponding Salesforce field.

Note: In this example, the Owner Role Name in column 40 is mapped to the Full Name field in Salesforce, the First Name field in column 1 is mapped to the First Name field in Salesforce, and so on.

Note: The CSV file must be organized in columns with header titles in the first row. Otherwise mapping does not work correctly.

11 Click **Next**.

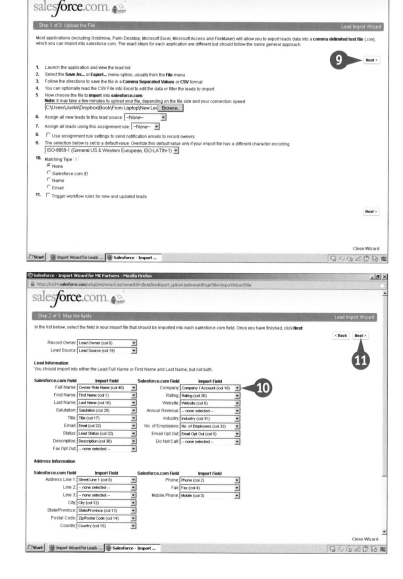

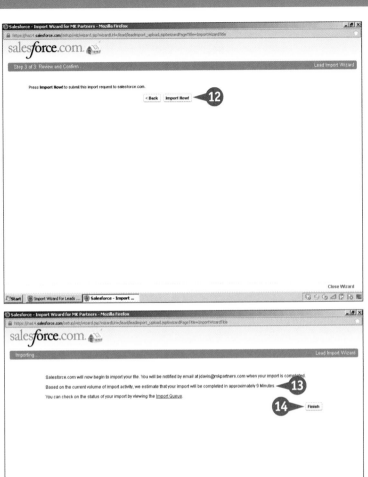

12 Click **Import Now!** to begin the import.

Salesforce displays a confirmation message.

13 Note the estimated time for the import.

14 Click **Finish**.

Note: Salesforce sends you an e-mail alert when the import is complete.

TIP

Can I apply automation rules to imported leads?

When using the Import Wizard, you can apply assignment, workflow, and validation rules to records. Click the **Trigger workflow rules for new and updated leads** check box, and then click **Next** in the Import Wizard window. Note that validation rules are always enforced.

Import Contacts and Accounts

You can import contacts and accounts with the Import Wizard. However, you must format the CSV file generated by your spreadsheet or database with contact and account information on a single row. During import, you can decide how to map the columns of data to fields in Salesforce.

Import Contacts and Accounts

1. Click your name.
2. Click **Setup**.
3. Click the **Data Management** ▼.
4. Click **Import Accounts/Contacts**.
5. Click **Start the Import Wizard!**.

6. Click **Next**.

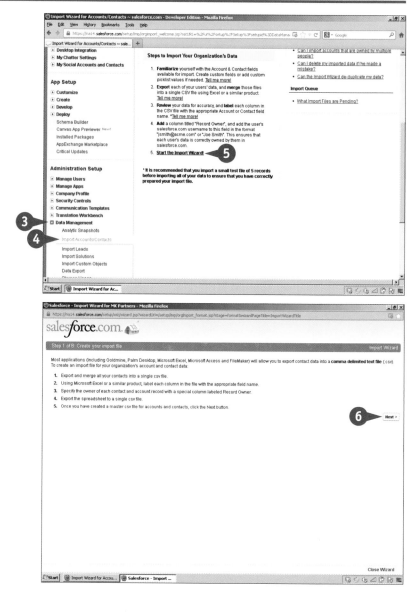

7 Click **Browse**.

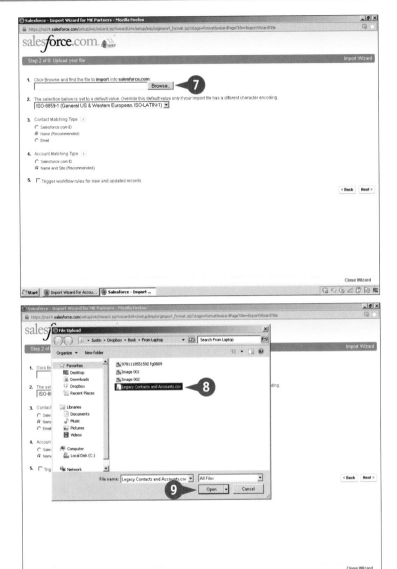

8 Select a CSV file for import.

9 Click **Open**.

Can I import data in other formats?

CSV is the preferred format. You must use CSV files to import leads, solutions, custom objects, or person accounts. For contacts and accounts only, Salesforce can accept data generated by Sage ACT! or Microsoft Outlook.

continued ▶

When importing contacts and accounts, the Import Wizard checks for duplicates. If it finds duplicated records, the Wizard sends you an e-mail with a summary of duplicated, merged, and new records.

Merging is a feature of the Import Wizard. If you do not want Salesforce to merge records automatically, use the Data Loader, which is discussed later in this chapter.

Import Contacts and Accounts (continued)

10 Click **Next**.

11 Use the drop-down lists to map columns in the CSV file to Salesforce contact record fields.

12 Click **Next**.

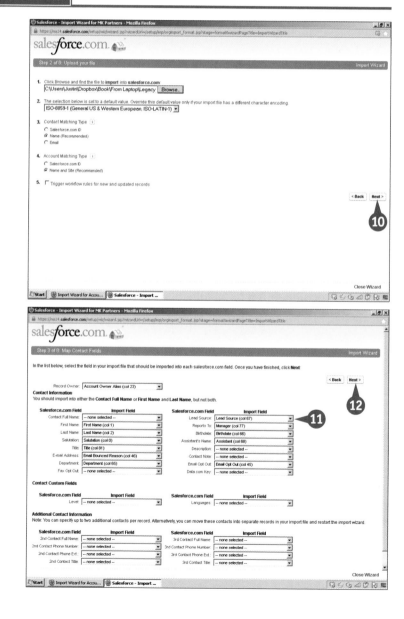

13 Use the drop-down lists to map columns in the CSV file to Salesforce account record fields.

14 Click **Next**.

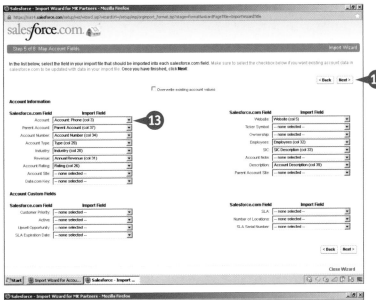

15 Click **Import Now!** to begin the import.

16 Salesforce generates an e-mail alert when the import is complete.

TIP

Can I import contacts and accounts to more than one owner?
Only system administrators can do this, and the CSV file must include an extra column with details of record owners. You can specify owners by Salesforce user name, or by each owner's full name.

Using Mass Delete

I f you are an administrator, you can mass delete up to 250 records at a time with the Mass Delete
Wizard. The Wizard can move records to a recycle bin for safety, or delete them immediately.

Optionally, you can select records for deletion automatically with rules called *filters*. You can apply
up to five filters at a time. This example mass deletes lead records.

Using Mass Delete

1 Click your name.

2 Click **Setup**.

3 Click the **Data Management** ▼.

4 Click **Mass Delete Records**.

5 Click **Mass Delete Leads**.

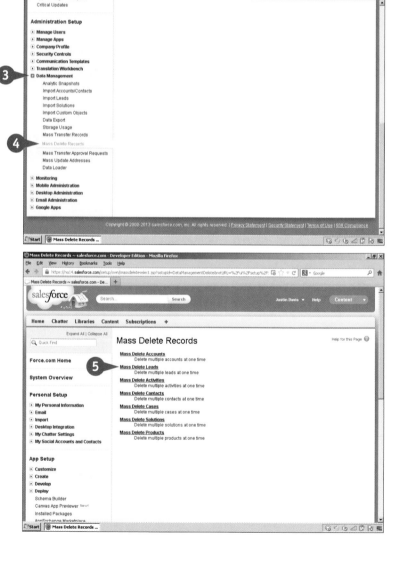

6 Click **None**.

7 Select a field from the drop-down list.

8 Type a value for that field.

Note: Salesforce tests the field against the value you type using the logical rule you select from the middle menu.

Note: For example, to delete all records for the Acme Company, filter on the Company field, type **Acme** into the value field, and leave the logical test set to "equals."

9 Click **Search**.

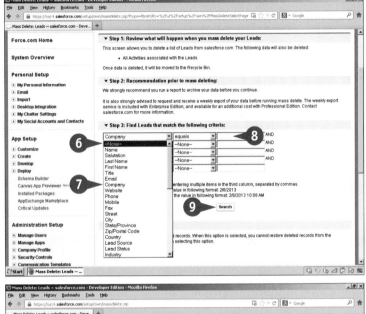

Salesforce displays records that match your criteria.

10 Click the check boxes to select the records you want to mass delete (☐ changes to ☑).

11 Click **Delete**.

Note: By default, records are moved to the recycle bin. To delete records permanently, click the **Permanently delete** check box at the top left (☐ changes to ☑).

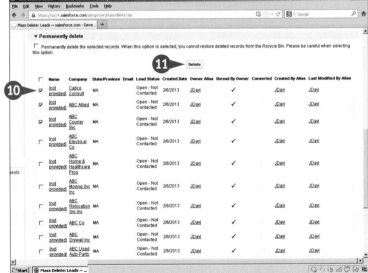

TIP

Can I undo a mass delete?
Yes. You should back up data before a mass delete by running a report and exporting the data to spreadsheet format. An administrator can then reimport the data if necessary. You can also use the Salesforce recycle bin to retrieve records. This keeps the last 5,000 deleted records for up to 15 days. To undelete records, administrators and users can navigate to the recycle bin from the sidebar and use the undelete option.

Install the Data Loader

You can use the Data Loader application to exchange data between Salesforce and a Windows computer. The Data Loader is more powerful than the Import Wizard. Where the Import Wizard can only import data and create Salesforce records, the Data Loader can also delete, update, and *upsert* records (a combination of update and insert), or export them to a CSV file.

You can use these options to back up data from Salesforce, exchange with it partners, load it into other software, mass transfer records, or import data from other sources into Salesforce.

Install the Data Loader

1 Click your name.

2 Click **Setup**.

3 Click the **Data Management** ▼.

4 Click **Data Loader**.

5 Click **Download the Data Loader**.

6 Click **Save File**.

7 Double-click **ApexDataLoader.exe**.

TIPS

What does upsert do?
Upsert combines update and insert operations. The Data Loader creates new records, and updates existing records with new data.

Are there alternatives to the Salesforce Data Loader?
The AppExchange provides a variety of solutions for data import, migration, and integration. The free Jitterbit Data Loader is a popular option for importing and exporting flat files or connecting to any ODBC or JDBC (Open/Java Database Connectivity) database. Popular pay-per-use data tool providers include Informatica and Pervasive. The paid tools offer advanced functionality, including complex data transformations, and support for both on-site and cloud-based execution.

continued ▶

Install the Data Loader (continued)

To install the Data Loader, you must run Windows 7 or Windows XP with 120MB of free disk space and 256MB of RAM available — more RAM is recommended. You must also have the Modify All Data permission enabled in your Salesforce profile to access the download link in the Salesforce Data Management tab.

Install the Data Loader (continued)

8 Click **I Agree**.

9 Click **Next**.

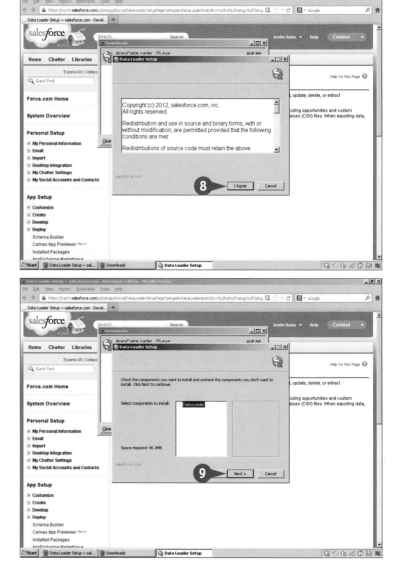

10 Click **Install**.

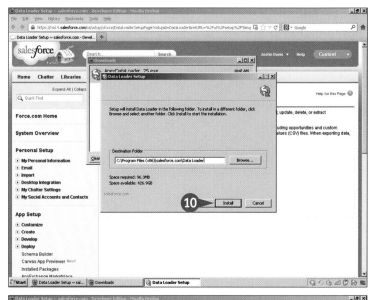

11 Click **Close**.

The installation is now complete.

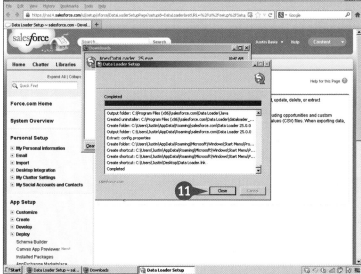

TIP

Can I run more than one version of the Data Loader?
Salesforce does not always delete old versions of the Data Loader when you install a new version. So in theory you can run older versions of the Data Loader. However, for the most reliable results, you should always remove all older versions, and then download and install the most recent version of the Data Loader.

Import Records with the Data Loader

To import records with the Data Loader, a user needs the create profile permission and access to the Salesforce API (Application Programming Interface).

Enterprise Edition and Unlimited Edition customers automatically have access to the API. Other versions do not. To use Data Loader, you must upgrade or order the API as an optional extra. For more details, contact your Salesforce.com account executive.

Import Records with the Data Loader

1 Click **Start**.

2 Click the **salesforce.com** folder.

3 Click the **Data Loader** folder.

4 Click **Data Loader** to start the program.

5 Click **Insert**.

6 Type your username.

7 Type your password.

8 Click **Log in**.

9 Click **Browse**.

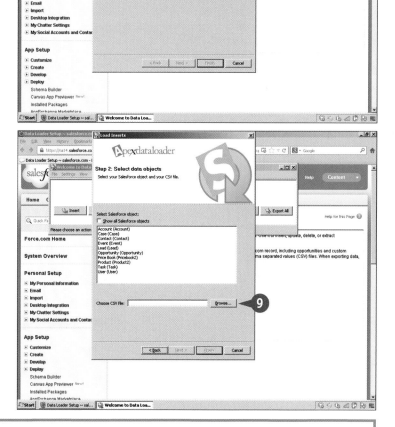

TIP

Why do I get an error when I try to log in to the Data Loader?

If you are attempting to log in from a new network, the Data Loader generates an error message. To access Salesforce, you must enter your password and your security token, discussed in Chapter 7. For example, if your password is *XMvbeSuw* and your security token is *9cQazynm*, you must combine them into a single "word": *XMvbeSuw9cQazynm*. Copy this text into the password field, and the Data Loader should allow you to log in.

continued ▶

Y ou can use the Data Loader from a Windows GUI (Graphical User Interface) or from the command line. Command line access allows batch loading, scripting, and timed running. For example, you can create a script that waits until a day's leads have been downloaded from a marketing source, and then runs Data Loader to upload them to Salesforce automatically.

Scripting is an advanced feature. To use it, you must know how to modify configuration files. The Salesforce help documentation includes a list of commands and parameter lists that are compatible with batch mode.

Import Records with the Data Loader (continued)

⑩ Select a CSV file for import.

⑪ Click **Open**.

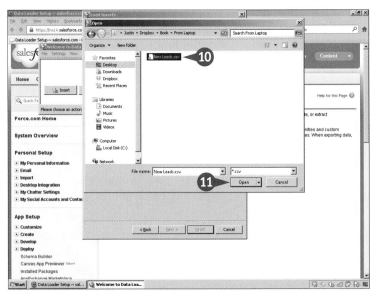

⑫ Click **Create or Edit a Map**.

⑬ Click **Auto-Match Fields to Columns**.

Note: You can create a customized mapping by following the instructions in the dialog box.

⑭ Click **OK**.

15 Click **Browse**.

16 Click **Desktop**.

Note: Data Loader saves error and success reports to this location after import.

17 Click **OK**.

18 Click **Finish**.

19 Click **Yes** to proceed with the data import.

TIPS

Do I receive an e-mail alert when the import is complete?

Salesforce does not send an e-mail alert, but generates two error and success files instead. The success file displays the status of the records modified, including their record IDs. The error file displays all columns from the import file with an extra column labeled ERROR that displays error details whenever a record is not inserted.

How do I fix Data Loader errors?

The Data Loader skips records with errors. You can speed up error recovery by modifying the source file to correct the error, and restarting import directly from the error file. Open the error spreadsheet and fix any issues, such as poorly formatted e-mail addresses or phone numbers. When you are done, click the **Insert** button on the Data Loader, select the error file as the import source, map fields as before, and restart the import.

Update Records with the Data Loader

Records often need updates. For example, you may want to update lists of prospects every quarter. To avoid duplicate records, supply the Data Loader with a list of existing record IDs when performing an update.

Update Records with the Data Loader

1 Launch the Data Loader.

2 Click **Update**.

3 Click **Lead**.

4 Click **Browse**.

⑤ Select a CSV file as a data source.

⑥ Click **Open**.

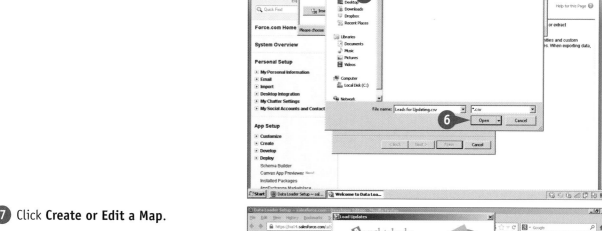

⑦ Click **Create or Edit a Map**.

Can I work with data in the sandbox?

You can use the Data Loader in test mode to work with data in a sandbox and avoid damaging your active commercial data. Open the Data Loader, click the **Settings** menu option. In the server host field, replace the word *login* with *test*, and then click **Save**. Enter your sandbox username and password. You can now work with sandboxed data.

continued ▶

Update Records with the Data Loader (continued)

U pdating duplicate records can create an error. To avoid this error, click the **Settings** menu option, select the batch size, reduce it from 200 to 1, and then click **Save**.

The Data Loader now updates one record at a time. Note this option increases API calls to 1 call per record rather than 1 per 200 records, so you can run out of API resources very quickly. Be sure to change the batch size setting back to 200 when the import ends.

Update Records with the Data Loader (continued)

8 Click **Auto-Match Fields to Columns**.

9 Click **OK**.

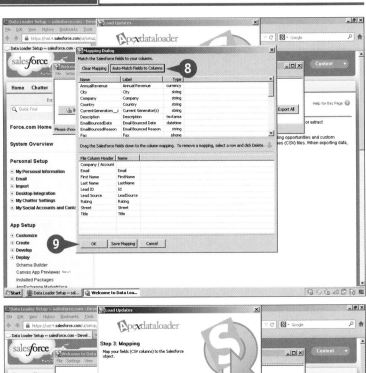

10 Click **Next**.

11 Select a directory for the error file.

12 Click **Finish**.

13 When the confirmation pop-up box appears, click **Yes**.

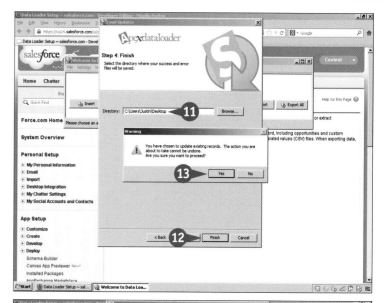

Salesforce displays the number of successes and errors.

14 Click **OK**.

TIP

What if I do not have record IDs?

Always keep track of unique IDs coming from legacy databases. For example, data.com provides a data.com key for all its records. When the time comes to run an update, the Data Loader knows which leads to update based on that unique identifier. If the legacy data does not have a unique ID, create one inside Excel prior to import. The best practice is to create a field on the target object called "legacy ID" or "unique ID." You can then map the field to the unique IDs created in your spreadsheet.

Delete Records with the Data Loader

You can use the Data Loader to mass delete leads as long as you have an ID for the records. To avoid deleting data by accident, create a report for the data you want to delete, including all records and record IDs, and export the report to a spreadsheet. You can keep the spreadsheet as a backup. Import it with the Data Loader and use the ID column to select records for deletion.

Delete Records with the Data Loader

1 Launch the Data Loader.

2 Click **Delete**.

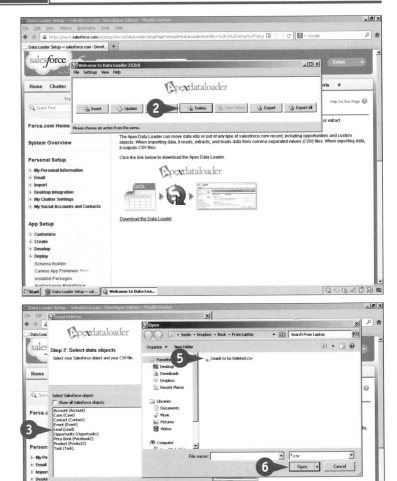

3 Click **Lead**.

4 Click **Browse**.

5 Click the CSV file that holds the ID numbers of the leads you want to delete.

Note: Create this file earlier by running a report.

6 Click **Open**.

7 Click **Next**.

8 Review the confirmation count, and then click **OK**.

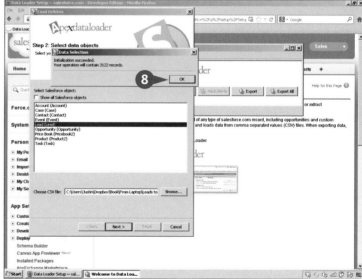

TIP

Can I delete records permanently?
Yes. The Data Loader has a Hard Delete button. Hard deleted records are not moved to the recycling bin, but rather deleted immediately. Click **Hard Delete** to remove records immediately and permanently. You can also use this option to delete test data. To use this feature, you must have the Bulk API Hard Delete permission enabled on your user profile.

continued ▶

Deleting records often changes the relationship between objects. For example, when records have a master/detail relationship, deleting a parent record automatically deletes its child records. If records are connected through a standard lookup field, the child records are not changed.

This can create broken relationships. Always check record relationships before a mass delete to make sure that child records are handled as you want.

Delete Records with the Data Loader (continued)

⑨ Click **Create or Edit a Map**.

⑩ Click **Auto-Match Fields to Columns**.

⑪ Click **OK**.

⑫ Click **Next**.

⑬ Click **Finish**.

14 Click **Yes**.

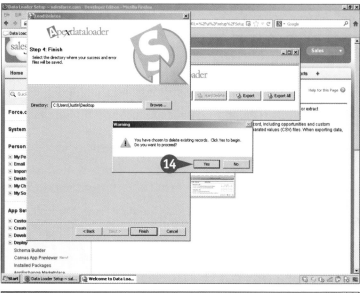

15 Click **Yes**.

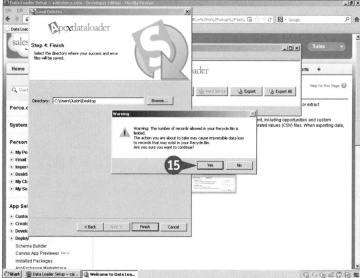

TIP

Can I fix broken relationships after a mass delete?
You can fix broken relationships if you know the record IDs of all the deleted records. As usual, the best backup option is to create a report and export it as a spreadsheet. Note that child record IDs are not listed automatically. You must add a formula to the report to find them and list them.

Export Records with the Data Loader

Y ou can use the Data Loader to export large volumes of data. Reports can time out if you try to work with too many fields and records. The Data Loader does not have this limitation.

Export Records with the Data Loader

1 Launch the Data Loader.

2 Click **Export**.

3 Click **Lead**.

4 Click **Browse**.

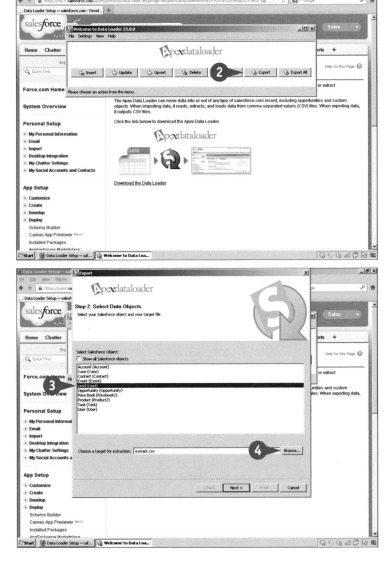

⑤ Select a target folder for the output file in the left-hand explorer pane.

⑥ Type a file name.

Note: Always add the .csv extension.

⑦ Click **Save**.

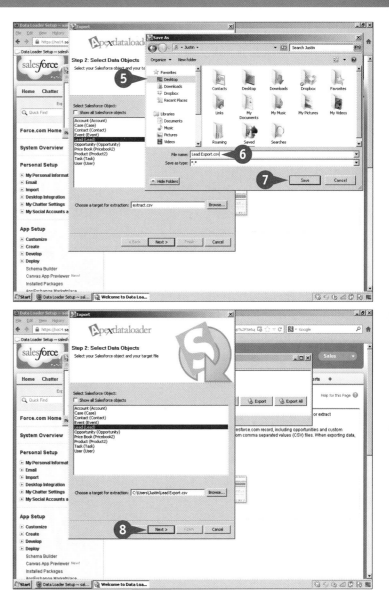

⑧ Click **Next**.

TIP

How can I recover lost data?

Salesforce.com backs up your data regularly, and restores lost records for a fee. Performing a data export regularly eliminates this time and expense, because you can restore lost data from your own backup.

continued ▶

The Data Loader provides a point-and-click interface for exporting basic record sets. It also supports SOQL (Salesforce Object Query Language) for more advanced record management.

You can use SOQL to search for specific strings in records, select specific fields for export, or create other custom filter criteria. For more information about using SOQL, see the Salesforce help materials.

Export Records with the Data Loader (continued)

⑨ Select the columns to include in the exported file (☐ changes to ☑).

⑩ Click **Finish**.

⑪ Click **Yes**.

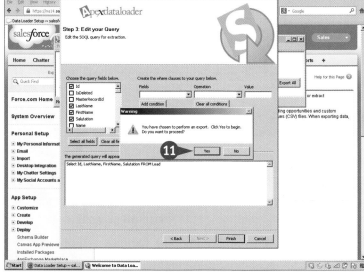

⑫ Click **View Extraction**.

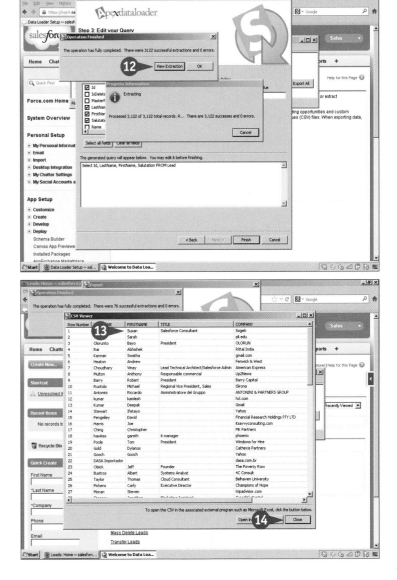

⑬ Salesforce displays the extract records.

Note: This example extracts leads.

⑭ Click **Close**.

TIP

How do I export archived records?

By default Salesforce archives some records automatically. For example, activities (tasks and events) with a due date more than 365 days old are always archived. To include archived records when exporting, click the **Export All** button in the Data Loader instead of the Export button.

Add a Field in the Schema Builder

The Schema Builder is a fast way to edit the fields and objects in records. You can use its dynamic, drag-and-drop interface to view record and field relationships graphically, and modify them with a minimum of effort. The full set of relationships is called a *schema*.

This example adds a check box named Active Customer to an accounts record. Note that if your schema holds a large number of objects and fields, the Schema Builder can load slowly.

Add a Field in the Schema Builder

1 Click your name.

2 Click **Setup**.

3 Click **Schema Builder**.

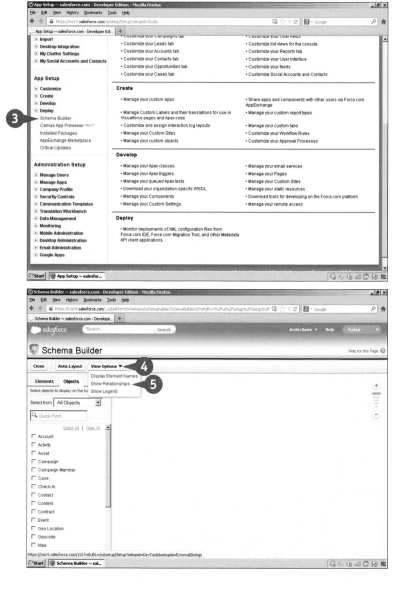

4 Click **View Options**.

5 Click **Show Relationships**.

⑥ Click **All Objects**.

⑦ Choose **Standard Objects**.

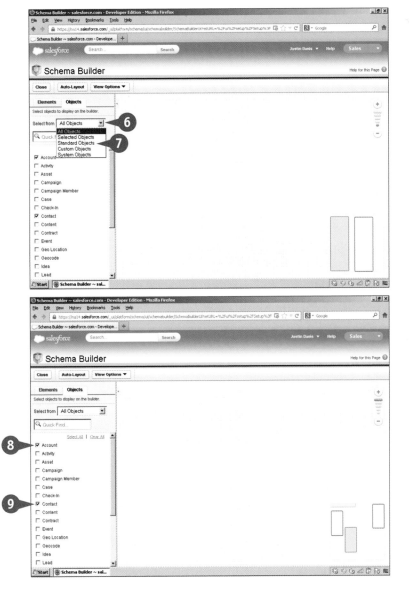

⑧ Click the **Account** check box
(☐ changes to ☑).

⑨ Click the **Contact** check box
(☐ changes to ☑).

TIP

What are other considerations when using the schema builder?
When creating custom fields using the schema builder, two additional steps need to be performed. Field-level security does not set automatically, so the administrator must modify the security of each field once created. The administrator must also modify page layouts to display the new fields.

continued ▶

The Schema Builder is a highly interactive tool. Clicking the sidebar drop-down list enables you to filter objects quickly. Hovering over an object on this list and clicking the magnifying glass jumps to that object on the canvas. Hovering over relationship lines reveals whether a standard lookup or master-detail relationship exists between objects.

Add a Field in the Schema Builder (continued)

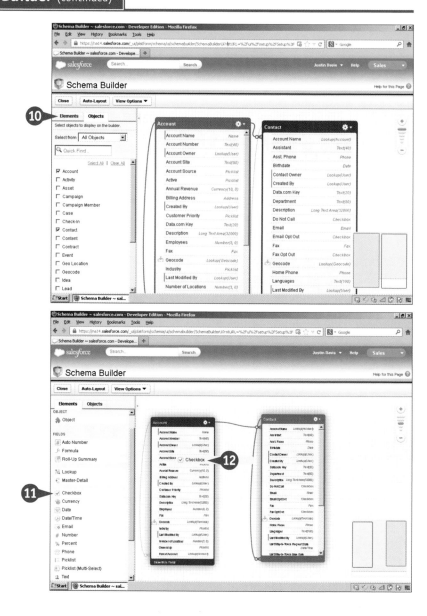

10 Click **Elements**.

11 Click **Checkbox** in the sidebar to add a new check box to the schema.

12 Drag and drop the check box item onto Account.

⓭ Type in a label for the field.

Note: Salesforce generates the Field Name automatically, adding the underscore characters. The Field Name should only be modified by a developer.

⓮ Click **Save**.

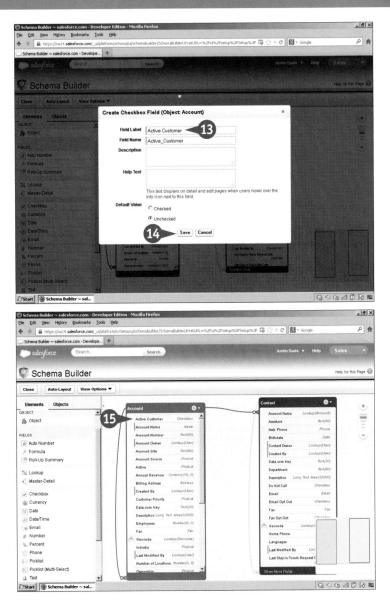

⓯ The new check box field appears in all account records.

TIP

What changes can I make with the Schema Builder?
You can use the Schema Builder to create custom objects; define lookup and master-detail relationships; add auto numbers, formulas, and roll-up summaries; and generally add every other available field type to records. Fields added must be enabled for viewing on user profiles prior to use.

Schedule a Data Export

You can schedule data exports to create regular backups and minimize the danger of data errors or accidental record deletions. If data is deleted accidentally, your organization can reimport it from the last exported file. Many Salesforce customers export data once a week. You can select monthly backups, but losing a full month of data is not recommended. A full export can take between 30 minutes and a day depending on the size and complexity of your records, so it is best to schedule exports during off-hours. You can also run a one-time export to save important data after a successful import. Click the **Export Now** button rather than the Schedule Export button.

Schedule a Data Export

1 Click your name.

2 Click **Setup**.

3 Click the **Data Management** .

4 Click **Data Export**.

5 Click **Schedule Export**.

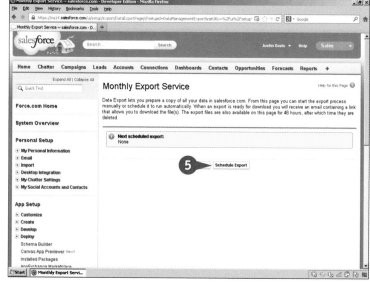

6 Choose a start date.

7 Choose an end date.

8 Choose a preferred start time.

Note: Scheduled exports begin on the start date, end on the end date, and run close to the preferred start time. The actual time may be delayed by half an hour or so.

Note: You can use the frequency option to select daily or monthly backups.

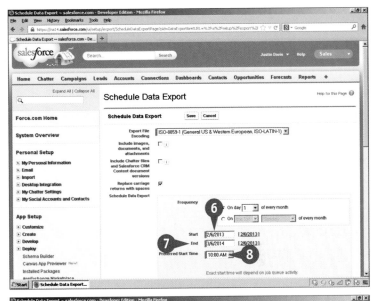

9 Check the **Include all data** check box (☐ changes to ☑).

10 Click **Save**.

What data format does Salesforce save to?

Data exports are Zip files of around 550MB. Salesforce does not keep these files indefinitely, so you should download and save them immediately to a local PC or server.

What security is in place to prevent unauthorized data export?

Only system administrators can schedule a data export. Salesforce.com can enable an optional CAPTCHA test on the export pages to minimize the danger of unauthorized malicious exports generated by scripts, Trojans, or viruses running on your network. The CAPTCHA system adds an extra layer of security by forcing an administrator to type two disguised words correctly before he or she is allowed to export data.

Create a Sandbox

Enterprise Edition and Unlimited Edition customers can use an environment for testing called the *sandbox*. Data in the sandbox can be copied from production and working data.

You can use the sandbox to test and implement new features and code without endangering valuable live information.

Create a Sandbox

1 Click your name.

2 Click **Setup**.

3 Click **Sandbox**.

4 Click **New Sandbox**.

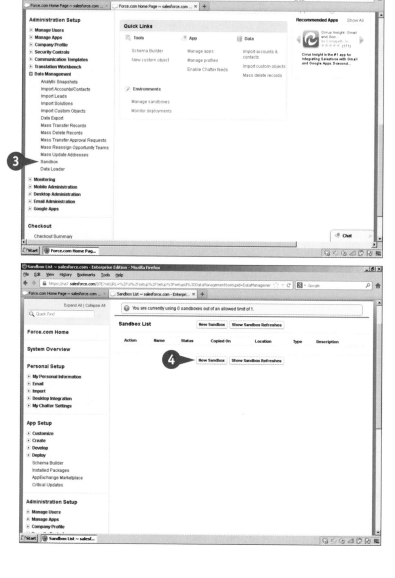

⑤ Type a name for this sandbox.

⑥ Select a sandbox configuration
(◯ changes to ◉).

⑦ Click **Start Copy**.

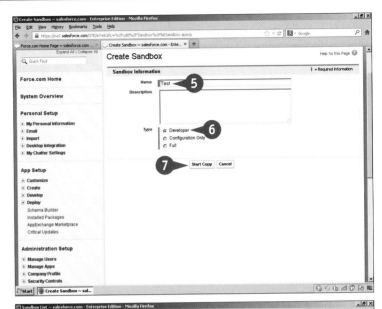

⑧ Salesforce displays a confirmation
message and begins copying data
to the sandbox.

What are the different types of sandboxes?
Salesforce provides three options for sandboxes.
A configuration-only sandbox copies all your
Salesforce reports, objects, dashboards, and
customizations. A developer sandbox adds Apex,
sites, and Visualforce pages. A full sandbox copies
everything, including all your production data.

How do I decide on the correct type of sandbox?
The developer option is usually the best choice.
The full sandbox is best for testing advanced
updates that need access to all your production
code and data.

Mass Transfer Records

You often need to mass transfer records from one user to another. A mass transfer feature that can transfer up to 250 records is included in all editions of Salesforce.

You can use this option to transfer all records, including accounts, leads, contracts, and custom objects. The user performing the transfer must own these records, or have access and sharing permissions. You cannot transfer records to inactive users. This example demonstrates how to transfer leads from one user to another.

Mass Transfer Records

① Click your name.

② Click **Setup**.

③ Click the **Data Management** ▾.

④ Click **Mass Transfer Records**.

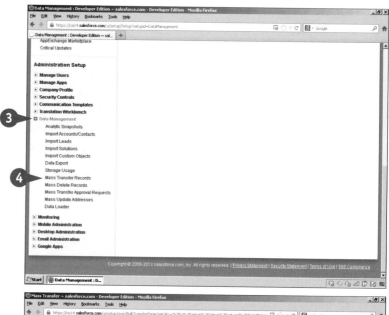

⑤ Click **Transfer Leads**.

6 Type the name of the person you want to transfer leads from.

7 Type the name of the person you want to transfer leads to.

8 Click **Find**.

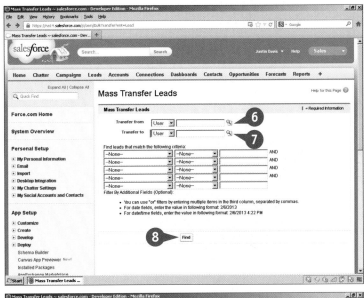

9 Check the check boxes next to records you want to include in the transfer (☐ changes to ☑).

10 Click **Transfer**.

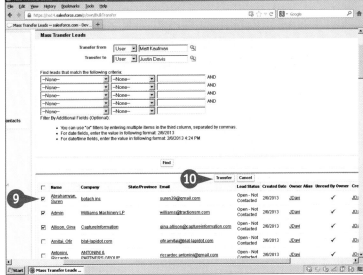

TIP

Are opportunities or cases transferred when parent records are transferred?
Yes. When transferring accounts, you can transfer either open or closed opportunities and cases. You can use the standard check boxes to select these options before clicking the **Transfer** button. Optionally, you can maintain the opportunity team by clicking the **Keep Opportunity Team** check box.

CHAPTER 9

Configuring Workflow

You can use workflow automation features to improve the speed and efficiency of your business processes. Automation has two elements. *Workflow rules* monitor records for specific changes. *Actions* send an e-mail, create a task, update a field, or connect to an outside system when a record is updated or created and a rule is triggered. Automation can add significant intelligence to your instance of Salesforce.

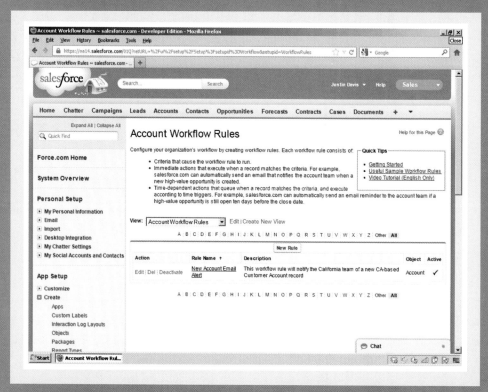

Using Workflow Rules

Workflow rules support business logic by triggering certain actions or reducing the number of clicks needed to perform a task. You can use workflow rules to automate common processes, including status and field updates, e-mail alerts, Salesforce messages, and task assignments. For example, you can create a new workflow rule task that runs whenever someone on the team brings in a new customer to assign the customer to that person automatically.

Understanding Workflow Rules

You can set up workflow rules to test for certain kinds of changes to records. For example, a rule can be triggered when the status of a sales lead changes, or a customer changes his or her contact details. Rules are bound to specific records; they can only access information in the record that triggers them, or in a parent record. More than one rule can be triggered at a time. You can add rules to all standard and custom objects. However, you cannot use rules to process records in bulk. Rules triggered as records are saved and you cannot apply them manually. To perform more complex record processing, you can use Apex technology or other custom code.

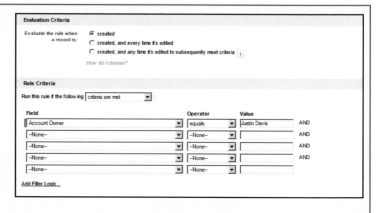

Viewing Workflow Rules

You can view rules on the App Setup page in the Create menu in the Customize area. Click the **View** drop-down list and then select **Account Workflow Rules** to view and edit rules.

Creating and Managing Workflow Rules

To create a new workflow rule, click the **New Rule** button. Each Salesforce instance can have up to 500 workflow rules, but resources are limited. For example, you can use rules to send up to 1,000 e-mails per day per standard Salesforce license, and up to 2 million e-mails across the organization as a whole. When you exceed the resource limit, Salesforce generates a warning e-mail, and eventually suspends your access to rule-based features.

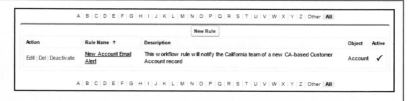

Creating Tasks, Field Updates, and E-mail Alerts

Rules check for changes to records. To make them perform a useful task, you must create supporting *workflow actions*. Actions typically include record field updates, e-mail alerts, and Salesforce tasks, which you can schedule to occur automatically for specific Salesforce users.

> Workflow Rules
>
> Approval Processes
>
> Flows
>
> Tasks
>
> Email Alerts
>
> Field Updates
>
> Outbound Messages
>
> Post Templates
>
> Settings

Linking Workflow Rules with Tasks, E-mails, and Field Updates

To make actions work with rules, link them together. You can either create actions separately and link them manually to one or more rules, or you can create a new action and add it to a rule immediately after creating it.

> Add Workflow Action ▼
>
> New Task
>
> New Email Alert
>
> New Field Update
>
> New Outbound Message
>
> Select Existing Action

Create a Workflow Rule

You can use workflow rules to create an automated response that is triggered when Salesforce users change or create records. For example, you might create a rule that assigns a new customer record created in a certain area to a relevant territory manager. Or you might set up an automated notification for sales managers, which is triggered when unusually large orders are booked. Rules are very flexible and powerful, and can significantly enhance your productivity.

Note that rules on their own simply check for changes. They do not create a response. To add a response, you must link a rule with a workflow action, as described later in this section.

Create a Workflow Rule

① Click your name.

② Click **Setup**.

③ Click the **Create** triangle (▼).

④ Click the **Workflow & Approvals** ▼.

⑤ Click the **Workflow Rules** link.

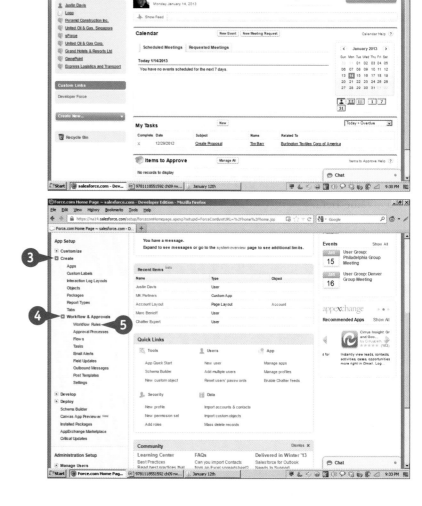

6 Click **New Rule**.

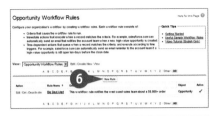

7 Click the **Select object** drop-down list and select an object.

Note: The workflow rule will be created for that object.

8 Click **Next**.

9 Type a name into the **Rule Name** box.

Note: Make the name unique and descriptive. If possible, suggest the business process supported by this rule.

10 Click a radio button to select one of the evaluation criteria (○ changes to ◉).

Note: This example creates a rule that runs when a record is created. You can also create a rule that triggers when a record is edited or when the edit operation meets further criteria.

11 Select a record field and an operator and type in a value.

Note: This example triggers the rule for billing addresses in California, as set by CA in the Value field.

12 Click **Save & Next**.

13 Click **Done** (not shown).

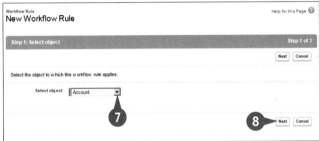

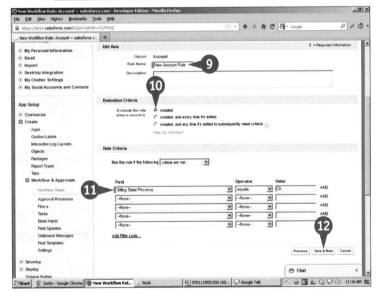

TIPS

Which editions of Salesforce support workflow rules?

Workflow rules are included in the Enterprise and Unlimited editions. You can purchase them as an optional add-on for the Professional Edition. You cannot add them to other editions.

Can I schedule an action to fire at a later date?

Once you have created the workflow rule, click the **Add Time Trigger** button to set up a future date and time for the actions. When attaching these workflow actions, remember to attach them in the time trigger action section, not in the immediate action section.

Create a Workflow Field Update

You can use a workflow field update to automatically change or update information in a record when a workflow rule is triggered. Depending on the structure of the records, the update may change the triggering record or its parent. For example, if a new won opportunity is created, you can set up a field update that changes the status of the parent account from Prospect to Customer when the opportunity closes. To make this possible, Salesforce allows you to select the relevant field on a parent record instead of the field on the child record that triggered the update.

Create a Workflow Field Update

1 Click your name.

2 Click **Setup**.

3 Click the **Create** ☑.

4 Click the **Workflow & Approvals** ☑.

5 Click the **Field Updates** link.

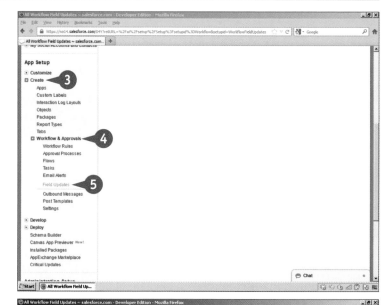

6 Click **New Field Update**.

⑦ Type a unique name for the update in the Name field.

⑧ Select the object you wish to create the update for from the Object drop-down list.

⑨ Select a target field in the Field to Update drop-down list.

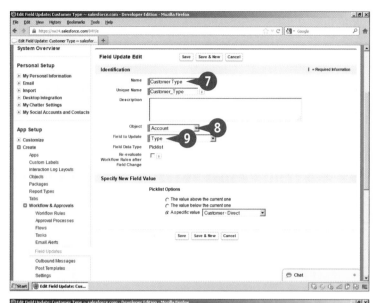

⑩ Click one of the Picklist Options (◯ changes to ◉).

Note: This example copies the Customer-Direct value of the record into the Account Type field.

⑪ Click **Save**.

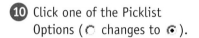

Can I use a field update to trigger a second workflow rule?

Yes. When you create the field update, click the **Re-evaluate Workflow Rules after Field Change** check box (☐ changes to ☑). If a field changes after an update, Salesforce evaluates the record again to see if further rules should be triggered.

What happens if I deactivate a workflow rule?

E-mails or tasks already queued by a rule are not deleted. You can remove them manually by navigating to the Monitoring area of Salesforce and searching for queued *time-based* workflow actions. Time-based actions occur at some point in the future. For example, Salesforce can generate an e-mail alert or task assignment one week after a workflow rule is triggered. If your search finds any time-based actions, you can delete them there.

Add a Field Update to a Rule

You can make a workflow rule and field update "live" by associating them. This tells Salesforce to perform the field update when the rule is triggered.

You must deactivate time-based workflow rules before you can add a new field update. Salesforce will not permit you to add workflow actions to active time-based workflow rules. This prevents any conflicts from taking places with workflow actions.

Add a Field Update to a Rule

1 Open the Account Workflow Rules page.

Note: For details, see "Create a Workflow Rule," earlier in this chapter.

2 Select the rule you want to link to an update.

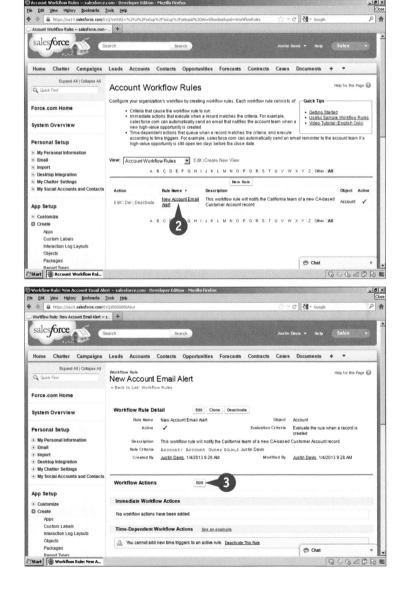

3 Click **Edit**.

④ Click **Add Workflow Action**.

⑤ Click **Select Existing Action**.

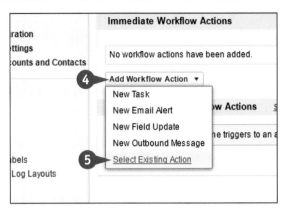

⑥ Select an action from the Available Actions list.

⑦ Click the **Add** arrow (▶).

Salesforce adds the action to the list of available actions and links it to the rule.

⑧ Click **Save**.

Salesforce now performs the update when the rule is triggered.

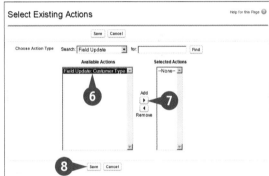

TIPS

What else do I need to know about field updates?

Field updates occur before e-mail alerts and task updates, but after case assignment, lead assignment, auto-response, and case escalation updates. Field updates do not follow the usual Salesforce validation rules, so a field update can create invalid data. Field updates are also not secure; a user can trigger a field update on a field they would not usually have access to. You cannot delete a field that can be changed by a field update; Salesforce generates an error if you try.

How do I disable time-based workflow rules?

You can disable time-based workflow rules in the same way as you disable standard rules; navigate to the workflow rule you wish to disable and click the **Deactivate** button. Salesforce deselects the Active check box (☑ changes to ☐) for the record to show that it is disabled.

Create a Workflow Task

You can use the workflow task feature to assign tasks to users when certain workflow rules are triggered. This is a powerful feature, because you can use this feature to automate standard business processes. For example, you can create a follow-up call task to remind a sales team member to call a lead a specific amount of time after the lead has been created.

Note that you must link a task to a workflow rule after creating it. Otherwise, Salesforce never assigns the task. For details, see the next section, "Link a Task to a Rule."

Create a Workflow Task

1. Click your name.
2. Click **Setup**.
3. Click the **Create** ▾.
4. Click the **Workflow & Approvals** ▾.
5. Click the **Task** link.

6. Click **New Task**.

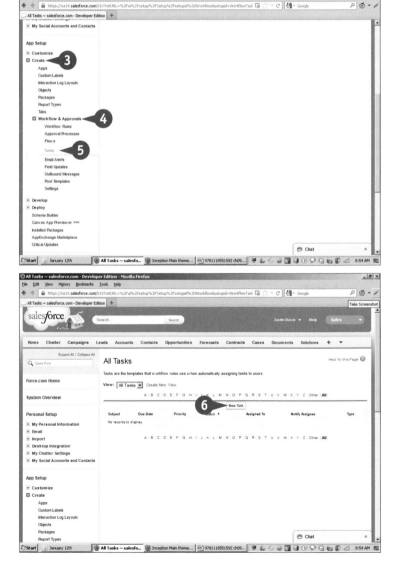

7 Select an object to be linked to the task.

8 Click **Next**.

9 In the Assigned To field, type the name of an active Salesforce user.

10 In the Subject field, type a name for the task.

Note: The name you enter appears under My Tasks on the user's home page. Make the name as descriptive as possible.

11 Click the Due Date drop-down list and select **Rule Trigger Date**.

Note: This option tells Salesforce to assign the task as soon as the rule is triggered.

12 Click **Save**.

Salesforce creates the task as soon as the rule is triggered.

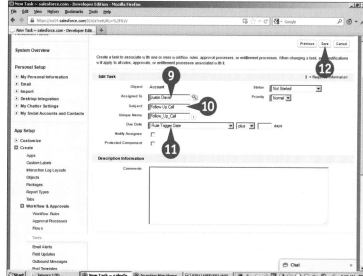

Can I choose the owner of this task dynamically?
Task assignment is fixed. You must specify a single Salesforce user. However, for certain rules you can set up tasks so the task owner is also the user who triggered a change to a record, or created a new record.

Can I defer a task?
Yes. You can use the Days field in the Due Date row to defer a task by a set number of days. Use this option to create automated reminders for follow-ups, or to assign reporting and sales summary tasks.

Link a Task to a Rule

Workflow tasks do nothing unless you link them to a workflow rule. Link creation is a straightforward process.

You can use tasks and rules creatively to automate processes and improve efficiency. For example, if a customer complaint is logged in Cases, you can create a follow-up call workflow task that is assigned 30 days later.

Link a Task to a Rule

1 Open the Workflow Rule page.

Note: For details, see "Create a Workflow Rule," earlier in this chapter.

2 Click **Edit**.

3 Click **Add Workflow Action**.

4 Click **Select Existing Action**.

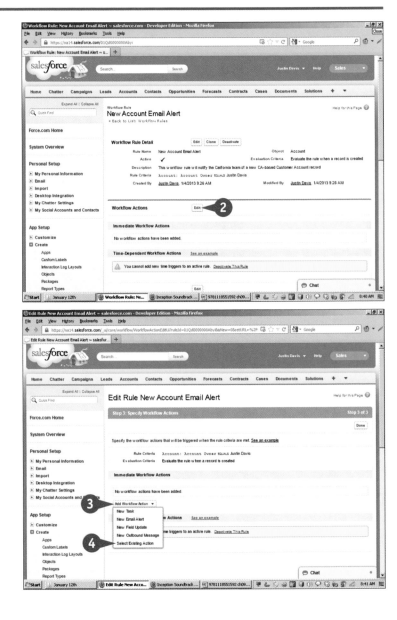

5 Select a task in the Available Actions column.

6 Click the **Add** arrow (▶) to move this task to the Selected Actions column.

7 Click **Save**.

8 Click **Done**.

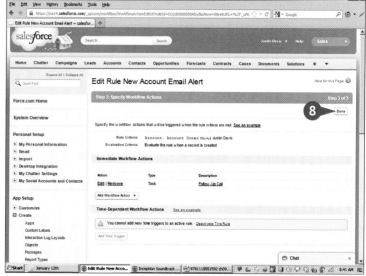

TIPS

Can the task owner be notified when the task is assigned?
Yes. Click the **Notify Assignee** check box (☐ changes to ☑) when you create a workflow task to force Salesforce to send an e-mail alert to the task owner. This is optional — tasks appear on each owner's home page, and they do not usually need additional e-mail reminders.

Can I add a task to an active workflow rule?
You do not need to deactivate a workflow rule to add a task to it. As with all workflow rules, associated tasks, alerts, and updates are only triggered when records change. Even though a rule is active, Salesforce does not scan its records to check if the rule already applies and a task should be created immediately.

Create an E-mail Alert

E-mail alerts can be sent to Salesforce users or to customers. You can also specify up to five e-mail addresses that do not belong to Salesforce users or customers. E-mails use predefined templates, which are covered in Chapter 2. You will need to navigate to the communication templates area during setup to create these e-mail templates before creating a workflow rule e-mail alert.

You can use the e-mail alert feature to inform users of significant events, notify management whenever a large sale completes, or remind customers to renew a contract or re-stock products.

Create an E-mail Alert

1. Click your name.
2. Click **Setup**.
3. Click the **Create** ▼.

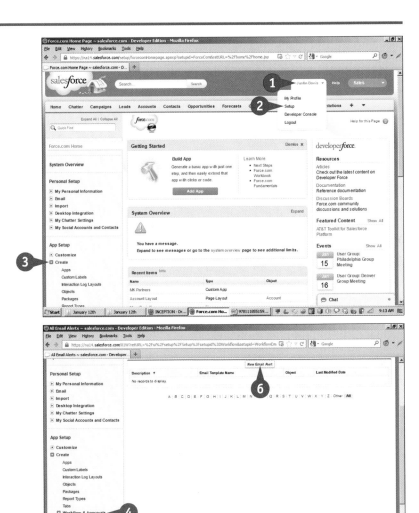

4. Click the **Workflow & Approvals** ▼.
5. Click **Email Alerts**.
6. Click **New Email Alert**.

7 Type a descriptive name for the alert in the Description field.

8 Click the **Object** drop-down list and select the object that generates the alert.

9 Click the **Email Template** drop-down list and select a template for the e-mail.

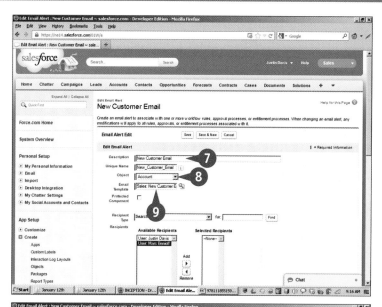

10 Select a user from the Available Recipients column.

11 Click the **Add** arrow (▶).

Note: You can add as many recipients as you like.

12 Optionally, type in up to five external e-mail addresses for recipients who are not Salesforce users.

13 Click **Save**.

Note: You must link the alert to a workflow rule before it goes "live." For more information, see the next section, "Add an E-mail Alert to a Rule."

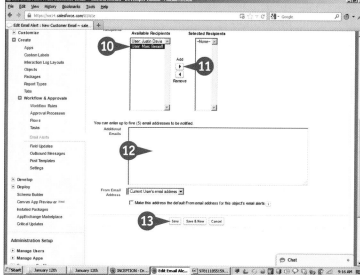

TIP

Can I send an e-mail alert to other addresses?
Yes. If you cannot see a recipient in the Available Recipients column, click the **Search** drop-down list to search further. Search the e-mail field to see a list of addresses included in the triggering record.

Add an E-mail Alert to a Rule

After you create an alert, you must add it to a workflow rule. This makes the alert "live" so it will be triggered by the rule. If you leave out this step, the alert remains on the system but does nothing. Alerts can be added to active or inactive rules; however, you should deactivate a rule before adding an e-mail alert.

Add an E-mail Alert to a Rule

1 Open the Workflow Actions page.

Note: For details, see the previous section, "Create an E-mail Alert."

2 Select the rule to which you want to add an alert.

3 Click **Edit**.

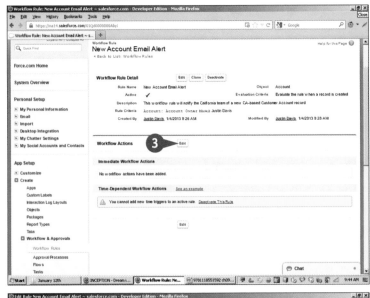

4 Click **Add Workflow Action**.

5 Click **Select Existing Action**.

6 Select **Email Alert** from the Choose Action Type drop-down list.

7 Select one of the e-mail alerts.

Note: This example shows a single alert. Typically Salesforce shows a longer list of alerts.

8 Click the **Add arrow (▶).**

9 Click **Save**.

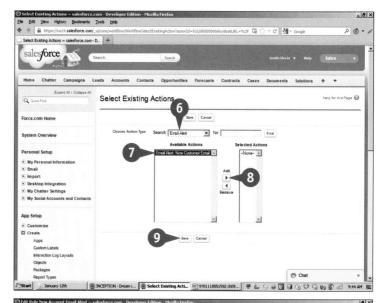

10 Click **Done**.

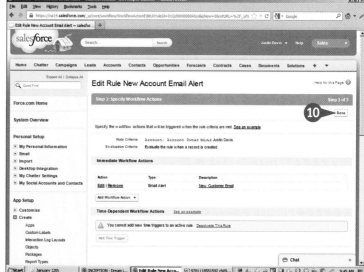

TIPS

Which From address does an e-mail alert use?
The default From address is noreply@salesforce.com. To change this, navigate to the Email Administration section of the Setup area and view the Deliverability option. Deselect the **Enable compliance with standard email security** check box (☑ changes to ☐). Alerts now show your usual work e-mail address.

Does an e-mail alert add a copy of the e-mail to a record?
Salesforce does not do this automatically, but you can add another workflow task to the workflow rule that triggers the alert. Do this when you need to track e-mails and confirm they have been sent in the record's Activity History Log.

Index

Symbols and Numerics

Read Less-Learn More®

Visual™

There's a Visual book for every learning level...

Simplified®

The place to start if you're new to computers. Full color.

- Computers
- Creating Web Pages
- Digital Photography
- Excel

- Internet
- Laptops
- Mac OS
- Office

- PCs
- Windows
- Word

Teach Yourself VISUALLY™

Get beginning to intermediate-level training in a variety of topics. Full color.

- Access
- Adobe Muse
- Computers
- Digital Photography
- Digital Video
- Dreamweaver
- Excel
- Flash
- HTML5
- iLife

- iPad
- iPhone
- iPod
- Macs
- Mac OS
- Office
- Outlook
- Photoshop
- Photoshop Elements
- Photoshop Lightroom

- PowerPoint
- Salesforce.com
- Search Engine Optimization
- Social Media
- Web Design
- Windows
- Wireless Networking
- Word
- WordPress

Top 100 Simplified® Tips & Tricks

Tips and techniques to take your skills beyond the basics. Full color.

- Digital Photography
- eBay
- Excel

- Google
- Office
- Photoshop

- Photoshop Elements
- PowerPoint
- Windows

...all designed for visual learners—just like you!

Master VISUALLY®

Your complete visual reference. Two-color interior.

- 3ds Max
- Creating Web Pages
- Dreamweaver and Flash
- Excel
- iPod and iTunes
- Mac OS
- Office
- Optimizing PC Performance
- Windows
- Windows Server

Visual Blueprint™

Where to go for professional-level programming instruction. Two-color interior.

- ActionScript
- Excel Data Analysis
- Excel Pivot Tables
- Excel Programming
- HTML5
- JavaScript
- Mambo
- Mobile App Development
- Perl and Apache
- PHP 5
- SEO
- Ubuntu Linux
- Vista Sidebar
- Visual Basic
- XML

Visual™ Quick Tips

Shortcuts, tricks, and techniques for getting more done in less time. Full color.

- Digital Photography
- Excel
- Internet
- iPhone
- iPod & iTunes
- Mac OS
- Office
- PowerPoint
- Windows

e **Available in print and e-book formats.**

For a complete listing of Visual books, go to wiley.com/go/visual